Exploring the Roots of Heartache

THE STORIES OUR PAIN IS TRYING TO TELL

Dr. Paula Davis

Copyright

Disclaimer

This book is offered as a reflective and educational resource. It draws on psychological theory, clinical experience, and personal narrative to explore the emotional meanings carried by pain and heartache. It is not intended as a substitute for professional counselling, psychotherapy, medical care, or crisis support.

Some material may evoke strong emotional responses, particularly for readers with experiences of trauma, loss, or relational wounding. Readers are encouraged to engage with the content at their own pace and to seek appropriate professional or pastoral support if distress arises.

The stories shared in this book have been altered to protect confidentiality. Any resemblance to actual persons or events is coincidental.

Scripture Quotations

All Scripture quotations, unless otherwise noted, are from:

Publication Details

ISBN: 978-0-6451179-8-1

First published as an e-book 2026 in Australia

To my granddaughters, with love and wisdom,

so that you may carry a piece of my heart with you wherever you go.

To my children, Mark and Rebecca and their partners,

the dreamers who refuse to let the world define them.

To my husband Barry, who taught me the value of storytelling

and was there with me through every word and every page.

Table of Contents

Index of Tables & Figures

Books by the Same Author

After the Breaking: Psychological Trauma and Collective Healing

Eating Water, Drinking Soup: Finding Nourishment in the Deepest Pain

A Safe Place: A Marriage Enrichment Resource Manual

Foreword

This foreword first appeared in *Eating Water, Drinking Soup: Finding Nourishment in the Deepest Pain* and is reproduced here because the themes apply equally to this volume.

In recent decades, neuroscience has illuminated incredible truths about the human brain - perhaps none more remarkable than its plasticity. We now understand that the brain is not fixed or static; it adapts, rewires, and regenerates, even in the face of deep trauma. This knowledge has ushered in a wave of research and literature exploring Post-Traumatic Stress Disorder (PTSD), with many approaches focusing on rewiring thought patterns, calming hyperactive nervous systems, and offering coping mechanisms rooted in cognitive science.

And yet, as vast and varied as this literature is, it often overlooks a foundational truth: we are not just brains and bodies, but souls - eternal beings made in the image of God. A purely clinical or cognitive approach, while valuable, is incomplete. It speaks to the symptoms but often misses the soul.

What our friend Paula offers in this book is deeply needed and refreshingly rare - a holistic path to healing that centres Christ and embraces the whole person. Rooted in empathy, naked bravery, and the transforming love of Jesus, this work dares to face trauma not as something to be erased, but as something that can be redeemed. Here, even the most painful experiences are stirred into something nourishing - like a healing soup, rich with meaning and grace.

This book is more than a collection of insights or stories. It is a sanctuary. A place where brokenness meets grace. Where theological depth and lived experience are held in holy tension. Paula has written with raw honesty and breathtaking vulnerability - not as one who stands above pain, but as one who has walked through it, hand in hand with the Healer.

Each chapter is a balm for the soul and a call to courage. Whether you are navigating deep sorrow, hidden shame, spiritual disillusionment, or the silent ache of unanswered questions, this book will meet you there - not with easy answers, but with sacred companionship.

Through Scripture, insight, and a heartfelt journey, this book offers a way to reconcile with shame, to see wounds not as permanent scars but as places where healing light can shine through. It doesn't just offer tools for coping, but an invitation to feel loved, being reinvented, and transformed - whole and free in Christ.

We pray that as you read, you will feel the gentle pursuit of the One who weeps with you, heals you, and calls you by name. And like Paula, may you too find nourishment in the places you never thought you could survive.

With love and gratitude.

Drs. Sam & Sanaa Labib, General Practitioners

Preface

This book is not a guide, a formula, or a prescription. It is a story, my story, offered in the hope that it might resonate with yours. Along the way, I have included glimpses of the journeys of others I've had the privilege to walk with in counselling. Their stories are not shared to instruct or impress, but to illustrate how heartache, healing, and hope often to move in ways that are both unexpected and tender. Names and identifying details have been changed, but the truth of their experience remains.

I have walked seasons where hope seemed to vanish, where fear whispered louder than faith, and where the wounds of my past felt too heavy to bear. In these pages, I share what I learned along the way, both from my own journey and from the stories of those who have trusted me with theirs. My hope is that reading these stories alongside my own might invite you to pause, to breathe, and to reflect on your own journey, recognizing that even in the places where heartache takes root, there is the possibility of growth, restoration, and grace.

Introduction

I didn't go looking for heartache. It came to me, quietly and without warning, in the middle of ordinary days that looked fine on the outside but felt hollow within. It showed up in my body first, in the exhaustion that no amount of sleep could fix, in the restlessness that followed me from room to room, and in the ache and emptiness that words could not reach. For a long time, I told myself to keep going, to pray harder, to stay strong. But heartache has its own language, and sooner or later it asks to be heard.

When I finally stopped long enough to listen, I began to see that what I was feeling had deep roots. It wasn't just about the present moment or a recent disappointment, it reached back into places I had long forgotten. Beneath the surface, I found layers of grief I had never named, losses I had minimized, and the quiet ache of needs that went unmet. What I had thought of as weakness or failure was often the body's way of remembering what the mind had tried to forget.

In my work as a counsellor, I have seen this truth mirrored again and again: the young woman who carries the shame of a childhood she could not control; the man who fears intimacy because love once brought only pain; the mother who silently mourns the relationship she never knew she could have with her own child. Their courage in naming their pain and stepping into the work of healing has taught me as much as my own journey.

This book was born out of that discovery. It isn't a map or a formula for healing, but a collection of moments, places where pain and grace meet in the same breath. As I began to trace my story alongside theirs, I noticed that God was not standing at a distance, waiting for me to be stronger. He was already there, in the very places I least expected Him to be, beneath the rubble, beside our fear, within the silence.

Each chapter marks a part of that journey. In the chapter, ***When Hope Disappeared,*** I write about the seasons when faith felt fragile and the light seemed far away. ***What is Depression Trying to Tell Me?*** explores how despair can emerge from unspoken grief, and loss. ***Buried Grief*** and ***Under the Broom Bush*** tell of the times I could no longer hold myself together and discovered that even in collapse, I was not abandoned.

There were moments of stillness too, times of shelter and reflection, like ***Under the Mango Tree.*** Yet healing has never been simple or straight. ***What is Stress Trying to Tell Me?*** and ***My Restless Mind*** describe the exhaustion of trying to manage what only grace can mend. In ***Holding My Fear*** and ***What is Anxiety Trying to Tell Me?*** I began to see how fear was not my enemy but a messenger, pointing me toward what needed care.

Later came chapters of deeper honesty. *Awakening Desire* **explores anxiety as a signal pointing toward the soul's deeper longing and** *The Monster Who Was Sorry* **brought me face to face with parts of myself, I had hidden away.** *What Is Anger Trying to Tell Me?* **taught me that anger, too, can carry truth. And when my strongholds began to crumble,** *Whose Voice Am I Hearing?* **helped me separate the voice of shame from the voice of love.**

Even then, healing was unfinished. ***Roots That Still Bleed*** reminded me that some pain lingers, not as punishment, but as a reminder to walk gently. ***When Regret Broke Me Open*** became a moment of surrender, where I finally let mercy have the last word.

By the time I reached ***From Mess to Message,*** I could see that my story, with all its jagged edges and tender places, had become something more than survival. It had become a kind of offering.

This is not a story about perfection. It is a story about God's presence, about what happens when we stop running from our pain and dare to meet Him in the middle of it. My hope is that as you read, you might recognize something of your own journey here too. And perhaps you'll find, as I did, that even the roots of heartache can hold the beginnings of hope.

CHAPTER 1

When Changing Touches Old Pain

"Grace doesn't change us overnight. It works slowly, like yeast in dough." ~ Eugene Peterson

"It is not imperfection that keeps us from growing; it is the fear of looking at ourselves honestly." ~ Thomas Merton

"I waited patiently for the Lord; he turned to me and heard my cry." ~ Psalm 40:1

There was a season when hope didn't vanish dramatically, it simply thinned out. I didn't wake one morning in despair. I kept functioning. I kept doing what was expected of me. From the outside, my life still looked steady, even purposeful. But somewhere underneath, something essential had gone quiet.

What I noticed first was not sadness, but effort. Everything felt harder than it used to. Practices I believed in no longer brought comfort. Rest felt restless. Prayer felt flat. Even habits I knew were good for me, reflection, stillness, gentleness, felt strangely irritating, as though my own body were resisting them.

What made this especially confusing was that I knew the truth. I knew the scriptures that spoke of life and freedom. I believed them. I could quote them. I had spent years helping others find their way back to hope through those same words. And yet, knowing the way did not mean I could walk it with ease.

Knowing the Way but Not the Capacity to Walk It

For a long time, I assumed the problem was me. I told myself I should be more disciplined. More grateful. More spiritually mature. I analysed what I was doing wrong and tried to correct it. When that didn't work, I pushed harder.

Only later did I begin to understand that what I was experiencing was not a failure of character or faith. It was my nervous system speaking, long before I knew how to listen. I have since learned that the brain does not move easily toward change, even when that change is good. It prefers what is familiar over what is new, because familiarity signals safety. Predictability tells the body, I have survived this before. My patterns, even the ones that were costing me, had once helped me cope, belong, or stay regulated. They were known. They were survivable.

When Familiar Patterns Feel Safer Than Life-Giving Ones

New ways of being, no matter how healthy or well-intentioned, felt uncertain. And uncertainty, to the body, often registers as threat. This helped me understand why scrolling late into the night felt easier than reading, even though I longed for nourishment. Why takeaway felt more natural than cooking, even when my body felt better afterwards. Why staying busy felt safer than resting, even when I was running on empty.

The familiar path required very little effort. The alternative asked my brain to build something new, a pathway that didn't yet exist. Each time

I tried to change, it felt like stepping off a clear track and pushing through dense undergrowth. Progress was slow. Resistance was loud. And I mistook that resistance for evidence that I was on the wrong path.

When Discomfort Is Mistaken for Danger

What I didn't yet understand was that discomfort does not always mean danger. The brain changes through a process known as neuroplasticity, forming new connections through repeated experience. But this process takes time. And more importantly, it requires safety. Pressure does not accelerate healing. It often delays it.

Still, when the discomfort persisted, I did what many of us do. I tried to fix myself. I analysed more. I tried harder. I told myself I would do better next time.

Learning That Growth Requires Safety, Not Force

Both psychology and spirituality eventually led me to a quieter, more unsettling truth: growth does not happen through force. The nervous system does not respond to pressure. It responds to safety. My patterns did not form because I was weak or careless. They formed because, at some point, they helped me survive.

That realisation began to loosen something, not hope yet, but harshness. It helped me see why emotional knots don't unravel when we try to cut them away. Suppressing feelings tightens the body. Avoiding conflict buries tension deeper. Overcompensating adds new strain to old wounds. These strategies can look productive, even virtuous. But underneath, they often keep the body braced, alert, vigilant, unable to soften.

Where This Book Begins

Healing, I would later learn, works differently. It begins not with fixing, but with noticing. Not with urgency, but with attention. Not with answers, but with presence. At the time, though, I wasn't there yet. Hope had not returned. Understanding had not arrived. All I knew was that something in me was tired of striving, and afraid of stopping.

Looking back now, I can see that this was the beginning. Not the beginning of healing, but the beginning of listening. Before hope can be restored, it must be allowed to disappear honestly. Before change can emerge, the body must be met where it already is. Before answers are found, pain must be trusted to be saying something true.

This book begins there, at the place where striving falters, certainty thins, and the roots of heartache start to show themselves.

Closing Thoughts

I am beginning to understand that when change feels harder than it should, something in me needs care, not condemnation. I have been shaped by experiences that taught my body how to survive. Knowing the truth does not always mean we can live it immediately. Sometimes the distance between what we believe and what we can embody is not disobedience, but fear waiting to be met with safety.

This chapter does not offer answers, only permission. Permission to stop striving. Permission to notice what feels heavy. Permission to trust that your pain is not meaningless but speaking.

Hope does not need to be strong to be real. It only needs space to breathe. The journey ahead will not rush you. It will begin by listening, to your body, your story, and the quiet places where God is already present. That is enough for now

Declarations

I declare that struggling to change does not mean I lack faith or truth. It means my body is learning how to feel safe enough to live what I believe.

I declare that knowing the way does not require me to walk it by force. God leads me with patience, not pressure.

I declare that my patterns were formed to help me survive. I can honour what once protected me while gently opening to something new.

I declare that growth happens at the pace of safety, not effort. I am allowed to move slowly and still be moving toward life.

I declare that even when hope feels thin, it is not gone. Listening is already the beginning of healing.

Prayer

God of gentleness,
I come without answers and without strength.
I am tired of striving and unsure how to stop.
You know the places in me that resist change,
not because I do not love the truth,
but because my body is afraid.

Meet me where I am.
Teach me how to listen.
Help me trust that your nearness is not withdrawn
when my hope feels small.
Hold what is fragile in me.
Make this place of thinning hope a place of beginning.

Reflection Questions

1. Where in my life does hope feel thin rather than gone, and what does that feel like in my body?
2. What currently feels like effort, even practices or truths I believe in, and how have I been interpreting that struggle?
3. Where have I tried to change by pushing harder or being more disciplined, and what has that approach cost me?
4. What patterns in my life might have once helped me survive or cope, even if they no longer serve me now?
5. If I stopped striving for a moment, what might my pain or resistance be trying to tell me?

Journal Prompt

1. Where in my life does change feel harder than it "should," even though I know what is good and true?
2. As I sit with this, what do I notice in my body, tension, tiredness, resistance, or longing, and what might these sensations be trying to protect?
3. If I let go of fixing or judging myself for a moment, what would it be like to simply listen to this place with kindness?

CHAPTER 2

When Hope Disappeared

"Why, my soul, are you downcast? Why so disturbed within me? Put your hope in God, for I will yet praise him, my Savior and my God." ~ Psalm 42:11

"The nature of the enemy's warfare in your life is to cause you to become discouraged and to cast away your confidence. Not that you would necessarily discard your salvation, but you could give up your hope of God's deliverance. The enemy wants to numb you into a coping kind of Christianity that has given up hope of seeing God's resurrection power."
~ Bob Sorge, Glory: When Heaven Invades Earth

"Despair is anger with no place to go."
~ Mignon McLaughlin

Navigating the Darkness of Depression

There are moments in life when the weight of the world feels so unbearable that hope seems to vanish altogether. In these seasons of despair, it can feel as though you are drowning in a deep, inescapable darkness. Depression is not just an emotional state; it seeps into every corner of your being, your thoughts, your body, your soul. It's a profound silence that replaces the rhythm of life, a void that makes even the simplest of tasks seem insurmountable.

In this chapter, I reflect on the experiences of depression, those times when the light of hope flickers and then fades. Through personal narrative and a journey of deep introspection, I will explore the nature of depression, its grip on both the mind and spirit, and the path toward healing. We will walk together through the moments of loss, confusion, and heartache, ultimately seeking a glimpse of restoration. For even when hope disappears, the journey toward its rediscovery is never truly over.

Breaking the Chains that Bind the Soul

There were days I hated myself. Days I didn't want to exist. Not die, exactly. Just… disappear. Evaporate, like a breath in winter, vanishing before anyone noticed.

It was a cry for help and attention, a slow, silent ache, invisible on the outside but relentless on the inside. I still got up, still smiled, still functioned. But underneath, something was crumbling. I wanted to curl up in a corner of the universe where I couldn't feel anymore. Where I could stop failing at life.

I was exhausted by my own inner critic, that harsh, moralistic voice that insisted I wasn't good enough, that I didn't try hard enough, that I should be stronger. I didn't have the language back then to name it. I only knew the shame. The soul-wearying shame of not being able to "snap out of it," of needing help, of feeling weak.

I'd lived my life by a spiritual script that said, "If you follow God, you'll be filled with joy." But when joy vanished and heaviness settled in, I turned the blame inward. Something must be wrong with me. Something unfixable. I was defective, emotionally untrustworthy, spiritually failing. That was the voice I heard in the dark, not God's voice, but I didn't know the difference yet.

I'd banish my shadow self, the part of me that felt afraid, ashamed, inadequate, into exile. I didn't want her to speak. I certainly didn't want God to see her. I thought healing would come through striving, through getting it right, through pretending I was fine. But the more I silenced the parts of me that were broken, the louder they cried for mercy.

Some might call it depression. Others would say spiritual oppression. I think it was both, a tangled knot of emotional pain, spiritual confusion, and shame woven through my nervous system. My body had absorbed messages long before my adult brain could reinterpret them. Messages like those mentioned earlier: You're too much. You're not enough. You don't belong. When you believe those lies deeply enough, you stop looking outward for rescue. You turn on yourself.

Suicide is the ultimate act of shame and self-loathing, a devastating expression of hopelessness and despair. Those who've never faced the will to die may struggle to understand the intensity of this inward collapse. But for those of us who have stood on that edge, or love someone who has, it is not about a desire to kill oneself. It is the aching belief that one's continued existence is a burden to others. That the kindest act is to disappear. To "relieve" the world of one's presence.

The following anonymous piece captures this torment in haunting beauty. It gives voice to the unspeakable, not to glorify it, but to help others understand the unbearable weight that can lead someone to such a final choice:

Goodbye my dear loved ones.
Shall I spend 2 years hugging each of you goodbye?
No it suffocates and stunts and binds
And anyway, I must go.
And anyway, I must go.

I cannot stay now.
I am empty, ashamed, hollow, and dead already.
The death in me already smells.
I can see your noses wrinkling at the stink and I love you all too much
to cause you such discomfort.

Do not shake your heads and say too bad.
This is best.
Those of us who do this really understand how broken we are; menaces.
This is my public duty.
It's a favour to you all.

Exhale relief: one less broken life to cope with.
Lift your hands and praise your Lord who has given you all life.
I will bow before Him and beg - my eyes down.
Should He lend me His hand to stand I will sing a new song.
If not, I will crawl ever downward from his presence understanding why.

What strikes me most in these words is not death, but longing. The longing to be free from the shame of one's own existence. The longing to be seen, cleansed, made whole. Even in the imagined presence of God, there is no expectation of embrace, only begging, crawling, hoping for mercy. This is what shame does. It doesn't just accuse, it isolates, condemns, and convinces you that even God wouldn't want to look you in the eye.

But here's the truth I'm still learning to hold with trembling hands: Jesus *does* look us in the eye. He doesn't turn away from our stench or shame. He touches lepers, lifts faces and enters locked rooms where despair has settled in like dust. He comes not with condemnation, but with scars of His own. Scars that speak of a suffering love, a love that joins us in the pit and refuses to leave us there.

I remember asking God: *Why do I feel so invisible? Why does no one see me?* But I didn't expect an answer. I didn't think I was worth one. What I couldn't yet see was that the ache itself was a kind of prayer. A longing to be known, held, restored. I didn't yet know that Jesus meets us in the dark. That He walks into locked rooms without knocking. That He doesn't despise our weakness but carries it, as His own. But something in me still longed for that kind of love. And maybe that's where Love enters the fracture.

The Silent Battle for the Soul

Depression often takes root in a shame-bound soul, weaving itself into the very fabric of one's being. For those who have never experienced it, clinical depression is difficult to describe. It is a dark, oppressive place of alienation and fragmentation, a liminal space caught between anger and grief yet marked by an unrelenting and inarticulate longing.

In this desolate place, the weight of life's losses pressed heavily upon me, yet shame whispered that I was too insignificant to grieve. I told myself: *"Doesn't everyone experience loss? What makes mine special?"* I convinced myself that my pain was unremarkable, that my suffering did not deserve acknowledgment.

But the greatest loss was one I could not name, let alone grieve: the loss of myself. Somewhere deep down, I had come to believe I was unworthy of existence, that deprivation and emotional abandonment were somehow deserved. Without realizing it, I had placed more faith in my capacity to fall than in God's power to lift me. That misplaced trust left behind an aching void, an unrequited ache that no effort seemed able to soothe.

Unanswered Questions

Curiously, telling this story now feels like describing someone else's life. That anguished, shame-bound woman is almost unrecognizable to me. Depression no longer defines or enslaves me, and it is this transformation that fuels my conviction that no one is beyond healing. Change is always possible.

Yet my experience left me with deep questions: *Why does depression strike? How does it manifest? And more importantly, what heals it?* What if depression is not simply a disorder, but a kind of spiritual and emotional signpost, pointing us toward unmet needs and long-overdue changes?

Although depression is treatable, reaching out for help often feels insurmountable. The ache can spiral into despair, convincing the sufferer that life will never improve and that the longings of their heart will never be met. In those moments, giving up can seem like the only way out.

This leads me to wonder: Is there a Biblical understanding of depression and its healing? Are there differences in how depression affects men and women? How does stress contribute? What role does loss play in its onset? And can depression become a sacred invitation to deeper healing and spiritual transformation?

Bio-Medical Insights into Depression

To begin with, it's important to acknowledge that clinical depression often requires medical attention. There are biochemical aspects that respond well to medication, particularly when combined with counselling. At its worst, depression can be so debilitating that a person can't function or even engage meaningfully in therapy. Medication can be a vital first step, bringing stability so that healing work can begin.

Unfortunately, some Christians reject psychiatric medications out of fear or misunderstanding, assuming mental illness is purely spiritual and should be treated solely with prayer and faith. But I believe deeply that a person can live a life of profound faith while also receiving psychiatric support.

Think of it this way: if a car runs out of power steering fluid, we might stop and pray, but we also refill the fluid or call for help. Likewise, when the brain is depleted of serotonin or other neurotransmitters, replenishment through medication can be a practical, even faith-filled, response to stewarding the body God has entrusted to us.

The fallout from COVID-19 left many vulnerable to depression. While genetic predisposition plays a role, environmental stress and loss, especially widespread during the pandemic, are often the catalysts.

Although depression is a normal part of grief, sometimes sadness deepens into something more persistent and misaligned, signalling that something inside us needs tending.

Responses to Depression

Tragically, those in helping roles, whether therapists or clergy, sometimes miss the deeper dynamics of depression. As Jones (1989) notes, therapy and religion often default to dispensing information, assuming that enlightenment alone leads to healing. But offering *"menu cards"* of insight to someone starving for emotional connection misses the point. Telling someone about *"the divine"* doesn't fill the soul any more than saying *"filet mignon"* satisfies a hungry belly.

This raises an important question: *What if depression is not a dead-end but a signpost, pointing us toward the parts of our lives that need healing, connection, and restoration?* What if the ache of depression, rather than something to flee, holds the potential to become redemptive? To that end, perhaps these questions might help guide our reflection:

1 Are there gender differences in how depression strikes us?

2 How is stress related to those gender differences?

3 What is learned helplessness, and how does it shape our experience of depression?

4 Can depression be understood through a biblical lens?

Each question opens a pathway toward deeper understanding, psychologically, practically, and spiritually. While this chapter will explore the first three, the final questions around a biblical perspective on depression will be gently unfolded in the chapter to come.

Are There Gender Differences in How Depression Strikes?

It's important to recognize that gender differences are general trends, not universal rules. Yet the impact of hormones on mood and mental health does seem to contribute to the prevalence and expression of depression in men and women.

Hormonal Influences

Before puberty and after menopause, men and women show similar risk levels for depression, which suggests that the hormonal fluctuations of a woman's reproductive years significantly contribute to increased vulnerability.

Gendered Expressions of Depression

Research by Piccinelli and Wilkinson (2000) highlights striking differences in how depression typically manifests in men and women:

- Men tend to blame others; women often blame themselves.
- Men may act out their depression; women internalize it.
- Men often express irritability or hostility; women are more likely to cry.
- Men may attack; women may withdraw.
- Men turn to distractions (for example, sport); women turn to friends.
- Women generally feel sadness; men may display anger.
- Women "feel" their depression; men "act it out."

This means male depression is often misdiagnosed or missed entirely, especially when it appears as anger, addiction, or aggression.

Different "Types" of Depression in Women

McEvoy, Payne, and Osbourne (2018) argue that what we label as *"depression"* may in fact be multiple distinct experiences or *"broken parts"* that present similar symptoms. For some women, hormonal shifts may be the primary cause, while for others, trauma, genetics, or social stressors may play the greater role. This highlights the need for personalized, compassionate care.

Estrogen and Women's Mental Health

Estrogen has a powerful effect on mood. Drops in estrogen, during PMS, postpartum, or perimenopause, can destabilize emotions for many women. These hormonal fluctuations don't affect all women equally, but for some, they're a significant factor in depressive episodes.

Testosterone and Depression in Men

By contrast, testosterone doesn't seem to have the same direct influence on male depression. Instead, men's experience of depression is shaped more by psychological, social, and behavioural dynamics.

Women: Disproportionately Affected

Globally, women are about twice as likely to experience depression as men (Gregory, 2018). This disparity is attributed to a complex mix of factors, hormonal, biological, psychological, and social, including abuse, gender-based oppression, and the internalization of suffering.

Interestingly, this pattern doesn't hold across all cultures.

A Global Perspective

In Amish and Orthodox Jewish communities, the rates of depression among women are much lower. Why? Rutz and Rihmer (2009) suggest several reasons:

1. **Emotional Expression:** Men are encouraged to express emotion, reducing repression.
2. **Social Support:** Strong familial and community ties act as protective buffers.
3. **Valued Roles:** Women's domestic roles are honored, which may foster identity and purpose.

These insights point to the importance of social connection, community meaning, and emotional freedom as buffers against depression.

How is Stress Related to Gender Differences in Depression?

Stress and depression often dance together. Stress can trigger depression, and depression can make us more vulnerable to stress. The sources of stress, external (for example, COVID-19, job loss) or internal (for example, shame, fear of failure), all place demand on our systems.

Understanding Stress

Stress is the mind-body's response to threat or demand. It can be positive (eustress) or negative (distress). Chronic stress, however, leads to overstress, in which the body can no longer return to a state of balance. Over time, this wears down both physical and emotional resilience.

Warning Signs

Stress and depression often manifest together with:

- Persistent overwhelm or hopelessness
- Physical symptoms like fatigue or digestive issues
- Emotional lability - irritability, anxiety, sadness
- Behavioural shifts - withdrawal, procrastination, unhealthy coping (for example, overeating, substance use)

Gender and Coping Styles

Men and women tend to cope with stress differently.

- **Women:** More likely to ruminate and use "tend-and-befriend" strategies, seeking connection and forming alliances (Brent et al., 2013).
- **Men:** More likely to distract, suppress emotions, or act out through aggression or avoidance.

What is Learned Helplessness?

Martin Seligman's concept of *learned helplessness* (1991) provides a powerful lens through which to understand the psychological effects of perceived powerlessness. His research showed that individuals repeatedly exposed to uncontrollable and painful circumstances often come to believe they are helpless, which deeply affects their emotions, thoughts, and behaviours.

Participants who developed learned helplessness believed that negative events would persist, affect every area of life, and were somehow their fault. They were more prone to depression, achieved less, suffered more physical ailments, and gave up easily. Their language reflected this mindset, they spoke in absolutes: *"always," "never," "everything," "nothing."*

But not everyone responded this way. One in three participants demonstrated resilience. Instead of collapsing under adversity, they maintained a sense of personal power and hope. Their language reflected a more flexible mindset, words like *"sometimes"* and *"this situation."* These individuals experienced better emotional and physical well-being, including stronger immune systems and higher motivation.

Locus of Control

Seligman's research also illuminates the idea of *locus of control,* the degree to which people believe they have power over events in their lives. Those with an **internal** locus of control tend to see themselves as responsible and capable of influencing outcomes. Those with an **external** locus often feel at the mercy of fate, others, or unchangeable circumstances.

People who develop learned helplessness often internalize failure and blame themselves. This self-blame erodes self-esteem and fosters self-dislike. In contrast, those with a hopeful, optimistic style externalizes setbacks without losing their sense of self-worth. They may acknowledge pain or difficulty, but they don't let it define them. Seligman observed that *hope is shaped by how we explain negative events*. Those who believe that adversity is specific and temporary, rather than global and permanent, are far more likely to remain hopeful.

When Learned Helplessness Becomes a Default

For much of my life, learned helplessness was my default response to adversity. When overwhelmed, I collapsed inward, emotionally and physically, shutting down, withdrawing, and feeling victimized. One example stands out vividly.

After returning from India some years ago, depleted and weary from intensive ministry, we were thrown into a painful family conflict. My daughter and her husband were at odds, and the emotional fallout was immense. Instead of supporting them from a healthy place, I felt drawn into the conflict in a way that felt punishing and overwhelming. I longed for my daughter to see my fragility, to care for *me,* but instead, I felt accused and emotionally ambushed.

I spiralled into helplessness: feeling hopeless, stuck, powerless, and persecuted. Old agreements surfaced instantly, like deeply carved grooves in my soul: *This always happens to me. Poor me. I have no right to express my needs. I will always be hurt and abandoned in close relationships.* And so, I disappeared, emotionally shut down, unreachable to those who love me. My husband, ever the gentle comforter, longed to reach me, but I had hidden myself away. It's what I do to survive, retreat deep within myself to recover from emotional shattering.

It took two months, and an angry confrontation with my son, for me to finally hear God whisper: *This isn't just about the current situation. This is about your default response to adversity.* That moment became a turning point. I began to see how learned helplessness, a destructive response, was really a spiritual stronghold, one God longed to dismantle in me.

Closing Thoughts

As we've explored throughout this chapter, depression is not merely a collection of symptoms or a set of biological markers; it is intricately bound up with our emotional, cognitive, and spiritual lives. Our response to life's hardships, especially when it feels like we're drowning, shapes how we see ourselves, how we relate to others, and even how we perceive God's presence.

Depression can feel like the slow suffocation of the soul, a grey mist that dulls joy, obscures meaning, and leaves us groping for a light we cannot see. And yet, even here, in this aching place, God does not abandon us. He is the One who bottles our tears, who sits with us in the dust, who speaks not in thunder, but in the still, small voice that reminds us: we are not alone.

Scripture does not shy away from sorrow; it gives voice to it. The Psalms cry out with raw anguish. The prophets grieve with broken hearts. Jesus

Himself weeps and sweats blood. The ache of depression is not a failure of faith. It is often a cry of the heart that dares to feel deeply in a fractured world. And if we let it, that ache can become the very thing that draws us back to the arms of the One who holds our sorrow and will one day wipe away every tear.

The notion of learned helplessness offers a profound lens through which to understand how we internalize suffering. When adversity strikes again and again, we begin to believe nothing will ever change, that we are powerless to alter our circumstances or even ourselves. But this mindset is not our destiny. Though deeply ingrained, these patterns are not permanent. What we have learned, we can unlearn, through grace, through reflection, and through the transforming power of God's love.

When I reflect on my own journey with learned helplessness, especially those moments when I've slipped back into old patterns of emotional collapse, I see a painful truth: it is often easier to retreat into familiar lies than to risk the vulnerability of healing. And yet I see a deeper truth too: that God is relentless in His pursuit of our restoration. He does not scorn us for our brokenness. Instead, He meets us there, with gentleness, patience, and an invitation to step out of the shadows and into His care.

Martin Seligman's research on resilience speaks profoundly into our spiritual lives. In contrast to those who succumbed to helplessness, resilient individuals believed adversity was temporary and could be navigated. They refused to surrender their sense of agency to their circumstances. In the same way, God invites us to reclaim our agency, not in isolation, but in co-labouring with Him in the work of renewal.

There will be times when we feel overwhelmed, when the darkness closes in, and hope feels far away. But even in those moments, we are invited to remember Jesus' words: *"Take heart, I have overcome the world"* (John 16:33). This is not a platitude. It is a promise, a deep, steadying truth we can hold onto in the storm. Our helplessness is never the final word. The cross stands as eternal proof that even in our deepest suffering, redemption is possible.

This chapter has shown us that depression, while complex and often debilitating, is not beyond hope. The journey from helplessness to healing is neither easy nor quick. It demands courage, vulnerability, and most of all, a deep trust in God's unfailing grace. As we begin to recognize and gently deconstruct our learned helplessness, we uncover a liberating truth: that in Christ, we are never beyond the reach of His redeeming love.

The path to healing is rarely linear, and it is never without pain. But it is a path that leads toward freedom, a freedom that restores our capacity to feel, to love, to hope, and to live fully once again. God meets us in our despair. But He never leaves us there.

In the next chapter, we'll turn more intentionally to Scripture and explore what the Bible reveals about depression. Through the stories of biblical figures who walked through deep sorrow, we'll discover a God who does not recoil from our pain but enters into it with us. *From Despair to Hope* invites us to see depression not as a spiritual failure, but as the very place where God's compassion meets our humanity, and where hope begins to rise.

Declarations

I declare that I am not bound by the limitations of learned helplessness. My identity is shaped by the love and power of Christ, who heals and restores every broken part of me.

I declare that I am not defined by my circumstances. I am more than a conqueror in Christ Jesus, who strengthens me in the midst of trials.

I declare that I will no longer be trapped by the cycles of despair and helplessness. With God's help, I will rise above my struggles and find hope in the darkest of times.

I declare that each step forward is a step toward freedom. I trust in God's promises of restoration, and I am empowered to live in the fullness of His grace and truth.

Prayer

Father God, Thank You for Your love and faithfulness. I surrender my heart, my thoughts, and my struggles to You. Help me to recognize the patterns of learned helplessness in my life and to replace them with Your truth and power. May Your healing touch restore every broken part of me, and may I find strength in Your promises. I choose to trust in Your ability to transform my pain into purpose. Fill me with hope, peace, and a renewed sense of power through Your Spirit. In Jesus' name, Amen.

Reflection Questions

1. In what areas of my life have I experienced learned helplessness?
2. How has this mindset impacted my emotional and spiritual well-being?
3. What lies or false beliefs have I internalized during difficult times that contribute to feelings of powerlessness or defeat?
4. How can I shift my perspective from seeing adversity as permanent to viewing it as temporary and changeable with God's help?
5. In what ways can I embrace the truth of my identity in Christ to combat feelings of helplessness and hopelessness?
6. How does my understanding of God's sovereignty influence my ability to trust Him through difficult circumstances?

Journal Prompt

Write about a time when you felt powerless or overwhelmed by a situation. Reflect on your emotional and spiritual responses. Let your pen move without censoring. See what flows out

CHAPTER 3

What is Depression Trying to Tell Me?

"There are wounds that never show on the body that are deeper and more hurtful than anything that bleeds."
~ Laurell K. Hamilton, Mistral's Kiss

"I waited patiently for the Lord; he turned to me and heard my cry." ~ Psalm 40:1

"The Lord hears his people when they call to him for help. He rescues them from all their troubles. The Lord is close to the brokenhearted; he rescues those whose spirits are crushed." ~ Psalm 34:17-18

From Shame to the Silence Within

Shame and depression are close companions. Where shame shouts, *There's something wrong with me,"* depression often whispers, *"There's nothing left of me."*

In the previous chapter, I described a triggering incident with my granddaughter that unearthed layers of generational shame. Shame has a voice, loud, condemning, relentless. But depression can feel like silence. It muffles joy, flattens emotions, and wraps life in a fog of meaninglessness. Shame that doesn't just sting but sinks into the soul. But even before that moment, before I had the language of shame or trauma, there was already a sadness in me that I didn't know how to name. It came early in life, silently, like a shadow.

I was too young to understand it, too well-behaved to express it, and too ashamed to ask for help. On the outside, I seemed capable and bright. But inside, I often felt hollow, like something vital was missing. There were days when life felt overwhelming, and I remember wondering, even as a teenager, *What's the point? Would anyone really notice if I disappeared?*

I never planned to end my life, but the ache was real, a quiet despair that made me feel both invisible and too much at the same time. Looking back, I can see how closely depression and shame were intertwined, each reinforcing the other, feeding me lies about my worth, my belonging, and even my right to feel.

This chapter is born from that ache, not as a clinical manual, but as a soul-deep reflection on what happens when sadness loses its way. Depression doesn't always look like despair. Sometimes it wears a smile. Sometimes it's highly functional. But underneath the surface, it is draining life drop by drop. I want to explore how depression can take root, especially in the lives of those who carry hidden wounds, and how it can drive even people of deep faith to the edge of hopelessness.

And yet, even there, even in the silence, God does not turn away. This is also a chapter about presence, not our strength to rise, but God's faithfulness to stay

Biblical Concepts of Depravity and Dignity

There is mystery in depression, but also a growing body of understanding, both theological and psychological. From a biblical perspective, depression can often be understood as a problem of misplaced dependency.

A healthy Christian holds a dual awareness of both depravity and dignity. In depression, however, there is often little awareness of either. Depravity reminds us of the sin that permeates all human life, we are all flawed, broken by the Fall. But dignity affirms our inherent worth as image bearers of God. In Christ, our dignity is restored; we are beloved, chosen, and empowered to live in dependent relationship with God, serving others with sacrificial love.

Earlier chapters explored the call of Mark 12:30-31:

> *"Love the Lord your God with all your heart and with all your soul and with all your mind and with all your strength... Love your neighbor as yourself. There is no commandment greater than these."*

Our fundamental starting point for loving God and others is not duty, but delight, God's own delight in us. This awareness of divine dignity often brings with it a deepened awareness of our depravity, the unearned nature of such love. But when dignity is missing or diminished, we lose sight of who we are in Christ. And this is often at the heart of depression: the absence of true identity, the pain of perceived worthlessness.

Depression becomes a core commitment to protect oneself from the unbearable pain of lost dignity, the belief that *"I have no value."* As Alan Jones (1989, p. 5) observed, *"When we forget our true worth, we forget where it comes from."* Sin becomes a sneaky way of forgetting how amazing we truly are in God's eyes. It tricks us into thinking we have to build and prove our own identity, to become our own *"soul-makers."* This burden is overwhelming. Ironically, even religious performance can become a way of forgetting, as the church sometimes encourages self-made righteousness in place of resting in God's grace.

The Desert Symbol

In Scripture, the desert often symbolizes trial, testing, and abandonment. In contrast, water, especially fresh, flowing, living water, represents God's grace, healing, and renewal (May, 2007, p. 119). Fresh water transforms barren wastelands into vibrant gardens. In Jeremiah 2:13, God laments, *"My people have committed two sins: they have forsaken me, the spring of living water, and have dug their own cisterns, broken cisterns that cannot hold water."*

A Personal Reflection

During my own depression, I found myself seeking fullness from *"broken cisterns"* - empty wells that held no water. I longed for others to affirm my worth, or for achievements to validate me. But I did not trust God to fill me as I worshipped and served.

Ironically, this relentless pursuit of self-protective autonomy led me to the very loss of dignity I feared. I was full of longing yet pushed in directions that left me empty. I became dependent on outcomes and people to define my value. When they inevitably fell short, because they were never meant to carry that burden, I experienced deep anger and rejection.

Over time, I came to see that these strong reactions were repetitions of early wounds: experiences of emotional withdrawal, unmet needs, and loss, especially the early emotional withdrawal of my mother. In a perfect world, I would have grieved that loss and turned to God for comfort. But I developed survival strategies: dogged efforts to earn validation and love. These efforts only deepened the emptiness.

I believe God's judgment in this was not punitive, but revelatory, allowing me to be turned over to my own resources so I could finally see the futility. I entered a dark place where nothing satisfied and where I felt no relational impact. As poet W. H. Auden (cited in Mendelson, 2007, p. 353) wrote, *"The garden is the only place there is, but you will not find it until you have looked for it everywhere and found nowhere that is not a desert."*

Anger, Misplaced Dependency, and Guilt

Even Freud (1917) recognised that hidden anger, often directed at God, underlies many depressive states. I've come to believe that anger lies at the heart of depression. Not only anger, but misplaced dependency.

In the darkness, I believed: *"He has not made my world come through to affirm my dignity. Therefore, I have none."* I was counting on my world to validate me, and when it didn't, I despaired. This wasn't appropriate grief; it was a distorted despair. I felt self-protective anger, even in my depressive thoughts: *"I have no value because of the way people treat me."*

Guilt also plays a powerful role in depression. Malan (1979) observed the inner conflict between love and hate, especially toward those we depend on. This conflict creates guilt, "Most frequently due to buried hostility against someone who is also loved" (p. 122). This love-hate tension sounds like: *"I love this person because I need them. But I hate them because they don't give me what I need. I can't express that anger, so I turn it inward."*

During my depression, I unconsciously defended against these unacceptable feelings. I couldn't tolerate anger toward those I depended on, whether in the present or the past. This repression caused anxiety and reinforced the depressive cycle (Malan, 2019).

Misplaced Dependency

Coming to understand misplaced dependency as central to my depression was like turning on a light in the dark. For years, I was trapped in patterns I couldn't name. But once I could see the dynamics clearly, my relationship to depression began to change. Arieti and Bemporad (1978, p. 307) offered insight into why I felt so disappointed and trapped:

> *"The depressive has had a narcissistic, need-fulfilling involvement with others... People have been important only to the extent that they could give praise or absolve guilt. There has never been an attempt to appreciate others as people in their own right...*
>
> *All their efforts are directed at the effect it will produce in others... They search for someone who can function as a surrogate source of self-esteem and absolve their guilt... bestowing this other with magical powers, modifying their own behavior to please them."*

This describes the exhausting cycle I lived in. At its core, depression isn't merely sorrow; it's a mix of displaced anger, distorted guilt, and a desperate hunger for affirmation from broken sources.

Closing Thoughts

Self-interest can be a good thing; it's part of taking care of yourself. But for someone who's depressed, self-interest often turns into pride. Not the kind of pride that makes you boastful, but the kind that comes from being entirely wrapped up in your own unmet needs and longings. It's a fixation on how others should come through for you. This mindset is the opposite of the joy Jesus describes - the kind that comes from giving yourself away.

At its core, depression seems to say: *"I love [this person] because I desperately need them, but I also hate [this person] because I feel trapped by my dependence on them for the approval I crave."* It's a heartbreaking cycle: *"I can't handle the shame of needing them so much or the guilt of resenting them when they don't meet my needs. I can't let myself get angry at them, so I turn that anger inward and direct it at myself."*

To put it simply, depression thrives on this dependent search for worth, whether it's through another person or some kind of achievement. But here's the hard truth: this constant striving is exhausting and self-consuming. Everything becomes about earning approval or recognition, and nothing feels like a genuine choice. When the approval doesn't come or the achievement falls short, despair sets in, and giving up feels like the only option.

Declarations

I declare that You, Jesus, are the Source of Living Water. I renounce my agreements with the enemy that I must look for life in my relationships or achievements.

I declare that I will turn to You, Jesus, in trust and dependence.

I declare that the bondage and power of depression is broken in my life.

I declare that I will live abundantly in the joy of Your presence through the power of the Holy Spirit.

I declare LORD, that You will restore my wasted years and my wasted efforts, in Jesus' name.

Prayer

Heavenly Father, I declare healing of depression over myself in the name of Jesus. Lord, You are my only true Source of Living Water. You are my good Father. Lord, You have given me a spirit of power and of love and of a sound mind. May courage flow from within me. May inner strength and self-control flow from within me, in Jesus' name I pray.

You promise to keep me perfect peace as I stay my mind on You. So, Lord, I pray that depression no longer has any dominion over my mind. I refuse to fear. I refuse despair and I lose the wrong thinking patterns behind my depression; in Jesus' name I pray.

Father, your thoughts towards me are thoughts and plans for my welfare and peace. I fix my mind on You and Your Word. I have the mind of Christ. I hold in my body, mind, and soul the thoughts feelings and purposes of Your heart. Lord, guide me along the paths I am to take every day.

Lord, I ask that now You will help me to lean into who I am in Christ. I rise from the ashes of defeat and depression. To become alive in You. From now on I want to radiate the glory of God and serve others from this place. In Christ I have been set free from every evil work. The joy of the Lord is my strength; in Jesus' Name I pray. Amen.

Reflection Questions

1. What role does your deep, unfulfilled longing or thirst play in turning away from the true source of Living Water?
2. How do you look to others or external circumstances for fulfillment?
3. In what ways can your self-interest be a positive thing, and how does it become distorted into pride for you?
4. How does your focus on unmet needs and a reliance on others for validation become a form of pride that undermines the joy Jesus describes?
5. How does depression create a cycle of love and resentment toward others, particularly when your worth and approval are tied to someone else's actions?
6. How does your depression thrive on a dependent search for worth, whether through other people or achievements, and what is the ultimate outcome of this pursuit for you?

Journal Prompt

Can you recall a time, early or recent, when you felt a quiet sadness settle over you? What were the thoughts, sensations, or beliefs that came with it? Without judging or fixing, gently name what was present in that moment.

CHAPTER 4

Buried Grief

"Grief can be a burden, but also an anchor. You get used to the weight, how it holds you in place."
~ Sarah Dessen, The Truth About Forever

"Life is full of grief, to exactly the degree we allow ourselves to love other people."
~ Orson Scott Card, Shadow of the Giant

"Blessed are those who mourn, for they will be comforted." ~ Matthew 5:4

Uncovering the Wounds We've Tried to Hide

Grief is a natural response to loss, yet it often doesn't unfold in predictable ways. Sometimes, it is buried so deep within us that we can no longer recognize it. We may think we've moved on, but beneath the surface, the grief remains, quietly shaping our thoughts, behaviours, and relationships. It shows up in unexpected moments, often triggered by memories, sights, or even small disappointments that seem disproportionate to the situation at hand.

In this chapter, I reflect on the grief we bury, whether from the loss of loved ones, the death of dreams, or unhealed wounds from the past. Buried grief can be isolating, leaving us feeling misunderstood or disconnected from others. Yet, it is often through acknowledging and facing this grief that we find healing. Together, we will journey through the layers of hidden pain, discovering how God's presence and healing grace can help us uncover and release the grief that has been silently weighing us down, offering a path to true freedom and restoration.

Ron's Story

Ron slumps heavily into the sofa as he begins to share his story. With each word, he sinks lower, his body folding in on itself until his gaze is fixed on the floor and his voice becomes little more than a mumble. His hopelessness feels tangible, almost contagious. Without realizing it, I find myself mirroring his posture, my shoulders rounding, my spirit absorbing the weight of his despair. But then I catch myself: *This is not your hopelessness; it is his.* I take a deep breath, straighten my spine, and ground myself, determined to stay present with him in his pain.

Ron is a remarkably gifted man. As he recounts his past, he speaks of his younger years in mission work, journeys that took him to some of the world's most dangerous places. On one particularly gruelling trip, he witnessed something that left an indelible mark on his soul: a grieving child trying to wake his dead mother. In that moment, something deep within Ron shattered. The suffering child inside him collapsed under the weight of that anguish, and he spiralled into a depression that would shadow his adult life.

His story is one of profound pain, yet even in the bleakest moments, there remains a flicker of hope. A possibility that healing and restoration are not beyond reach.

This chapter explores some of the deeper questions that arise when reflecting on the pain of depression:

- What triggers depression?
- How are loss and depression connected?
- Does early loss predispose someone to depression?
- Can depression truly be overcome?

What Triggers Depression?

As Ron's story illustrates, depression is often triggered not by the severity of an event itself, but by how it connects with internal wounds and longings. It might be a personal insult, a job loss, or the crumbling of a long-held dream. These events awaken deep, unconscious beliefs that whisper: *"Once again, the world confirms I have no worth, and there's nothing I can do to change it."*

Those caught in the grip of depression are not usually aware of the subtle strategies they use to have their needs met. Instead, they're painfully attuned to the aching absence of those needs. Ron was keenly aware of his longing for connection and affirmation. Yet beneath that longing was a belief seeded in early pain: *"I will always be left empty and alone, even by God. Does He really love me?"* Dan Allender (1999), in *The Cry of the Soul*, writes:

> *"...is a refusal to embrace loss as a deepening of the hollowness that makes more room for God... It flees to an illusionary safe harbor where, isolated, it holds onto whatever pleasure comes from the fantasy of non-existence."*

That illusionary harbor can seem safer than hoping again. Ron's despair became a shield, a way to protect himself from confronting his own sense of inadequacy. His self-image was stark: *"I see myself as garbage, having no value. I don't make any impact on the world. Life would be better if I were gone."*

Ron's anguish wasn't imagined. It was real and deep. Yet his story invites us to gently confront the lies that despair feeds on and to hold fast to the truth, that the God who formed us can fill even the hollowest places with His healing presence.

How are Loss and Depression Connected?

We live in a broken world, where none of us experience the fullness of Christ this side of eternity. Loss is part of that reality. But why do some people respond to loss with sadness and growth, while others spiral into depression?

Some psychologists suggest that depression can be understood as grief that has been bottled up, unfelt, unprocessed, and unreleased (Malan, 2019, p.118). And grief isn't always obvious. It doesn't only follow death or

visible tragedy. It can stem from the loss of a dream, a defence mechanism, or a sense of safety in relationships.

In my own experience with depression, I often felt quietly cheated by life. Helpless, especially in the face of relational loss. The world had let me down again, and I couldn't see a way forward. I had little awareness of how I might have subtly demanded or manipulated others to meet my needs. I simply absorbed the pain. My thoughts spiralled: *I'm of no value. I've lost my dignity. Nothing draws me anymore.* That spiral eventually led me into the dark cave of suicidal ideation.

Looking back, I can see how I internalized a core lie: *I have no strategy to regain what I've lost, so why try?* Depression became a place to retreat, a kind of temporary refuge. Ironically, it even gave me a fleeting sense of power. A way to say: *You've hurt me, and now I'll make you see it.* It brought attention, even pity, but not healing. Those small consolations only deepened the cycle and prevented me from confronting the deeper pain of loss.

In the realm of psychoanalysis, there's a compelling idea that depression isn't simply sadness, it's often a form of denied grief. A quiet shield we raise to protect ourselves from the unbearable weight of unmet longings and shattered dreams. Depression, then, becomes a survival strategy: it preserves a fragile psychological equilibrium, but at a steep cost. We trade away joy, spontaneity, motivation, and authenticity. We retreat from life to avoid disappointment, especially the painful risk of setting boundaries and reclaiming our sense of self.

True mourning is not just about feeling sad or reacting to emotional blows. It's a courageous and conscious process of facing the deeper wound beneath our triggers. Without this kind of intentional grieving, we remain trapped in a cycle of longing and disappointment, hoping, hurting, retreating, without resolution.

But there is hope. When we dare to grieve consciously, we begin to move through the numbness. We start to encounter clarity, connection, and healing. We stop merely surviving and begin to reclaim the life God still has for us, even in the aftermath of loss.

Understanding the Link Between Grief and Mental Health

Many researchers link early maternal loss to later depression (Malan, 2019). For a child to develop emotional health, they need to build trust, a core belief that *"There is a solid foundation outside of me I can rely on."*

A warm, accepting mother is central to that trust. One who delights in her child, responds with joy, holds them closely, and embodies emotional security. This doesn't foster selfishness, but freedom, the freedom to live without being absorbed in self-concern. But Ron's early years lacked this warmth. His mother was dutiful, self-sacrificing, and efficient, but emotionally distant. She struggled with intimacy, having learned through her own life that emotional closeness can lead to pain. As Ron moved from infancy into toddlerhood, his mother withdrew further, finding comfort in control and duty rather than closeness. Ron felt cared for but not deeply known or emotionally safe.

He came to see her as a kind of nanny in a starched uniform, present but disconnected. This early emotional absence left him with a silent, internal ache: *"I had something once... and now it's gone. I must not lose it again."* To cope, Ron developed patterns of deep dependency and subtle manipulation, strategies to try and regain what he'd lost. These patterns followed him into adulthood, showing up in anxiety, difficulty with intimacy, and depression. Yet understanding this helped Ron release shame and begin to heal. He began to see his pain not as failure, but as a cry from the child inside him, longing for connection.

Two Styles of Relating

Children respond differently to emotionally distant parenting, often falling into two broad styles of relating:

1. Early Loss During Dependency: The Manipulative and Dependent Style

If a typically nurturing mother withdraws early in life, the child may develop a dependent and manipulative style of relating. This child unconsciously believes: *"I can't perform well enough to win approval, but I have to find a way to get what I need."*

This style centres around earning love while avoiding disapproval. As Arieti and Bemporad (1978) describe, behaviour is shaped by two powerful drives:

- **Self-enhancing:** trying to regain what was lost
- **Self-protecting:** guarding against future loss

Every action becomes filtered through the lens of: *"What will others think? Will they love me, or reject me?"* The result is a child (and later, adult) trapped in an exhausting cycle of emotional survival.

2. Later Loss: The Performance-Oriented Style

If emotional withdrawal happens later in childhood, the child may shift into a performance-based identity. Their belief becomes: *"I am only worthy if I succeed."* These children often become hyper-responsible, trying to manage family conflict or live up to adult expectations. Arieti and Bemporad (1978) note that depressed children often carry the unspoken burden of making the family happy. They learn to gain approval not by being, but by doing.

Addiction to Dependency or Performance

- **Early loss** leads to an addiction to dependency, seeking connection through manipulation or emotional over-investment.
- **Later loss** fosters an addiction to performance, seeking worth through achievement and visibility.

Adult Loss

In adulthood, when we encounter loss, whether through disapproval, failure, or broken relationships, those early wounds get reactivated. We may not realize it, but we're no longer responding to just the present pain. We're reliving the old one.

What cuts deepest is not simply what we've lost, but what the loss seems to say about who we are. And yet, the pain of depression is not just a psychological pattern. It's real. It's valid. It reveals a soul still longing for healing.

The Courage to Grieve the Fantasy

In contrast to depression's numbing withdrawal, true grieving is an act of courageous confrontation, an intentional journey into our depths. It requires deep awareness and radical permission to feel. To express a full-bodied release of pain for the loss of a cherished fantasy: the dream of the perfect upbringing we needed, longed for, but never truly had.

This longing isn't foolish or naïve. It's deeply human. I hoped against hope not because I was stubborn, but because something in me knew how things should have been. The yearning for unconditional love, nurturing presence, and reliable guidance is imprinted into our very DNA. It appears across cultures. Somewhere inside, I held the hope that my Fairy Godmother would arrive, even if all I knew was the Wicked Witch.

Raised by emotionally unavailable and dysfunctional parents, my childhood became a swinging door between fantasy and reality. I caught glimpses of what could be, in a teacher, a friend's parent, or a storybook character, but they were only glimpses. The ache remained.

Through conscious grieving, I finally began to peel back the protective layers of denial and touch the rawness underneath. When I allowed myself to feel the full weight of that loss, I was no longer stuck in it but honoured it. Yes, it was sad. It was unfair. But it was what it was.

This grief asked me to surrender the fantasy, not as failure, but as freedom. I let go of the illusion of a perfect past and began to accept reality, and myself, as it truly is. I stopped demanding what could not be given, and in doing so, I reclaimed my energy, my boundaries, and my future.

And here's the paradox: once I truly grieved what could never be, a peace began to take shape. I realized that in mourning my unmet needs, I had done the brave work. In the quiet aftermath of weeping, I laid it all at the feet of Jesus, the sorrow, the longing, the ache that no earthly parent could soothe. I surrendered my grief to the only One who fully sees, fully knows, and fully loves. He did not turn away. He wept with me.

In that sacred exchange, I discovered something deeper than tenacity: I found rest. Not in answers, but in His presence. Understanding this sacred process of grief not only brings spiritual healing but also sheds light on the deep connection between grief and our mental health.

Can Depression Be Overcome?

Jesus reminds us of our complete dependence on Him: "Without Me, you are nothing" (John 15:5), and "Apart from Me, you can do nothing" (John 15:5; 16:4–6). These truths reveal that we lack the power to overcome the bondage of depression and the lies of the enemy on our own. Left to ourselves, we are powerless to break free.

But Scripture offers a profound contrast: "I can do all things through Him who strengthens me" (Philippians 4:13). Our strength and victory come not from ourselves but from Christ, who empowers us.

The Gentle Invitation of Jesus

In Matthew 11:28–30, Jesus extends a deeply personal invitation:

> *"Come to me, all who labor and are heavy laden, and I will give you rest. Take my yoke upon you, and learn from me, for I am gentle and lowly in heart, and you will find rest for your souls. For my yoke is easy, and my burden is light."*

Here, Jesus offers rest for the weary and burdened. He invites us to exchange our striving and despair for His gentle guidance and sustaining strength. In Him, we find the power to face depression, reject the enemy's lies, and discover the soul-rest we long for.

Treasures in Ruins

It has been said that "treasures are hidden in ruins" (Rumi, n.d.). In earlier times, gardens often featured a secluded, shaded corner meant for quiet reflection, a space to sit with sadness, confront the ache in the soul, and engage with the shadowed parts of our emotions. Today, we often avoid such introspection, distracting ourselves with social media, entertainment, and busyness.

But what if we embraced our sadness instead of trying to eliminate it? Imagine creating a sacred space, physical or emotional, where we could slow down, soften our hearts, and truly listen to the parts of ourselves that dwell in the shadows. Perhaps depression is less a problem to be solved and more a signal to rest, reflect, and reconnect with our souls.

A Twofold Cure: The Insight of Larry Crabb

This perspective echoes Christian psychologist Larry Crabb's understanding of a twofold cure for depression:

1. Awareness of our ungodly, self-serving beliefs and strategies.
2. Embracing our legitimate dignity.

This isn't just about clinical recovery; it's about soul restoration.

The Turning Point: Losing My Life to Find It

For me, healing began when I acknowledged both the depths of my sinfulness and my stubborn clinging to a false sense of dignity. Christ's teaching that "the path to life is to lose it" struck me profoundly. I saw how deeply entrenched my self-protective strategies were, how I had organized my life around demanding fulfillment on my own terms. Repentance came when I stopped chasing empty wells and turned to the Source of Living Water.

The turning point was recognizing my demand for life to come through for me and how my survival strategies kept me locked in self-preoccupation. For the depressed person, self-protection often takes the form of pride, a relentless focus on unmet longings. This is the antithesis of Jesus's call to joy, which invites us to give ourselves away. As Fyodor Dostoevsky wrote, "What is hell? I maintain that it is the suffering of being unable to love."

Misplaced Thirst

A depressed person is profoundly thirsty, often demanding that others or circumstances provide what they need to function: "You must come through for me; my life depends on it." This misplaced responsibility burdens others and resists the true Source of Living Water. Depression, at its core, is often a state of being dependently committed to finding fulfillment in the world, blind to the self-consuming nature of this pursuit.

Tribulation and loss are meant to cultivate patience and maturity. Yet in depression, if I recovered what I believed was lost, a job, a relationship, a sense of direction, my depression would lift, but for the wrong reasons. I might feel better, but I would miss the opportunity to grow. If my strategy succeeded, it would only reinforce denial and distorted thinking.

Strength in Surrender

True maturity comes when we lose what we depend on and are forced to reorient ourselves toward God. If we look closely, we can see incredible strength in depressed individuals, a tenacity to survive. But that strength is often misplaced, relying on external sources to provide life. A holy undoing unfolds when we surrender these dependencies and allow our losses to deepen our maturity and align us with God's purposes. As Maggie Young cries, "I am done looking for love where it doesn't exist. I am done coughing up dust in attempts to drink from dry wells."

Repentance and the Inner Child

My healing journey has been marked by both repentance and restoration. When I asked God's forgiveness for seeking life everywhere but in Him, I began to see my depression for what it truly was, a helpless cry from the little girl within me, longing for the love and connection she never received.

I think of my infant granddaughter. When she's hungry, she cries, protests, and sometimes seems to lose all control just to get my attention. If I were to respond with resentment or feed her in anger, I would inflict a wound far deeper than hunger. She would learn that those she loves cannot be trusted to come through for her, that she must face life alone. Is that the message I want to send? Absolutely not. I have infinite compassion for her helpless state.

Offering Compassion to Ourselves

So, what if I extended that same compassion to myself, to the desolate, hurting child within me? When the young, needy parts of me cry out for attention, do I really want to repeat the pain of the past by pushing them away with resentment or condemnation? No. I don't wish to perpetuate what was once done to me.

Instead, I choose to acknowledge and soothe that weeping child. To comfort and understand her. To listen with tenderness. And when I befriend that empty, vulnerable part of myself, I find myself falling to my knees, seeking from my Heavenly Father the love and connection I have always longed for. This is where true repentance and restoration begin.

Restored by the Compassion of God

Scripture reflects this recurring theme of renewal and healing: "Restore to me the joy of your salvation and uphold me with a willing spirit" (Psalm 51:12). "I will restore you to health and heal your wounds," declares the LORD (Jeremiah 30:17). In these promises, I'm reminded that God alone offers hope when everything else feels hopeless. He meets us in our helplessness, not with condemnation, but with infinite compassion and the power to restore what is broken.

Closing Thoughts

Depression can feel like an endless winter, a barren landscape where hope is buried, and joy feels like a distant memory. But even in the bleakest seasons, God does not abandon us. He draws near to the brokenhearted. He sits with us in the dust. He waits, not with impatience, but with tender love.

In my own journey, I've learned that healing doesn't come by fixing ourselves but by surrendering, by letting go of our strategies for survival and turning instead toward the gentle, unhurried presence of Jesus. He does not shame us for our sorrow. He does not reject us for our neediness. Instead, He calls us beloved. He enters our pain. He leads us, slowly, steadily, into life.

Depression may not disappear overnight, and the road to restoration is rarely linear. But it is holy ground. It is where we come to know the God who weeps with us, walks with us, and whispers to our souls, *"You are not alone."* And so we keep walking, imperfectly, sometimes falteringly, but always in the direction of light. We keep returning to the One who alone can restore our joy. The One who transforms our wounds into wellsprings. The One who makes all things new.

But what happens when even that light feels unreachable? When our prayers echo back in silence, and our souls feel too numb to respond? What happens when we, like Elijah, find ourselves under a broom bush, too weary to go on, begging God to take it all away?

In the next chapter, *Under the Broom Bush: Finding God in Desolation*, we'll enter the sacred story of a prophet who, in the depths of exhaustion and despair, encountered the tender care of God. His story is not just ancient history, it is a mirror for our own moments of collapse. Together, we'll explore what it means to be met by God not in strength, but in desolation, and how His gentle presence can begin to breathe life into the most withered places of our souls.

Declarations

I declare that I am no longer ruled by depression, emptiness and despair.

I declare, in the name of Jesus, healing and restoration of every broken, hidden part of my body, heart, mind, soul, and spirit where I have been trapped because of past trauma. I forgive the sins of those who first opened the door to the sin back in my family line.

I declare forgiveness over them for the effects their sin has had on me and release myself from every generational bondage.

I declare that I am filled with all the fullness of Christ to live an abundant life.

Prayer

"Lord, you know the hopes of the helpless. Surely you will hear their cries and comfort them" (Psalm 10:16-17). God I'm so aware of how limited my perspective is. I give You my eyes - would You show me what You see. I give You my limited understanding - would You give me Your Divine perspective? I give You my discouragement - would You give me Your hope?

O Christ Jesus,
when all is darkness
and we feel our weakness and helplessness,
give us the sense of Your presence,
Your love, and Your strength.
Help us to have perfect trust
in Your protecting love
and strengthening power,
so that nothing may frighten or worry us,
for, living close to You,
we shall see Your hand,
Your purpose, Your will through all things.
(By Saint Ignatius of Loyola)

Reflection Questions

1. How has your depression stemmed from a painful or seemingly insignificant event that struck at unresolved wounds within?

2. In what ways did early maternal loss play a significant role in shaping your depression, particularly by disrupting the development of basic trust?

3. What is your self-enhancing relational pattern, and how does it relate to striving to reclaim what was lost?

4. What was your self-protecting relational pattern that developed as a way of shielding yourself from further loss, and how does this affect your relationships?

5. How has loss experienced in adulthood reactivated earlier wounds, amplifying feelings of helplessness and pain

Journal Prompt

What is my soul trying to tell me through this sadness, and how might Jesus be inviting me to respond? Without judging or fixing, gently name what was present in that moment.

CHAPTER 5

UNDER THE BROOM BUSH

"You have to keep breaking your heart until it opens."
~ Rumi

"Only the heart that hurts has a right to joy."
~ Lewis Smedes

"A quiet voice asked, "So Elijah, now tell me, what are you doing here?" ~ God (1 Kings 19:13, MSG)

Finding God in the Wilderness of Despair

Elijah's story is one of triumph and struggle, of faith and doubt, of mountaintop victories and deep valleys of despair. After experiencing God's incredible power in defeating the prophets of Baal, Elijah finds himself fleeing for his life, overwhelmed by fear and exhaustion. It is in the wilderness, under a solitary broom bush, that he collapses in despair, praying for death.

In this chapter, we will journey with Elijah into the depths of his emotional and spiritual exhaustion. Under the broom bush, we witness a man at the end of his rope, yet it is in this very place of desperation that God meets him. The story of Elijah's encounter with God is a powerful reminder that even in our darkest moments, God is near, offering rest, renewal, and a fresh vision for the journey ahead. As we explore Elijah's experience, we will reflect on how we, too, can find God in the wilderness of our own despair, discovering that hope is often born in the most unexpected places.

Quieted By Love

It was the quiet that settled me. The sunlight filtered gently through the gum trees. A warm breeze stirred the air as I sat in the garden, listening to the soothing sound of the water feature trickling nearby. My granddaughter curled up next to me on the wicker chair, weary after a big day. She didn't speak. She didn't need to. I stroked her hair in slow, rhythmic movements and softly sang a tune from her baby days. Within minutes she was asleep, curled against my chest, her breathing deep and even.

There was something sacred in that moment, an intimacy beyond words. Her little body at rest in mine. Her nervous system regulated by my presence; her heart quieted by my song.

Across the table, a single pansy grew in a small pot. Its deep violet petals opened towards the sun, its centre forming the shape of a cross, a gift of beauty hidden in plain sight. In that peaceful garden moment, I felt strangely aware that I was being offered something more than a fleeting calm. There was healing here. A glimpse of God's tenderness that I didn't even know I needed.

Later that evening, a verse came to mind from Zephaniah 3:17:

"The Lord your God is with you,
he is mighty to save.
He will take great delight in you,
he will quiet you with his love,
he will rejoice over you with singing."

This verse had carried me through many seasons, but now it felt achingly personal. I realised I had not allowed myself to be quieted in God's love. I had not rested against his chest like my granddaughter had rested against mine. It had been too long since I felt held.

Even now, as I write, the ache returns. I've known the dark weight of despair. The numbness. The loss of motivation. The soul-weariness that lingers even after rest. It doesn't always come from a single cause. Sometimes it's the build-up of years, grief upon grief, responsibility upon responsibility, sorrow upon sorrow. There have been times I felt like joy had left me. Like I was barely functioning. Times I could not pray and barely believed. Sorrow and despair can rob us of memory, of who we are, of the God we once trusted, of the hope we once held. Elijah knew this too.

Elijah's Descent from Victory to Despair

Elijah's life took a dramatic turn, from a position of significant ministry and effectiveness in serving God to a state of fleeing for his life. He had recently prayed for rain, which broke a seven-year drought, a miracle that demonstrated God's power and faithfulness. Alongside this, Elijah had called down fire from heaven, leading to a national revival in Israel, with the people turning back to worship the one true God. In a powerful confrontation, he had executed 850 prophets of Baal, showcasing God's authority over idolatry.

However, after these monumental achievements, Elijah faced an ominous threat from Jezebel, the queen of Israel. Furious over Elijah's influence and the events that transpired, she vowed to kill him. This threat sent Elijah into fear, causing him to flee from his life of ministry and success into the desert.

Blindsided by Fear and Burnout

Instead of leaning into God's power, which he had just witnessed in spectacular fashion, Elijah was blindsided by fear. Jezebel's threat triggered a deep emotional crisis. Elijah, filled with fear and despair, fled into the desert, overwhelmed with thoughts of ending his life. Beneath a solitary broom tree, he collapsed, praying for death: *"I have had enough, Lord. Take my life..."* (1 Kings 19:4).

In his moment of complete exhaustion, Elijah poured out his heart to God:

> *"I have zealously served the Lord God Almighty. But the people of Israel have broken their covenant with you, torn down your altars, and killed every one of your prophets. I am the only one left, and now they are trying to kill me too" (1 Kings 19:10).*

How could he forget so quickly what he had just witnessed on the mountaintop?

God's Gentle Intervention

In his despair, God asked Elijah a profound question: *"What are you doing here, Elijah?"* (1 Kings 19:9). This inquiry wasn't a rebuke but an invitation for Elijah to shift his perspective, to see that God was still in control. God gently reminded Elijah that he was not alone in his struggles, there were seven thousand others in Israel who had remained faithful (1 Kings 19:16-17). This revelation not only comforted Elijah but also showed him that God was sovereign and had already prepared others to continue His work.

Instead of offering judgment, God extended care. *"Then he lay down and slept under the broom tree. But as he was sleeping, an angel touched him and told him, 'Get up and eat!'"* (1 Kings 19:5). Elijah's physical, emotional, and spiritual exhaustion required rest and nourishment, which God provided in abundance. Through this tender care, Elijah was reminded of his purpose and received the guidance necessary to continue on his journey.

The Question That Awakens: "What Are You Doing Here?"

When we find ourselves in desolate places, emotionally exhausted or overwhelmed by despair, God does not leave us there. Instead, He seeks us out, just as He sought out Elijah, to ask, *"What are you doing here?"* It is not a question of condemnation, but one that invites us to reflect on where we've been and where we need to go. In the depths of emotional and spiritual struggle, God calls us to look beyond our immediate pain and see His hand at work, even in our most difficult moments.

Elijah's journey from despair to hope was not instantaneous, but it was deeply transformative. God gently guided him, provided him with rest, and renewed his sense of purpose. This story reminds us that God's care for us is not just about miraculous interventions; sometimes it comes in the form of rest, nourishment, and a timely reminder of His sovereignty. We are not alone in our struggles, and God's presence is often most apparent in the quiet moments of restoration.

Meeting Us in Our Desolate Places

Just as God met Elijah in his desolation, He meets us in our own dark and hopeless places. Whether our despair is rooted in the weight of past trauma, spiritual exhaustion, or the overwhelming challenges of life, God is there. He does not condemn us for our brokenness; rather, He extends compassion and calls us back to Himself. The question, *"What are you doing here?"* is not about judgment, but about an invitation to move from isolation to community, from despair to renewal.

How Did Hope and Joy Find Me?

Reflecting on my own journey, I ask myself, how did hope and joy find me? The answer seems intertwined with the process of shedding everything that does not represent my true self. In many ways, emotional healing is about releasing false identities, the ones we construct as shields to protect us from pain and embracing the authentic truth of who we are in Christ.

This journey of self-discovery prompts me to reflect on the teachings of Jesus, who warns that we may gain the world but lose our soul in the process. True fulfillment cannot be found in external achievements or relationships, but in the alignment of our hearts with the truth of God's love and the values that shape our identity. As we shed our false selves, we make space for God to fill us with His joy, hope, and healing.

Emotional Healing in Sri Lanka

In a course I'm teaching in Sri Lanka focused on developmental attachment, we begin by sharing personal stories. By day two, many participants feel emotionally adrift, numb, lost, and distant from themselves. It's as if an unspoken pact has been made to avoid pain by shutting down desire. I recognize this emotional state; I've known what it is to grow cold and hard in an effort to stay safe. But I've also known the deep joy that comes with emotional healing.

A Story of Scars and Redemption

I share my own story, my journey from numbing to feeling, from surviving to healing. I want them to see a God who can take the worst parts of our story and somehow bring forth something redemptive. A God who transforms wounds into wisdom. As I stand before them, I let them witness my scars. Not as badges of shame, but as signs of healing in progress.

I acknowledge the truth we all live: Hurt people hurt people. But I also speak of the other truth, that healed people can become wounded healers. That our pain doesn't have to define us; it can shape us into vessels of hope.

One by one, they begin approaching me during the breaks, tentatively, with raw eyes and trembling voices, asking for a moment to talk. Their hearts are ploughed up and tender. Barry and I have shared honestly how our own wounds nearly destroyed us, how the enemy tried to take us out. But we've also shared the hope we now carry. They see it. And they want it.

I tell them that healing requires sitting with the pain a little longer. Not rushing past it, not numbing it, not pretending it doesn't matter. Because it's in this slow sitting that empathy is born. It's in this space that transformation begins. I tell them, *"Your mess will become your message."*

Childhood Photos and Sacred Names

On the final day, many participants have brought childhood photographs. I invite them to hold these images in their hands as we gather for prayer. We pray healing over those young, wounded parts of themselves. We pray they will renounce the old names, old messages, old self-talk that kept them bound. And we ask God to sing new names over them, names that breathe life, names that restore, names that reflect His original design.

Because that's what love does. It doesn't rush the breaking. It honours it. It brings wounds to the Healer. And in that sacred exchange, restoration begins.

A Picture Tells a Thousand Words

A young woman stands at the front of the room, holding a picture she's drawn. The room stills. The image is powerful: darkness on one side, light on the other. She has drawn herself standing in the light. Slowly, through tears, she shares how Jesus gently invited her to step out of the shadows and into His embrace. At first, she resisted, afraid to open her bruised heart again. But His invitation was steady. And eventually, she surrendered.

As she speaks, her tears flow freely. Her heart has cracked open, not in despair, but in love.

A Child's Betrayal

Another young woman steps forward, clutching her picture. Her voice shakes. The day before, she had shared the pain that shaped her life. She had grown up believing her father worked overseas. At ten, she accompanied her mother to a Buddhist temple. What happened next shattered everything she believed: in a moment of despair, her mother tried to stab the temple priest. She was restrained by monks, and in that chaotic moment, the girl discovered the truth, her father was a monk. A man whose children were never allowed to acknowledge him.

A flame of hatred ignited in her heart that day. And when her mother left to work abroad, promising to return, she was devastated. After two years, her mother came back, only to leave again. The abandonment was too much. Her heart shut down.

She tells us how she spiralled into depression, consumed by hatred and grief. But today, something has shifted. Over the past two days, Jesus has come for her heart. And she has let Him in. Her face shines. The darkness has lifted.

As she speaks, my tears spill over too. We lock eyes, both streaked with tears. And in that holy moment, we see one another, broken to broken, mended to mended. We are sisters now. Bound not by shared trauma, but by shared redemption. I will carry her with me always.

Reclaiming Worth

A man takes the microphone. His voice is low and humble. He speaks of the message of worthlessness that once took root in his soul. The despair. The self-contempt. And then, slowly, the shift. The small shoots of surrender, pushing up through hardened soil.

I tell him how brave he is. Brave to be seen. Brave to stop apologizing for who he is. Brave to silence the enemy's lies. For when we abdicate our true selves, we shut out the Lover of our souls. But in reclaiming his worth, he is swinging open the door to grace.

Others speak too. Their gratitude is real. And my heart swells. I see now how my former pain, my depression, my numbness, has become fuel for healing. For tending to this small corner of the world.

As I gather my things and tuck them into my suitcase, I gather my joy too. I'm going home full. Robert Alden's words echo again in my mind:

"There is not enough darkness in all the world to put out the light of even one small candle." Now I understand why I'm here.

Life Continually Robs Us of Our Expectations

The dynamics of depression often leave us wrestling with frustration, guilt, and a deep sense of loneliness and inadequacy, which can trigger a wide range of personal struggles. In our desire for relief, many of us search for a *"cookbook"* solution, a simple, step-by-step guide to follow until the problem is resolved. The longing for practical solutions sometimes leads us to reduce God's principles to mere techniques, driven by an underlying fear of failure.

We also tend to resist the hard work of deep reflection. We want quick fixes; answers we can apply immediately. A Christian blog on mental illness humorously captured this mindset: *"I like the part where Paul said he has a thorn in the flesh that God won't take from him. I think I have a thorn, it's people!"* This quip highlights how often we seek simple answers while avoiding the challenging, but necessary, work of building meaningful relationships. Healing from depression can never be reduced to a list of steps, it requires engagement: with us, with others, and with God. It's a process, one that calls for understanding, discernment, and wisdom.

Life, in its brokenness, continually robs us of our expectations. It reminds us that the most important things in life often resist our attempts to control them. Yet, it is often through our wounds that God speaks most profoundly to us. While acknowledging the need for medical intervention when it comes to biochemical or clinical depression, I resonate deeply with Richard Rohr's insight in *Broken and Blessed* (1987):

> *"Deep woundedness rarely fully disappears. It still hurts, you still remember it, and you often carry your hurts to your grave. There are great graces given, and the burdens are gone. But what I see is that when people pray through their hurts and pains, what goes away, or the grace that is given, is their power to destroy them and their power to let them*

> *destroy other people... The Godliest people I know are wounded healers. They carry great pain, but they've learned it is OK to have the wounds because somehow our wounds are our redemption."*

Our wounds, in the hands of God, become the places where we can experience deep healing and transformation. As we learn compassion for our own wounds, as we forgive ourselves and extend patience to our inadequacies, we draw closer to God. In this way, we understand the nature of mercy as we learn to be merciful to ourselves. The most profound healer, Nouwen points out, is the wounded healer. There's a mystery to owning our vulnerability.

We need to bring the dark parts of our souls before the Lord, surrendering them to Him for healing. This surrender often brings an awareness that we have a wound, even as it is healed. And we don't need to be afraid of our wounds, because they are the very things that remind us of our dependence on God. When we live under the illusion that we are not needy, we fall into the trap of false self-sufficiency.

Healing means that our wounds no longer define us. Depression no longer dictates our identity. It doesn't have the power to destroy us or others. Our strength is found not in the weight of our hardships or the scars they leave behind, but in our refusal to allow those hardships to determine who we are or who we become.

What Am I Doing Here?

After a restless night, I rose early and went to the local park, seeking some clarity in the quiet of the morning. Sitting among the trees, I began to reflect on my unmet expectations. I started to see these expectations not as a longing for deeper fulfillment, but as a way of avoiding further discomfort. My mind, weighed down by the effects of depression, revealed a painful truth: I had been consumed by self-preservation, by a need to shield myself from negative emotions, a tendency I had often criticized in others close to me.

I realized that healing is not about avoiding pain or discomfort, but about releasing those false safeguards and engaging with the reality of life and relationships. True brokenness stopped me in my tracks, preventing me from chasing after people and things for the wrong reasons. This led me to a period of immobilization, a necessary space to reflect and allow God to speak. At my lowest point, I could no longer rely on my own strength.

That surrender was the turning point; it marked the end of my self-sufficiency. In that moment, I confessed to God: *"I cannot control what matters most to me. It may never happen in this life."* Stripped of all my supports, I cried out, echoing Crabb (2005a): *"But God, what will I do with this pain?"* The terror of being unable to make life work felt like being torn apart.

But still, I clung to faith, a faith that anchors hope. Crabb (2005a, 2005b) identifies two possible responses when we realize, "I can't make it happen": 1) a pressure-driven effort to force outcomes, or 2) trust in God, which alleviates that pressure and frees us to give our best effort while depending on Him. As May (2007, p. 133) observes, when our usual supports are gone, we are left vulnerable. But in that vulnerability, we are more open to grace than ever.

For many, letting go of coping mechanisms is a profound struggle. Some abandon their families in search of fleeting pleasures; others leave ministry, convinced that Christianity is too burdensome. Malan (2019, p. 10) describes this as rejecting what we truly desire.

I realized I had a choice: to shut down my desires or to trust God, even without any guarantees of improvement (Crabb, 2005a). Choosing trust ignited a new passion in me. I found freedom and confidence in knowing that I had nothing to fear when I had nothing to lose. I learned to accept the uncertainty of life, recognizing that only God remains steadfast.

May (2007, p. 128) captures this paradox beautifully: "*Freedom is purest when our addictions have completely defeated us, leaving us with no choice. In this state of complete powerlessness, we actually have the most real power. There's nothing left to force us to make a choice. So, our choice becomes a genuine act of faith.*" In my surrender, I discovered the freedom to trust in God's grace, and through that trust, I experienced a deeper freedom than I had ever known.

Refuge in the Wilderness

In Hebrew tradition, the broom bush is a desert shrub that offers shade and symbolizes refuge in the wilderness. Under this tree, God sustained Elijah, offering him solace and protection. I too have experienced a growing awareness of God's presence and a deepening relationship with Him.

This awareness has fostered newfound perseverance and courage, helping me face life's challenges without succumbing to despair. I have learned that it's possible to endure pain without being overwhelmed by depression. This realization brings a profound sense of freedom, grounded in the unshakable assurance that nothing can separate me from God's love in Christ Jesus.

This freedom has released me from the need to prove myself, from the need to protect myself. I no longer demand immediate fulfillment or blessings from God. Instead, I seek to glorify Him and become a source of joy for Him and for others.

In response to depression, I came to a pivotal realization: *"God, I cannot demand anything from You. Forgive me for seeking fulfillment in others and in achievements instead of in You. Even if nothing changes, I will pursue You, because of who You are."* This shift in perspective deepened during my three months in Uganda, Africa.

As I've learned, true spiritual growth involves taking deeper and deeper risks. My time in Uganda was filled with ministry, teaching, counselling, and supporting others. It was a season of profound healing and grace, where I experienced beautiful co-creation with God. Through this journey, I learned that surrendering to Him and seeking His presence, even in uncertainty, leads to the deepest restoration and hope.

The Journey Home

I often ask myself that same question that God asked Elijah: *What am I doing here?* When despair lingers. When I feel lost in the fog. When joy feels far away. And then I remember: He comes to us in our exhaustion. He meets us when we've had enough. He sings over us. He quiets us with His love. He sends companions for the journey. He offers bread and rest and presence.

Depression is complex, layered with emotion, shame, exhaustion, spiritual struggle. But it does not disqualify us from God's care. In fact, it can become the very place where He meets us most tenderly.

I'm still learning to rest against His chest. To let Him hold me. To believe I am not alone.

Sometimes, this is where it turns when we remember who we are, and whose we are. Just like my granddaughter, curled up in the quiet of the garden, I am safe. And I am held.

Closing Thoughts

After a period of intense ministry, Elijah finds himself weary and deeply troubled. Fleeing from threats, he seeks refuge under the shade of a broom bush. In this moment of despair, God meets him and gently asks, *"What are you doing here?"* This question reflects God's compassionate desire to meet us in our brokenness and guide us toward restoration.

Rather than removing our wounds entirely, God often works to heal their destructive power, ensuring they no longer harm us or those around us. In the face of life's disappointments, we can take comfort in the promises of Isaiah 61:1–3, where God offers to exchange beauty for ashes, joy for mourning, and praise for despair. These transformative promises remind us of His unwavering commitment to bring healing and hope. But how do we begin to receive that healing? What does it look like to live into God's restoration, not just in moments of crisis, but in the quiet, ordinary rhythms of our lives?

In the next chapter, *Under the Mango Tree: Rest, Reflection and Restoration*, we'll explore the sacred invitation to slow down, to rest in God's presence, and to reflect on how our souls are being shaped. Like Elijah, we need spaces where we can pause, breathe, and be nourished, not only by physical food, but by God's gentle voice. Sometimes we begin to mend, not in the fire or the whirlwind, but in the stillness under a tree.

Declarations

I declare that though I have fallen, I will rise. Though I sit in darkness, You, Lord, are my light and will bring me into Your Light. You confront despair in my life, ensuring it won't prevail.

I declare that I have abundant life in Christ Jesus.

Prayer

Jesus is the Good Shepherd. Pray David's poetic praise to God in Psalm 23 (adapted from The Passion Translation):

You, Lord, are my best friend and my shepherd.
I always have more than enough.

You offer a resting place for me in your luxurious love.
Your track takes me to an oasis of peace, the quiet brook of bliss.

That's where you restore and revive my life.
You open before me pathways to God's pleasure
and leads me along in your footsteps of righteousness
so that I can bring honour to your name.

Lord, even when your path takes me through
the valley of deepest darkness,
fear will never conquer me, for you already have!
You remain close to me and lead me through it all the way.

Your authority is my strength and my peace.
The comfort of your love takes away my fear.
I'll never be lonely, for you are near.

You become my delicious feast
even when my enemies dare to fight.
You anoint me with the fragrance of your Holy Spirit;
you give me all I can drink of you until my heart overflows.

So why would I fear the future?
For your goodness and love pursue me all the days of my life.
Then afterward, when my life is through,
I'll return to your glorious presence to be forever with you!

Reflection Questions

1. Take a moment to become quiet in God's presence. Reflect on a previous experience when you felt a profound sense of closeness and connection to God. Dedicate a few moments expressing gratitude for that experience and acknowledging the aspects that you appreciate.

2. Subsequently, without self-judgment, allow yourself to become aware of your depression and/or despair in your current life. Quietly sit with God and observe the emerging emotions and thoughts.

3. Without judgment or attempting to resolve these issues immediately, invite God to reveal His perspective and desires.

4. Ask God to enter this space and communicate His will for you and Him to address these matters.

Journal Prompt

Reflect on a time when you felt broken or overwhelmed. How did God meet you in that moment, and what healing or transformation did you experience? Without judging or fixing, gently name what was present in that moment.

CHAPTER 6

Under the Mango Tree: Rest, Reflection and Restoration

"We must be willing to get rid of the life we've planned, so as to have the life that is waiting for us."
~ Joseph Campbell, Reflections on the Art of Living

"Starting over is never easy, but it can be the first step toward a life filled with renewed purpose and unexpected grace. Rebuilding your life is possible." ~ Thom Singer

"God can do anything, you know, far more than you could ever imagine or guess or request in your wildest dreams!"
~ Ephesians 3:20 (MSG)

A Sacred Pause

In Uganda, the mango tree was more than shade; it was sanctuary. Set a little apart from the buildings where I taught or counselled, it became an unspoken gathering place. People came not because I called them, but because something in our gathering drew them. Mothers who had lost children, young men broken by war, teachers burdened by the pain of their students, one by one, they found their way to the tree.

I never set out to create a "ministry space" under that tree. I went there to catch my breath, to pray, to reflect. But in time, others joined me. We sat in silence. We wept. Sometimes we spoke softly of things too painful to say aloud indoors. The mango tree became a sacred meeting ground where trauma, hope, and God's quiet presence intertwined.

Looking back, I see now that it was not my words that mattered most. It was my stillness, my willingness to be present without fixing. Something happened in those slow, shaded conversations, a kind of healing that doesn't rush or demand but waits, listens, and honours the soul's deep ache. Under that tree, I became less a teacher and more a companion. And in that place of shared humanity, God moved.

A Journey Back to Mukono

The Ugandan people have a deep appreciation for storytelling, and the story I am about to share is particularly significant to me. With only a few days remaining before Barry joins me and we depart from this region, which has become a second home, I have relished the slower pace of recent days, reconnecting with old friends and acquaintances. In Uganda, they often say, *"Slowly, slowly."* This period has provided me with a much-needed opportunity to rest and recuperate.

One day, I hired a driver and travelled to Mukono Christian University, where I had previously resided for an extended period while teaching a module on trauma counselling. Wilberforce, my driver, has a smile that can brighten any situation. He is a kind-hearted man, and together we made efforts to overcome the language barrier and occasional cultural misunderstandings. It was evident from his eyes, frequent head nods, and broad smile that there were times when he did not fully understand what I was saying.

A Visit to Peace and Divine

My first stop was to visit Peace and her daughter Divine. Peace had come to me for counselling in my modest campus home. I remember our sessions vividly, sitting on old couches, her head bowed in pain. She spoke of losing her husband in a fire and struggling to raise a disabled child amidst scarce services and rejection. Her deep depression was palpable. With compassion, I helped her confront her grief and begin healing. Her resilience amidst desolation inspired me deeply.

A year later, she opened her compound's iron gates as we arrived. We embraced warmly. Her single room was filled with basic necessities, and the worn furniture reflected her poverty. She served tea in a tin cup, but it was a grainy beverage with seeds. I felt guilty for having so much.

Divine, using crutches, moves about with an independence that belies her physical limitations. Her misshapen body is hunched over. I took some groundnuts served with the tea, but I stopped chewing when Divine chided me for not praying over my tea. I acknowledged my mistake with a smile. She lowered her head and prayed a simple, seven-year-old's prayer over the tea. I marvelled at her hospitality, reflecting on the economic divide between us.

Later, I slipped a sum of money into Peace's hand, feeling the weight of the complex emotions that both of us might experience in that exchange.

A Quiet Place of Healing and Presence

We made our way to Mukono University, and as we reached the campus, warm memories flooded my mind. I still loved being here. I met Hope, the coordinator of the Counselling Psychology degree program in which I had taught. She was genuinely thrilled to see me, having anticipated my visit. She was well-informed through the grapevine about my recent activities and asked about each one. We slowly walked to the shade of the mango tree, a popular meeting spot. She recalled me as the *"Muzungu"* (slang for white person) who rode a bicycle around campus, a memory shared by many at the university because it was so unusual.

Hope greeted Peace and Divine, who had found acceptance on campus. We walked to the grass and sat. I called Grace, my former house-girl, who joined us, tearfully grateful for the gift of her school fees. I rang

Annie's office, but she was busy, so we waited under the mango tree. Eventually, Annie arrived, and we celebrated our friendship and shared memories. As always, parting was difficult, but I promised to return if possible. I was deeply moved by these rich life encounters.

We dropped Peace and Divine back to their home. After warm embraces and farewells filled with unspoken pain and deep love, I prayed for Peace and Divine, who once again dutifully assumed the prayer position. I smiled. On the drive back to Kampala, Wilberforce was unexpectedly warm and tender. He told me that while I had been occupied with my friends, he had chatted with Peace under the mango tree. He said she was overwhelmed with gratitude to God that this *"Muzungu"* would come from afar just to visit with her. My heart could not contain its joy. Now I was the one who felt humbled by the gratitude, realizing that the privilege was truly mine.

Discovering My True Self

My East African friends call me *Nyamungu*, meaning *"Daughter of God; daughter sent from God."* Returning to Uganda helps me understand this name as I discover my true self, significant, secure, and resilient. On a path to goodness, I love God above all and others for His sake. Leaving the broom bush to sit under the mango tree, God has turned my mess into His message.

Life often shatters our expectations. Control slips from our fingers. We live in a broken world, but it's through our wounds that God often speaks, and the journey of transformation begins.

In the following section, I explore the wounds of depression and despair through the Biblical lens of Isaiah 61.

The Anointed One

In Isaiah 61, the prophet Isaiah describes the Messiah, referred to as the *"Anointed One,"* who would bring healing and restoration. Jesus references this passage in Luke 4, indicating His mission to address the consequences of sin and the Fall. Isaiah 61:1-3 explains that Jesus' purpose was:

> *"...to comfort all who mourn,*
> *and provide for those who grieve in Zion,*
> *to bestow on them a crown of beauty instead of ashes,*
> *the oil of joy instead of mourning,*
> *and a garment of praise instead of a spirit of despair."*

This passage offers profound hope for those struggling with despair and brokenness. It promises not only deliverance but also transformation, turning ashes into beauty and mourning into joy.

A Crown of Beauty and a Garment of Praise

In ancient Israel, ashes were a public sign of grief and lamentation. But Isaiah tells us that God replaces these ashes with a *"crown of beauty"* - a symbol of dignity and joy. The shift is radical: from disgrace to honour, from sorrow to strength.

The *"garment of praise"* contrasts with the *"spirit of despair."* This despair, sometimes translated as "heaviness," can feel suffocating, like a thick fog that blinds the soul. Depression often arrives like this: wordless, heavy, and relentless. Yet God offers a way through, not by pretending the pain isn't real, but by inviting us to choose praise in the midst of it.

Confronting the Spirit of Despair

Some scholars interpret this *"spirit of despair"* as more than an emotion, it is a spiritual oppression, a force that crushes the human spirit. I have known it. In my own experience with depression, the heaviness felt demonic, a dark fog that sought to extinguish my light. But Isaiah 61:3 offers a weapon: the garment of praise. To wear it is an act of war. It requires faith. It declares: *God is still worthy, especially now.*

David praised God in his despair. Paul and Silas sang from their prison cell. Habakkuk, seeing only barren fields, still declared, *"Yet I will exult in the Lord; I will rejoice in the God of my salvation"* (*Habakkuk 3:17–18).* To praise in pain is not denial, it is defiance. It is a holy rebellion against despair.

The Oil of Joy for Mourning

The *"oil of joy"* in Isaiah 61:3 is another powerful symbol. Some scholars suggest this oil represents the Holy Spirit, who brings healing and transformation to those in mourning (Legge, 2011). There are also two contrasting pictures associated with this oil. In one perspective, oil symbolizes honour and celebration, as seen during festive occasions like weddings (Psalm 45:7, Luke 7:46). In contrast, at funerals or times of grief, oil was not used, as it was reserved for joyful events (Barnes' Notes on the Bible, n.d.).

Jesus, however, transforms sorrow. He pours out the "oil of joy" to replace the mourning of the brokenhearted, turning grief into gladness. This beautiful exchange demonstrates the transformative power of God's love and grace.

Prayer of Healing for the Spirit of Heaviness

Spirit of heaviness,
I bind you in the name of Jesus.
You have no place in me.
Holy Spirit, come, fill every place where despair once lived.
Clothe me in the garment of praise.
Make me an oak of righteousness,
planted by the Lord for the display of Your splendour.
In Jesus' name, Amen.

Prayer of Healing for the Oil of Joy

Lord, You are worthy of praise.
You have poured on me the oil of joy for mourning.
Forgive me for letting grief cloud my gaze.
Help me look to You as my rescuer and restorer.
I choose to praise You,
and to glorify You, even here.
In Jesus' name, Amen.

The Restorative Cycle in Psalm 77

Walter Brueggemann (1984), a renowned Old Testament scholar, proposed a deeply insightful framework for understanding the emotional and spiritual movement in the **Psalms.** Let's briefly explore the five movements of the restorative cycle found in Psalm 77, which echo not only Elijah's journey and my own, but also the universal human experience of moving through despair toward renewal.

1. *Illusion* – *"Everything will turn out all right..."*

The Psalm begins in a place of unrest. The Psalmist calls out to God, but comfort doesn't come immediately. He recalls the idealized belief that things would always be okay, that God would always feel near, prayers would be answered, and suffering would be short-lived. Illusion offers a false sense of security, one that often cannot withstand the storms of life. Many of us live here until pain disrupts the narrative.

2. *Disillusionment* – *"My life was an open wound that wouldn't heal..."*

This is the wilderness moment. The Psalmist plunges into anguish and doubts the goodness of God. *"Has his salvation promise burned out?"* he asks. The honesty of this raw pain is staggering. I too entered this phase when the old wound reopened after India, disoriented, betrayed, and spiritually numbed. In this place, there are no easy answers, only the ache of unmet expectations and silent nights.

3. *Orientation* – *"Once again I'll go over what God has done..."*

Something begins to shift. Though his pain remains, the Psalmist recalls past faithfulness—acts of God that once stirred awe. He begins to reorient, not by denying the pain, but by choosing to remember what is still true. This is the point in my own story where I opened my heart to the Spirit again, not because I felt strong, but because I needed to remember who God had been to me before.

4. *Re-orientation* – *"You're the God who makes things happen..."*

Now, the Psalmist's perspective broadens. God is no longer absent, but active, even in the storm. The chaos of the sea trembles before Him. This stage doesn't erase the trauma, but it reframes it. God is seen not only as the One who once acted in history, but as the One who still walks *"through roaring Ocean,"* hidden, but present. Recovery starts here, not with clarity, but with a reawakened trust.

5. *Reality* – *"You led your people like a flock of sheep..."*

Finally, the Psalmist reaches a grounded reality. Not a return to illusion, but a new place of confidence. It is quiet and unglamorous: God, the Shepherd, leading gently, invisibly. The cycle comes full circle, not to naïve certainty, but to rooted faith that can weather life's storms. My journey, like Elijah's and like David's, didn't resolve into perfection, but it brought a deeper awareness of God's faithful presence, even in the silence.

Ongoing Transformation Through the Restorative Cycle

The restorative pattern seen in Psalm 77, and echoed throughout the Psalms, is not a one-time event. It is a rhythm of the soul, a sacred dance of breaking and remaking. We don't move through illusion, disillusionment, and back to reality just once; we do it again and again. Each time, we are invited to deeper intimacy with God, greater honesty with ourselves, and more profound compassion for others.

In trauma recovery, this cycle becomes especially vital. Trauma shatters the illusion that the world is safe, that we are in control, or that God will always protect us from harm. Disillusionment can feel like a spiritual collapse. We may find ourselves asking, like the Psalmist, *"Has God forgotten me? Has He left me just when I needed Him most?"*

But healing rarely comes through quick answers. It comes through presence, God's presence in the pit, and the presence of those who don't try to fix us but dare to sit with us. Re-orientation doesn't erase the past; it makes space for it to be held in the compassionate hands of God. It allows our stories to be retold in the context of His love and redemptive purpose.

Spiritual growth, then, is not linear, it is cyclical, spiralling. With each cycle we are formed more into Christ's likeness. We descend into the darkness of confusion, grief, or shame, and rise into new light. But we do not rise as we were. We are changed. Our illusions drop away. Our souls are enlarged. Our capacity for empathy deepens. As we return to orientation and reality, we carry with us a truth hard-won: God is faithful *even here.*

This cycle reflects the very pattern of Christ's own journey, His descent into suffering and death, and His rising into resurrected life. We are invited to join in this pattern, not just once at salvation, but every time we face the losses and longings of life. The restorative cycle becomes a rhythm of resurrection.

I think of the words from Psalm 30:5, *"Weeping may endure for a night, but joy comes in the morning."* Not the joy of denial or perfection, but the joy of knowing we are not alone in our sorrow. The joy of discovering God's nearness in our undoing. The joy of rising again, even with our scars, and finding that we are somehow more whole than before.

Stirrings of Freedom

There was once a poultry farmer who received an eagle's egg as a gift. Curious to see what would happen, he placed it among the eggs that a hen was incubating. In due time, the eagle hatched alongside the chicks and grew up with them in the confined space of the barnyard. Though it was inherently different, it adapted to their behaviours and believed itself to be one of them.

One day, around its first year, the young eagle saw a majestic bird soaring high above. Something deep within stirred, an ache, a recognition. But just as quickly, a rooster barked at it to stop daydreaming and return to its chores.

Ending One: The Conformist Path

The young eagle lowered its gaze and obeyed. It lived out its days in the barnyard, confined by expectations, never tasting the wind or glimpsing the world beyond.

Ending Two: The Soaring Spirit

But in this telling, the eagle lifts its eyes again. Inspired by the vision of freedom, it stretches its wings and takes flight. Leaving the familiar behind, it rises into the sky, discovering a boundless world it was made to explore.

On Purpose and Aspiration

We are called to live a life of abundance, not to be confined to mediocrity. We were not made for the barnyard; we are made to soar with Christ. The Gospel invites us into a passionate union with God, yet so often we settle for control instead of surrender, familiarity instead of freedom.

May God awaken within us a longing for more, for truth, for transformation, for the heights we were made to inhabit. Ask Him to call forth that holy longing.

> *"Those who hope in the Lord will renew their strength.*
> *They will soar on wings like eagles;*
> *they will run and not grow weary,*
> *they will walk and not be faint."*
> (Isaiah 40:31)

Closing Thoughts

The story of the eagle is a beautiful picture of what it means to awaken to the fullness of life, what it means to step out of the confines of what's familiar and soar to the heights for which we were created. Yet, so often, we find ourselves living in the barnyard, trapped in patterns of stress, exhaustion, and emotional depletion. We may long for freedom, but the weight of our circumstances pulls us back into the barnyard, where stress becomes a way of life.

When we live with the constant pressure to meet demands, please others, or keep everything under control, we can feel like the eagle, destined for more but unable to break free. As we explore in *Living on Empty: When Stress Becomes a Way of Life*, the consequences of living on empty are profound. The burden of stress wears down not only our bodies but our spirits, too. In this chapter, we'll look at how stress can become a way of life, how we lose sight of the abundant life we're meant to live, and how God offers us rest, not as a quick fix but as a lifeline to our souls.

It's time to recognize that we are called to soar, not to be weighed down by the endless cycle of stress. God is waiting to meet us in our weariness, offering His strength to carry us, renew us, and set us free. But we must be willing to surrender our need for control and step into the freedom He provides. As Mark Nepo writes in his poem (2013, p. 143):

It's as if what is unbreakable -
the very pulse of life - waits for
everything else to be torn away,
and then in the bareness that
only silence, suffering, and
great love can expose, it dares
to speak through us and to us.

It seems to say, if you want to last,
hold on to nothing. If you want
to know love, let in everything.
If you want to feel the presence
of everything, stop counting the
things that break along the way.

Declarations

I declare that my depression is lifting.

I declare that as a child of Light, darkness cannot overcome me.

I declare that hopelessness and despair do not belong to God; instead, I choose to embrace hope.

I adorn myself with a crown of beauty and wear a garment of praise.

I declare that my mourning will turn into dancing, and I am now clothed with gladness (Psalm 30:11).

Prayer

Lord, I confess, in agreement with God's Word, that You, Lord, are worthy to be praised. You have empowered me with the oil of joy for mourning. Forgive me for allowing the enemy to focus me on grief and negativity and not looking to You to rescue me. Give me strength to praise and glorify You. In Jesus' name, Amen.

Reflection Questions

1. How do the crown of beauty, the garment of praise, and the oil of joy described in Isaiah 61 speak to your own journey through depression, and how might they offer a biblical framework for overcoming the pain you face?
2. How have King David's Psalms resonated with your own feelings of depression?
3. What have you learned from his raw expressions of anguish and his unwavering hope in God's faithfulness?
4. Why is it important for you not to fear or rush through the ache of depression, and what might God be revealing to you through this painful season that can lead to personal growth and deeper understanding?
5. In your times of pain and suffering, do you believe God has a purpose for these moments and how might He be using them to shape you, bring healing, or draw you closer to Him?
6. Take a few moments to sit with God in this space. What is He stirring in your heart as you reflect on these questions, and how might you invite Him into the depths of your emotional journey today?

Journal Prompt

Take a moment to reflect on how God's promises of beauty, joy, and praise can reshape your understanding of depression and lead you toward healing and transformation. *Without judging or fixing, gently name what was present in that moment.*

CHAPTER 7

What is Stress Trying to Tell Me?

"Every morning in Africa a gazelle awakens knowing it must today run faster than the fastest lion or it will be eaten. Every morning a lion awakens knowing it must outrun the slowest gazelle or it will starve. It matters not whether you are a gazelle or a lion, when the sun rises you had better be running." ~ African proverb

"No matter where I run, I meet myself there."
~ Dorothy Fields

"Do not be anxious about anything, but in every situation, by prayer and petition, with thanksgiving, present your requests to God. And the peace of God, which transcends all understanding, will guard your hearts and your minds in Christ Jesus." ~ Philippians 4:6-7

When Giving Out Drains What's Within

There comes a point, quiet, often unnoticed, when the soul begins to run dry. Not from a lack of love or calling, but from pouring out beyond what was replenished. In those seasons, I've found myself still showing up, still giving, still ministering… but on the inside, I was running on empty.

In Uganda, surrounded by stories of unimaginable loss and enduring resilience, I gave of myself wholly. My heart was present, my hands were busy, and my prayers were earnest. But slowly, the weight of sorrow I was holding for others began to seep into my own spirit. I would smile, teach, counsel, listen, but return home numb or weeping, unsure what part of me had disappeared along the way.

This chapter is an honest reckoning with the cost of compassion. It's about recognizing the signs of emotional and spiritual depletion, not as failure, but as invitation. God does not call us to be reservoirs that never dry up, but to be honest, human vessels that return often to the Source. "Running on Empty" is not the end of the story; it is the point where we are invited to stop, surrender, and be filled again.

A Highly Sensitive Person

I'm a Highly Sensitive Person (HSP), a trait shared by around 20% of the population. Research suggests both genetics and early parental warmth play a role in shaping this trait and how it expresses in adulthood. Documented by Drs. Elaine and Arthur Aron (1997), HSPs are often drawn to quiet environments, a love for nature, a desire to help others, and a deep inner life. As an HSP, my intuitive and perceptive nature allows me to empathize deeply, often experiencing intense reactions to both external and internal stimuli.

Highly sensitive people pick up on feeling tones, unspoken dynamics, energy shifts. Our senses are so finely tuned that it often feels as though we absorb others' emotions beyond conscious control. These responses tend to be more intense, more deeply felt, making joy richer, sorrow heavier, and the world a more overwhelming place at times. Many HSPs end up feeling different, misunderstood, or *"too much."*

One of the most challenging parts of being highly sensitive is distinguishing between my emotions and the emotional energy of others. Carl Jung (1966) once observed that emotions are contagious. When we experience another person's suffering as our own, we may unintentionally double the burden of pain in the world (Poulin et al.,

2013). Watching the nightly news can flood my system with helplessness. Crowds, loud noises, bright lights, or even scratchy clothing can overstimulate me. Yet I'm also moved to tears by beauty, in nature, in art, in poetry, in Scripture, in stories of human courage and tenderness. These moments stir something sacred within me.

Someone once said, *"Sometimes I think I need a spare heart to feel all the things I feel."* That captures it well. My inner life is rich and intricate. I need regular solitude to recharge. I feel things deeply, joy, grief, love, loss, and I'm highly attuned to the emotional atmosphere in any room. This sensitivity is a gift in my work as a therapist, but it comes at a cost. I have to watch my energy closely. I tire more quickly than others and must structure my calendar to preserve well-being. That doesn't always sit well with those who have different expectations of my availability. Sometimes I disappoint others to honour the boundaries that protect my emotional and physical health. So how does high sensitivity become holy compassion? And can I extend that same compassion toward myself?

I often ask God to write 1 Peter 5:7 into the depths of my being, *"Pour out all your worries and stress upon him and leave them there, for he always tenderly cares for you."* Healing and wholeness require ongoing surrender to the Spirit, courageous honesty about painful memories, and openness to receive the gifts hidden in our struggle.

Stress as a Response to Threat

Stress (including HSP predispositions) is a natural, built-in survival mechanism. Whether it's a physical threat, like escaping a burning building, or a psychological one, such as an overwhelming workload, our body's response is strikingly similar. The moment we perceive danger, our sympathetic nervous system kicks in, triggering the *"fight, flight, or freeze"* response.

Adrenaline floods the system. Our heart rate spikes. Muscles tighten. Blood pressure rises. Blood flows away from digestion and toward vital organs and limbs. Endorphins increase, temporarily numbing pain and enhancing our ability to act fast.

Ideally, once the threat has passed, the body enters recovery mode, rebalancing, resting, and preparing for the next challenge. But what happens when there is no pause? No recovery? What happens when we live in a perpetual state of activation?

That's what this chapter explores. Because stress, when chronic and unrelenting, erodes health from the inside out. By understanding how stress works, we gain the power to make different choices, to manage it, rather than be mastered by it.

Controllable and Uncontrollable Stress

Stress falls into two broad categories: controllable and uncontrollable. *Controllable stress,* like planning a wedding, preparing for travel, or starting a new job, can be managed with tools like deep breathing, rest, and healthy routines. It may challenge us, but it's often infused with purpose and hope.

Uncontrollable stress, by contrast, often feels like a heavy, persistent weight. Think of caring long-term for a mentally ill or disabled family member or navigating a crisis with no end in sight. These situations activate the body's stress systems continuously. Over time, the wear and tear become visible, physically, emotionally, spiritually.

The line between these types isn't always clear, and both can become chronic. But it's the cumulative load that does the most harm. Prolonged stress raises the risk of high blood pressure, heart disease, sleep problems, anxiety, and depression. Since the 1930s, scientists have known that continuous activation of stress hormones, especially glucocorticoids, depletes the body. Without time to reset, we wear down. We live on empty.

Understanding the Stress Response

Let's look at the physiological chain reaction stress sets off:

1. **Fight-Flight-Freeze Response:** The body's automatic survival system when faced with threat.
2. **Adrenal Glands:** Perched on the kidneys, these glands release cortisol and adrenaline.
3. **Adrenal Cortex:** Produces glucocorticoids (about 50 kinds), fuelling our survival responses.
4. **Glucocorticoids:** Help the body maintain balance during stress, supplying energy for action.
5. **Adrenaline:** Increases heart rate, opens airways, sharpens attention.
6. **Cortisol:** Known as the "stress hormone," it raises blood sugar, suppresses immunity, and fuels metabolism. Chronic elevation can damage memory and shrink the hippocampus.
7. **Serotonin:** Regulates mood, sleep, and appetite. When depleted, we feel more anxious, irritable, or depressed.

Under stress, the body burns fat for fuel. But too much cortisol weakens the immune system and disrupts brain function. If left unaddressed, chronic stress behaves like a festering wound, it deepens over time, affecting every part of our being. Eventually, cortisol and adrenaline begin to do more harm than good. They contribute to hypertension, memory problems, reproductive dysfunction, and even impaired creation of new brain cells (neurogenesis). Without intervention, this biochemical wear-and-tear quietly erodes our vitality.

Stress, Distress and Stress Disorder

Stress isn't always the problem. It's when stress becomes distress, and then disease, that we get into trouble.

Consider Bob. He's under pressure at work. A critical team member is sidelined by an accident. Bob steps in, pushing himself hard to meet the deadline. When he misses it, the client graciously offers an extension. But the toll on Bob has already begun, his anxiety increases, his blood pressure spikes, his cholesterol rises. Still reversible. Still manageable.

But then another deadline looms. And another. And the stress becomes his new normal. His adrenal system never gets a break. Eventually, his body starts breaking down, his immune system falters, his memory weakens, his mood declines. This is no longer just stress. This is stress disease. Strategic dying.

The good news? Bob has choices. Even now. He can slow the deterioration. He can alter the path. But it requires awareness, intention, and a willingness to make radical changes to how he lives, works, and relates.

The Cost of Chronic Stress

As Bob's stress becomes entrenched, his endorphins drop, leaving him in pain. Serotonin dips, increasing depression. Anxiety becomes constant. He starts drinking more, exercising less, eating poorly, and sleeping irregularly. His relationships fray. And his physical body reflects the toll, chronic fatigue, inflammation, weakened immunity.

This spiral is not inevitable. But it is predictable. Unless interrupted, it becomes a cycle of depletion and decline.

Flight-Fight-Freeze Continuum

In the animal kingdom, fighting and anger are instinctive defensive responses to threats or danger. Anger signals dominance, compelling the other party to back down. It marks the beginning of an attack, often escalating into a consuming form of anger. This is revealed through intense facial expressions, loud vocalizations, and bared teeth. These signals communicate, *"I'm ready to take you out, so submit."* This *"take no prisoners*" mentality stems from a deep need for dominance or survival, often tied to securing resources like food.

Humans exhibit similar patterns. When we perceive a threat, our reactions can become combative, mistrustful, blaming, impulsive, controlling, or judgmental. Though the circumstances may differ, the underlying drive to assert dominance or protect ourselves remains deeply embedded in our biology.

On the other hand, the flight or fear response drives us to escape, putting as much distance as possible between ourselves and the danger. Healthy fear can serve as protection, making us alert and cautious. But it can also lead to avoidance, turning away, hiding, or freezing in an attempt to go unnoticed. Fear surfaces when we face a threat more powerful than ourselves, one capable of causing harm.

Fear and Memory

One of fear's primary effects is on memory. It shifts our focus from the immediate threat to the broader context surrounding it. For example, I recall very little about a car accident where I had to veer off the road and into the scrub. But what stands out are seemingly irrelevant sensory details, like the tiny yellow flowers by the roadside and the sound of bushes bouncing off the car. This scattering of focus illustrates how fear imprints specific, contextual elements of a traumatic event, even when the core experience fades from memory.

Interestingly, the Cape Grysbok, a small and cautious antelope, has a unique flight response to threats. When chased, it bolts in a zigzag pattern, making it almost impossible for a predator to follow. Similarly, humans exhibit various flight responses. We might avoid confrontation, display ambivalence, resist engagement, remain silent, create emotional or physical distance, or withdraw entirely. Like the Grysbok's unpredictable zigzag, these behaviours serve as strategies to evade perceived threats and protect us from harm.

The freeze response, embedded in our reptilian brain, is an ancient survival mechanism. Nature enthusiasts may recognize this behaviour in animals. Predators often overlook prey that remains perfectly still, instinctively avoiding what they perceive as a rotting carcass that could carry disease. In the final moments of a chase, when neither fight nor flight is viable, the prey may *"play dead"* in a freeze response, commonly known as *"playing possum."* For example, when a mouse is caught by a cat, it often freezes. The cat, distracted by boredom, might release the mouse, giving it a chance to recover and escape.

Humans experience this too. When faced with overwhelming threats, our autonomic nervous system may trigger a freeze response, causing us to become immobilized. The phrase *"frozen with fear"* captures this reaction perfectly. A deer caught in headlights reacts the same way. This automatic, unconscious response occurs when the threat feels inescapable.

Trauma victims often grapple with feelings of shame and confusion about their inability to act during moments of danger. As Uher (et al., 2014, p. 169) explains, trauma occurs when our body's natural fight-or-flight response doesn't function properly, it's as if the body's alarm system is stuck on high, and we can't calm down. In such situations, the freeze response may be the body's best attempt at survival, manifesting as frozen terror, panic, caution, suspicion, disinterest, inability to concentrate, or retreating inward.

Role of the Autonomic Nervous System (ANS)

Our Autonomic Nervous System (ANS) is made up of three main parts:

1. **The sympathetic nervous system (SNS)** - think of it as the accelerator.
2. **The parasympathetic nervous system (PNS)** - this one's the brake.
3. **The enteric nervous system** - it's in charge of managing digestive functions.

The ANS works with the somatic nervous system to control our body's automatic responses in two main situations:

1. Emergencies when we need to fight, flee, or freeze.
2. Non-emergencies, when our body can rest and digest.

The best part? The ANS works without us even thinking about it. Picture this: It's a beautiful sunny day, and you're out for a peaceful walk in the park. Suddenly, a big, angry Rottweiler jumps in your way. Do you fight, flee, or freeze? That's the SNS kicking in, getting your body ready to survive. You feel your heart race, your blood pressure spike, and your digestion slow down, all in a split second.

Now, imagine it's the same sunny day, but instead of a dog, you decide to lie down on the grass and relax. This time, your PNS takes over, slowing everything down. Your heart rate drops, your blood pressure goes down, and digestion gets back to normal.

These two systems are opposites but work hand in hand. The SNS revs you up when you need excitement, fear, or energy (the accelerator), while the PNS calms you down, promoting peace, relaxation, and contentment (the brake). Together, they help keep everything in balance. But when the ANS gets "stuck" in one of these modes, it can lead to hyper-arousal or numbness.

Take Bob, for example. His SNS was stuck in high gear. He didn't make time for relaxation or rest, and eventually, it started to catch up with him.

Bob began to experience chronic anxiety, restlessness, difficulty sleeping, racing thoughts, panic attacks, irritability, and an ever-present feeling of being on edge. His thoughts and emotions were constantly on overdrive, and he felt overwhelmed by it all.

Eventually, his body just couldn't keep up anymore. One day, Bob hit a wall and had to leave work early. Exhausted from living in that high-stress state, his body switched into a sort of shutdown mode. For days, he felt numb, avoiding emotions, losing interest in things he once enjoyed, and feeling disconnected from others and from life itself. His body felt heavy, his muscles sluggish, and he couldn't seem to sleep or experience any joy.

Bob's story is a reminder of how important balance is for the ANS. When stress sticks around for too long, it can send us into cycles of being too revved up or too numb, affecting our mental and physical health. The key is finding that sweet spot where both the SNS and PNS can work together in harmony.

Who Fares the Best?

Helen Keller, who was both blind and deaf, once said, *"Although the world is full of suffering, it is also full of the overcoming of it."* I think there's something profound in that. A study by Tedeschi and Calhoun (2006) found that people can actually experience growth after going through significant trauma, and they identified five main ways this happens:

1. They develop a deeper appreciation for life.
2. Their spiritual beliefs become more meaningful.
3. They feel stronger, more resilient, and more capable.
4. They build stronger connections with others.
5. They find themselves on unexpected new life paths.

The researchers also found that those who cope well with adversity often share some key traits:

- They seek support from others.
- They work hard toward goals that matter to them.
- They collaborate and get along with people.
- They nurture themselves rather than fall into self-pity.
- They are proactive, taking charge of their lives, rather than letting things just happen to them.
- They find meaning in their suffering.
- They draw strength from adversity, using it to build resilience for the future.

Interestingly, the study found that people who allow themselves to feel their emotions, like anxiety, fear, or sadness, are often the ones who do the best. This kind of emotional engagement without letting it take over is called *"active surrendering."* It's not about avoiding tough feelings but giving yourself the space to experience them while holding onto hope.

Signs of Chronic Stress

Just like Jesus' disciples grew weary, we too can find ourselves with nothing left to give. Chronic stress can leave us feeling disillusioned, helpless, and totally drained. The constant pressure takes its toll, sometimes causing us to lose the sense of fulfillment and satisfaction we once had in our work. This sense of fulfillment, what we call **compassion satisfaction**, is the positive emotional reward we get from feeling competent in our professional roles, especially when helping others. According to Stamm (2009), compassion satisfaction is all about having positive relationships with colleagues and feeling that our work contributes meaningfully to the well-being of others and society. It's that sense of pride and purpose we get from making a difference.

But when stress becomes chronic, compassion satisfaction can turn into something much more exhausting, **compassion fatigue**. This happens when constant stress leads to a mix of vague, unexplained symptoms like fatigue, anxiety, sleep problems, aches, and digestive issues. It's like your body is stuck in a fight-flight-or-freeze mode, always on alert and never getting a break. Over time, this ongoing stress can erode our ability to empathize, leaving us emotionally drained and disconnected from others. It can lead to a sense of emptiness and a loss of purpose.

Burnout

The term "burnout" was first introduced by American psychologist Dr. Herbert Freudenberger in 1974. It describes a gradual progression of emotional exhaustion and withdrawal, often triggered by an overwhelming workload or institutional stress. Unlike trauma-related conditions, burnout doesn't stem from a single traumatic event but results from prolonged, cumulative stress over time.

Signs of burnout include chronic exhaustion, emotional disengagement, cynicism, and a loss of motivation and hope. Daily tasks may feel either monotonous or impossibly overwhelming. People experiencing burnout often report that nothing they do seems to make a difference or is appreciated. Emotional numbness, deep sadness, and a sense of futility can set in, affecting every part of life, work, relationships, and health. Burnout depletes emotional, physical, and mental reserves, leaving a person feeling ineffective, disconnected, and overwhelmed.

Bob's Experience of Burnout

Bob had reached burnout. The effects were profound. His frontal lobes, responsible for planning, prioritising, and problem-solving, essentially shut down. He found himself mentally sluggish, emotionally flat, and deeply weary. The temporal lobes, which help us process memory and emotion, also seemed affected. Bob was unable to feel pleasure, joy, or hope. His emotional world became bleak, and his thinking clouded. He couldn't escape the cycle of cynicism and exhaustion, even when he tried.

He began saying things like, *"I can't think straight. It takes me forever to do what I used to do easily."* But when Bob began to recognise the depth of his burnout, he took a crucial step: he asked for help. With support, he began to reengage his thinking brain. Slowly, his problem-solving abilities returned, his emotional numbness began to lift, and a sense of purpose re-emerged. His path to healing began with a single courageous step, acknowledging the truth of where he was.

Healing Chronic Stress

What if Bob had ignored the signs? As Parker Palmer (in Fox, 2018, p. 56) wisely observes, *"Self-care is never a selfish act, it is simply good stewardship of the only gift I have."* Ignoring self-care depletes our energy and leaves us unable to serve others well.
Bob had to learn how to break the cycle of chronic stress. Stress management involved more than coping; it required rethinking how he lived, worked, and related. Recognising early signs allowed him to pause and reset before his stress spiralled out of control.

Bob's Story: A Multi-Dimensional Approach to Recovery

Bob's History

Bob's resilience helped him reinterpret his stress not as a sign of failure, but as a potential spiritual awakening. This shift in mindset allowed him to view his burnout not as the end, but as a call to something deeper. Had he believed he was powerless to recover, despair might have taken over. But Bob had a realistic understanding of how he'd arrived at this place, and that clarity empowered him to take steps toward healing. It reminded him that his story wasn't over.

Bob's Workload

People often leave jobs not because of the work itself, but because of the environment (Conte, 2012). Bob learned the value of setting boundaries. He spoke with his supervisor about restructuring his tasks to include more variety. He built peer debriefing into his schedule, reclaimed lunch breaks, and took short walks between clients. Weekends became sacred again, reserved for family, rest, and restoration.

He also reframed his thinking: *"Even though my workload is heavy, I choose to work here because..."* By celebrating small wins and remembering his reasons for staying, Bob shifted from pessimism to gratitude. He started noticing what was good again.

Bob's Physical Fitness

Bob prioritised sleep and exercise, realising that chronic stress had depleted his body. He learned deep-breathing techniques to counteract the shallow breathing stress had triggered. Intentional breathing brought oxygen back to his brain and helped him feel grounded.
He and his wife began evening dance classes, something that brought joy and rhythm back into his life. The movement had a calming effect on his nervous system and created space for shared laughter and connection.

Bob's Spiritual Fitness

Ruth Haley Barton (2008) writes that we fail young leaders when we encourage them to dream big without first asking who they are becoming. Bob realised he'd lost touch with his core values and longings. He began to make prayer and reflection a regular practice, learning to separate his needs from those of others. Most importantly, he learned to extend grace to himself.

Mother Teresa once said, *"To keep a lamp burning, you have to keep putting oil in it."* Bob discovered that true success wasn't solving every problem, it was staying present in distress while drawing strength from God's grace. Relying on divine resources, rather than his own, became a new way of life.

Bob's Emotional Fitness

Humour became a sign of healing. Bob made space for laughter and play, whether tossing a ball with his kids, playing with the dog, or enjoying a cup of tea with his wife in the garden. He realised that joy doesn't erase hardship, but it nourishes the soul.

Bob's Mental Fitness

Bob likened his stressed mind to a runaway stagecoach, horses racing wildly while the driver sat frozen. To regain control, he had to pull the reins. He focused on what mattered and let go of what didn't. He learned basic relaxation techniques: breathing deeply, counting slowly, saying the word *"relax"* on each exhale.

He also practiced naming and challenging his self-defeating thoughts. Over time, these practices calmed his overactive mind and helped him rebuild mental clarity and confidence. He even stopped to smell the roses, literally. The scent of flowers shifted his brain patterns, a gentle reminder of the healing beauty in God's creation.

Bob's Social Connections

A wise teacher once illustrated the difference between illness and wellness by circling the "I" in illness and the "we" in wellness. Bob had stopped attending church and drifted from his family. Work took over, and he slowly isolated himself. Without close relationships, Bob became vulnerable to loneliness, depression, and unhealthy coping strategies.

Research shows that loneliness can significantly impact physical and emotional health. Bob eventually realised that healing required reconnection, with God, his family, and his community. He began rebuilding those connections, rediscovering the gift of belonging. He also learned to lean into trustworthy friendships, allowing others to speak truth and grace into his life. As Ann Voskamp (2019) puts it, love is not about changing others, it's about changing ourselves. For Bob, healing began with this kind of inner transformation. Through intentional care, honest reflection, and spiritual surrender, he began to reclaim his life and rediscover joy.

Closing Thoughts

As we reflect on Bob's story, we begin to see the deep connection between burnout and the soul's cry for rest. Burnout teaches us that the solution is not in doing more but in being more, being more present with ourselves, our needs, and our God. Yet, for many, even when we slow down, we find our minds still racing, overwhelmed by worry, fear, and unease. This is where anxiety often enters, the restless, nagging voice that never seems to let us be at peace.

In *The Restless Mind: Understanding Anxiety*, we will explore the ways in which anxiety takes root in our minds and hearts, distorting our ability to rest, to trust, and to find peace. It's a struggle that many of us face, and it's one that often comes alongside burnout, feeding off our weariness and contributing to our sense of being out of control. Understanding anxiety is the first step in healing from it. Just like with burnout, healing doesn't come from striving to manage anxiety but from learning to face it with grace, compassion, and the understanding that God is present with us, even in our restless moments.

As we delve into this chapter, let us remember that in the midst of anxiety, God is still inviting us to find rest in Him, to let go of the burden of perfection, control, and constant worry, and embrace His peace that surpasses understanding.

Declarations

I declare that my body is the temple of the living God.

I declare that You, God, have united me to Christ and clothed me in Your righteousness.

I declare that Your dwelling place is within me - my body is a temple where the Most Holy One dwells.

I declare that I will nurture and care for my body.

Prayer

Let this season be for me
a time of gathering together the pieces into which my busyness has broken me.
O God, enable me now
to grow wise through reflection,
peaceful through the song of the cricket, recreated through the laughter of play.
Most of all, Lord,
let me live easily and grace-fully for a spell,
so that I may see other souls deeply, share in silence unhurried,
listen to the sound of sunlight and shadows, explore barefoot the land of forgotten
dreams and shy hopes, and find the right words to tell another who I am.

(Ted Loder, *A Summer Praye*r)

Reflection Questions

1. How do you recognise the difference between motivating stress and chronic stress in your own life, and how does each impact your physical, mental, and emotional health?
2. When you feel threatened, how does your body react, and how do you ensure that you allow time for relaxation and recovery once the threat is gone?
3. How do you make time for rest and recharge in your life?
4. What self-care strategies can you incorporate into your routine to avoid burnout and compassion fatigue?
5. What are the warning signs of stress in your life?
6. What proactive steps can you take to manage stress before it becomes overwhelming?

Journal Prompt

Reflect on a recent challenge you faced. How did it shape your perspective on your own resilience and faith? Without judging or fixing, gently name what was present in that moment.

CHAPTER 8

My Restless Mind

"It's not what you eat that gives you indigestion, it's what's eating you." ~ Mark Twain

"Anxiety is suffering that is yet to find its meaning." ~ Carl Jung

"My anxiety is silent. You wouldn't even notice a change on the outside but I'm honestly so stressed I can't even manage simple tasks. People call me lazy when, in reality, I'm just overwhelmed." ~ Samantha Gluck

"I am the bread of life. Whoever comes to me will never be hungry..." ~ John 6:35

When Worry and Anxiety Take the Reins

There are seasons when my mind refuses to rest, when thoughts circle endlessly, scenarios play out like unwelcome dramas, and peace feels just out of reach. I know the promises of God. I've taught them, clung to them, whispered them over others. But there have also been nights when anxiety hijacked my body, and worry etched itself into my chest like a weight I couldn't lift.

In the wake of trauma, worry often finds fertile ground. The mind, once a place of reflection and imagination, becomes a battleground of fear and "what ifs." Even when the world is relatively calm, the echoes of past chaos or future dread keep the nervous system on high alert. I've known this restlessness not just clinically, but personally. I've prayed through it, wrestled with it, and slowly learned to befriend it, without letting it rule me.

This chapter is a gentle exploration of how worry and anxiety shape the restless mind, and how the Spirit of God invites us into stillness, even when our thoughts won't quiet easily. It's not about quick fixes, but about learning to listen differently, to breathe deeply, and to anchor ourselves in the truth that even when our minds are unsettled, we are held by a God who never slumbers.

Healing in the Light: Stories, Bread, and the Ache of Anxiety

They stand, one by one, and it's impossible to stem the flow. Stories and tears, streaming like a waterfall, pour from husbands and wives alike. Earlier that day, as the Sri Lankan heat climbs, Barry and I shift our chairs to face each other, sharing our story. The uncontained pain of abandonment. The chasm of despair. The desperate ache of being misunderstood and unheard. Robert, our friend and translator, stands nearby, gently relaying our words.

Though my gaze stays fixed on Barry as we converse in front of the crowd about our relationship, I hear the pain in the room: sobbing, sighing, hearts cracking open. This is a holy space. A safe space. A space where secrets, buried under cultural layers of shame, begin to surface. In this moment, our suffering meets theirs. The wounded ones, us, become participants in healing, not just helpers. Love spills into the room, disrupting the silence of sorrow, breaking suffering into fragments, shards of fear, anxiety, worry, and grief, now exposed to the Light. This is where what was buried begins to rise: in the raw honesty of shared pain, and the radiant hope that comes from being seen and heard.

Sleeping With Bread

It reminds me of *Sleeping with Bread*, a beautiful metaphor and book by the Linns (1995). During the bombing raids of World War II, thousands of children were orphaned and left starving. Though some were rescued and brought to refugee camps where they received food and care, their nights were still filled with terror. They feared waking up to hunger, homelessness, or the absence of everything familiar.

Then someone had an idea; give each child a piece of bread to hold as they fell asleep. With that bread in hand, the children began to sleep peacefully. The bread whispered a quiet promise: *Today I was fed. Tomorrow I will be fed again.* Even in the presence of trauma, a crust of bread became their anchor, physical proof that provision had been made.

I often picture these war-weary little ones, sleeping with bread tucked into their hands, and I think: *Jesus knew I would need the same.* When life is bewildering and grief crushes me, I need to sleep with bread too, a reminder of God's provision, a tangible grace that still speaks, even in the dark.

The Ache of Anxiety

Worry, a component of anxiety, is temporary. Anxiety, however, is persistent. It lingers, even when its roots seem irrational. Anxiety compromises our ability to function, fogs our judgment, and often spins worst-case scenarios.

There's an old story I've always found hauntingly true:

Death was walking toward a city, and a man stopped him and asked,
"What are you going to do?"
"I'm going to kill ten thousand people," Death replied.
"That's terrible!" the man cried.
"That's just what I do," Death shrugged.

Later that day, the man met Death again. "You said you'd kill ten thousand, but seventy thousand died!"

"I only killed ten thousand," Death answered. "Worry and fear killed the rest."

This story holds a mirror to the way anxiety can consume us. Worry expects the enemy to act. Faith expects God to act.

My Battle with Anxiety

During the early days of COVID-19, my anxiety surged. As the death toll in Italy rose, I stood before my wardrobe and thought *I might never wear these clothes again.* I lay awake night after night, catastrophizing. I worried about my unborn granddaughter. What if I died? What if Barry died? What if my daughter grieved alone?

Anxiety was a straitjacket. My thoughts spiralled. Hope shrank. It reminds me of a famous quote by naval commander Oliver Hazard Perry (National Park Service, n.d.): *"We have met the enemy, and they are ours."* Later, cartoonist Walt Kelly twisted it beautifully: *"We have met the enemy, and he is us."*

Anxiety is often an enemy within, one of Satan's most potent weapons. It can cloud our capacity to think, rob us of peace, and isolate us in shame. Yet anxiety is not a weakness. It is the most common mental health condition in Australia. According to Headspace (2015), 1 in 4 people, 1 in 3 women and 1 in 5 men, will experience anxiety in their lifetime.

And still, many are too ashamed to seek help.

Understanding Anxiety: A Broader Picture

Anxiety is not just personal; it's also profoundly human. In fact, it's the most common mental health condition in Australia and the most prevalent issue experienced by young Australians (Headspace, 2015). On average, one in four people, one in three women and one in five men, will experience anxiety at some point in their lives (ABS, 2008). That's a staggering statistic, and yet many suffer silently, unsure of how to name what's happening within them.

Interestingly, while English offers only one word for anxiety, other languages offer nuanced terms that reflect its many faces (Iliesco, 2018). That matters. Naming the kind of anxiety people carry can be the first step toward finding the remedy we need.

Anxiety is not always pathological. Sometimes it functions like a divine smoke alarm, a warning system built into our bodies to grab our attention when something's not right. In the right dose, it helps us prepare, respond, and protect ourselves. But when left unacknowledged or untreated, anxiety can overwhelm, turning into a constant hum of distress that interferes with everyday life.

There are many types of anxiety disorders, each with its own texture:

- **Specific phobia** (for example, fear of spiders, flying, heights)
- **Social anxiety disorder** (fear of judgment or embarrassment)
- **Panic disorder**
- **Agoraphobia** (fear of being in situations where escape might be difficult)
- **Generalized anxiety disorder** (persistent worry about various life areas)

At its core, anxiety is a kind of depressive illness. While depression often centres on sadness and a loss of pleasure, anxiety involves relentless, fearful thoughts that often seem to come from nowhere. It's like being caught in a podcast that never pauses, racing thoughts, tightening chest, sleepless nights.

For some, anxiety presents mildly: chronic tension, restlessness, irritability, difficulty concentrating, or feeling threatened in new situations. For others, it escalates into full-blown panic attacks, heart racing, sweating, shaking, and a sense that something terrible is about to happen. Actor and comedian Gary McDonald (ABC, 2015) once said:

> *"The anxiety would paralyze me with fear... like a sort of wall, almost like a straitjacket... Suddenly there was this thing sapping me of all energy and cognitive skills, it was terrifying... and then you start to get suicidal."*

His words reflect what so many experience in silence.

And yet, anxiety is not a character flaw or spiritual weakness. Like depression, it can be inherited. It can also be a secondary symptom of medical or psychological conditions. Medication, therapy, body-based interventions, and spiritual support can all play a role in restoring balance, especially when used in tandem.

What Causes Anxiety?

Anxiety has multiple roots. It may be **biological, psychological, social, spiritual**, or some mixture of these.

Biological Anxiety

There is clear evidence of biochemical underpinnings in severe anxiety (Martin et al., 2010). Stress is often the trigger, over-activating the adrenal system and flooding the body with cortisol, epinephrine, and glucocorticoids. Chronic stress impairs the brain's tranquilizing systems and depletes immunity.

It's also important to rule out medical causes, including:

- Mitral valve prolapse (MVP)
- Hyperthyroidism
- Hypoglycemia
- Cardiac arrhythmias
- Vitamin B12 deficiency

Even substances like caffeine, alcohol, cannabis, amphetamines, and asthma medications can trigger anxiety.

That's why a thorough medical check-up is crucial. Medication, while not a cure, can help ease symptoms enough for the person to engage in deeper healing work, emotionally, psychologically, and spiritually.

Psychological and Spiritual Anxiety

Some anxiety disorders are clearly learned or stem from early trauma. Phobias and panic disorders, for example, often begin in childhood or adolescence. Environmental stressors and unresolved losses can awaken anxious patterns later in life.

But anxiety doesn't just live in the body or mind, it also inhabits the soul. Anxiety may raise spiritual struggles: *Why do I feel so distant from God? Why can't I trust? Why do I feel unprotected, unloved, unworthy?*

Spiritual practices, like prayer, silence, Scripture meditation, and worship, can gently realign us with God's presence. Healing often begins when we bring both our **biology** and **spirit** into the light of Christ's compassion.As I've learned in my own healing journey, and in the sacred space of ministry among the wounded in Sri Lanka, we don't heal by pretending. We heal by naming what hurts, by breaking bread together, and by clinging to the One who says, *"I am the Bread of Life."* Even when anxiety clenches the chest and darkens the mind, I sleep with bread in my hand.

Childhood Experiences and Attachment Wounds

Many forms of anxiety have deep roots in childhood, especially when a child's basic needs for safety, emotional attunement, and soothing are unmet. Attachment wounds, caused by inconsistent caregiving, emotional neglect, or trauma, can leave a residue of chronic unease. This unease is often carried into adulthood as a vague sense that the world isn't safe, that love is conditional, or that we are somehow not enough.

As a child, I often lay awake at night, my little heart clenched with worry. I couldn't have articulated it then, but I felt the world was teetering on the edge of something dreadful. I carried an invisible burden, watching over the well-being of others with the hypervigilance of someone far too young. Only much later did I understand these were early signs of anxiety shaped by unresolved sorrow and emotional isolation. My nervous system had learned to stay on high alert, preparing for the worst.

That kind of early imprinting doesn't simply vanish with adulthood or faith. It takes time, and often trauma-informed care, to rewire those neural pathways. But it also takes love. The kind of love that is steady, kind, and deeply present. I began to find that love not just in therapy or safe relationships, but in the God who was with me in the night watches, whispering, "You don't have to carry this alone."

Faith and Fear: A Spiritual Battle

Anxiety is not just a psychological issue, it's also a profoundly spiritual one. It strikes at the core of our trust. When anxiety floods in, the soul often trembles with unspoken fears: *What if I'm not safe? What if God doesn't show up? What if I'm left alone again?* It's here that fear becomes more than emotion, it becomes a battleground for the heart.

Scripture doesn't shame our anxiety. Instead, it meets us in it. Paul's words to the Philippians offer a way through, *"Do not be anxious about anything, but in every situation, by prayer and petition, with thanksgiving, present your requests to God..."* (Phil. 4:6). This isn't a demand to suppress our feelings. It's an invitation to relationship. Prayer becomes the turning point, where we shift from spinning in fear to anchoring in Presence. And the promise follows, *"...the peace of God, which transcends all understanding, will guard your hearts and your minds in Christ Jesus"* (v. 7).

That peace isn't passive. It *guards,* like a sentry at the door of our hearts and minds. It doesn't always remove the storm, but it anchors us in the One who holds us through it. When I'm in the grip of anxiety, my prayers aren't eloquent. They're raw. A whisper. A sigh. Sometimes just, *"Help."* But something shifts in that moment of turning toward Love. I've come to believe that anxiety, when brought into the light of grace, can actually draw us closer to God. It becomes a place of encounter. A place of healing.

The Journey Toward Peace

For much of my life, I didn't realise that what I was experiencing was anxiety. I had no name for the tightness in my chest, the restlessness that kept me on edge, or the sudden wave of dread that would crash in for no clear reason. I simply assumed I was weak, overly sensitive, or not praying enough. I told myself to *"get on with it,"* to push through, to do more.

But anxiety doesn't respond to pressure. It grows in the shadows of silence and self-blame.

Looking back, I now see that my anxiety had deep roots. Some of it was inherited, woven into my biology. Some was shaped by childhood experiences where I felt unsafe or unseen. And some arose later in life, in moments of exhaustion, fear, and loss, when I felt overwhelmed by responsibilities or wounded in relationships.

As a clinical counsellor and trauma educator, I came to understand how anxiety lodges itself not just in the mind, but in the body and soul. It tightens the muscles, shortens the breath, distorts thinking, and disconnects us from God's peace. Theologically, I wrestled with what it meant to trust God when my body felt out of control. I wondered: *Can faith and anxiety coexist?*

For me, healing didn't come all at once. It came through layers, learning to recognise the signals my body was sending, naming what was happening without shame, and gradually allowing God's truth to displace the inner lies that had taken root. I needed a renewed mind, yes, but I also needed safety, compassion, and grace. And I needed to stop running from the very ache that was asking to be heard.

What I discovered is that peace isn't the absence of anxiety, it's the presence of God in the middle of it. It's learning to breathe again, to trust that I am held even when my world feels shaky, to take refuge in the One who whispers, "Do not fear, for I am with you."

Learning to Listen to My Anxiety

For many years, I treated my anxiety as an enemy. I feared its arrival, tried to suppress it with busyness or spiritual effort, or scolded myself for not having enough faith. I didn't understand that anxiety wasn't trying to destroy me, it was trying to speak to me.

Anxiety often signals that something deep within us needs tending. It might be pointing to a buried fear, an unmet need, an internal conflict, or a wound that hasn't healed. It might be alerting us to our over-functioning, our people-pleasing, our inability to say no. It might be echoing early relational pain, the kind that taught us love had to be earned, or that our safety depended on constant vigilance.

When I began to see anxiety not as a flaw, but as a signal, my relationship with it started to change. I still remember the first time I sat with it, not fighting, not fleeing, but asking, *"What are you here to show me?"* That small shift, though uncomfortable, marked the beginning of a deeper healing journey. I began to see how my body had carried fear for years, and how my soul longed for rest. I began to notice how often my thoughts were rooted in scarcity, in not enough - not safe enough, not strong enough, not spiritual enough.

In those moments, the words of Jesus became more than just a promise. They became a lifeline. *"Peace I leave with you; my peace I give you. I do not give to you as the world gives. Do not let your hearts be troubled and do not be afraid"* (John 14:27). This peace, His peace, isn't fragile. It doesn't depend on the absence of pain or the presence of control. It's a peace that anchors us when the waves rise. A peace that says, *"You are not alone in this storm."* A peace that slowly, gently rewires our nervous system and our self-concept until we know, in the marrow of our being, that we are safe in Love.

Becoming Bread for Others

All this begs the question: *How can I be bread for others?* I see the war-weary and broken ones standing before us, hungry for that which truly sustains. Jesus declared:

> *"I am the bread of life. Whoever comes to me will never be hungry, and whoever believes in me will never be thirsty... I am the living bread that came down from heaven. Whoever eats of this bread will live forever"* (John 6:35, 51).

What does He mean?

Perhaps a clue is found in 1 Corinthians 11:23–24, *"The Lord Jesus, on the night when he was betrayed, took bread, and when he had given thanks, he broke it and said: 'This is my body, which is broken for you.'"* Jesus, knowing the pain and betrayal that lay ahead, gave thanks, broke the bread, His body, and offered it to His disciples. What strikes me most is that **He gave thanks first.** Before the breaking. Before the offering. Thanksgiving preceded suffering.

I am convinced, as I stand before these courageous souls, that what gives life meaning is not simply surviving, but receiving grace with gratitude, and then offering it freely. I am blessed to bless. Holding onto what gives me life, I can come alongside others as they move more fully into who they are meant to be. Not because I am strong, but because I carry the Bread of Life in my outstretched, trembling hands.

Surrounded by abundance, we in the West often live famished lives, anxious, restless, and fearful of scarcity. The panic-buying of toilet paper during COVID-19 exposed this collective fear, even in times of relative abundance. But the antidote to scarcity isn't more, it's giving.

True Abundance is Found in Self-giving

Sharing bread with a broken world, whether literal or metaphorical, is an act of faith. A quiet rebellion against fear. In the giving, we are not depleted but made whole. Our lives become meaningful not through accumulation but through allowing God to use our brokenness to nourish the hunger of others.

The fan whirs, steady and rhythmic, as voices fill the humid room, sharing burdens that weigh heavy. Sweat trickles down my back, mingling with the weight of the moment. War-trauma stories spill forth, unbidden, relentless, each a sacred testament to pain, resilience, and survival. I am bone-weary. The kind of exhaustion that seeps beyond body into soul. Yet in this holy space of raw honesty and broken hearts, I feel the profound privilege of presence.

This is Holy Ground

This is where bread is broken and shared. What we offer, our words, our listening, our very presence, is not symbolic. It is sustenance. A gift of hope. A quiet defiance against despair. In those moments, healing feels possible, not dramatic or instant, but tender and real. A flicker of light, steady enough to keep walking.

Later in the year, we reflect with quiet joy on our final days in India. Our last workshop, held for the tireless JanPragati staff working with children in the slums, leaves an indelible mark. The leader's openness, his willingness to be unhidden alongside his beautiful wife, astounds us.

Their honesty becomes a final, unexpected gift, an embodiment of all we came to witness: truth-telling as transformation.

On my birthday, we attend church in Lucknow. Physically and emotionally spent, we are met by God's quiet presence. The worship leader invites us to lay our joys and victories at the foot of the cross, reminding us they belong to Him too. In that sacred moment, I feel the bread in my hand replenished. A deep sense of gratitude wells up, gratitude that does not erase the pain but redeems it.

Over these five weeks, we have been broken open, poured out, and offered as bread, for comfort, for courage, for hope. The distant ache of our own past has been transformed into a kind of communion: our story becoming nourishment for others. As the psalmist declares,

"Praise the Lord... He heals the brokenhearted and binds up their wounds" (Psalm 147:1, 3).

In becoming bread for others, we discover an unmatched joy. Not fleeting happiness, but a joy that flows from the privilege of giving ourselves away in love**.** It is this joy that sustains us as we prepare to return home, body weary, but spirit renewed.

We think of our children and dear friends waiting to embrace us. There is quiet anticipation, not just of reunion, but of returning with fuller hearts and deeper faith. We come back changed. Stronger. Softer. The unmistakable blessing of God rests on our lives and our marriage.

Imprinted on our souls are the faces of those we met, men and women who, despite unimaginable suffering, cling to the Bread of Life with tenacious hope. They are our teachers. Their stories and faith live within us now, shaping how we choose to live and love.

And so, we walk forward, carrying these words from
Habakkuk **3:17-19** like a psalm in our hearts:

"Though the fig tree does not bud
and there are no grapes on the vines,
though the olive crop fails
and the fields produce no food,

though there are no sheep in the pen
and no cattle in the stalls,
yet I will rejoice in the Lord,
I will be joyful in God my Savior.
The Sovereign Lord is my strength;
he makes my feet like the feet of a deer,
he enables me to tread on the heights."

Closing Thoughts

As we reflect on the journey of being broken and poured out, there's a truth that becomes clear: healing doesn't always come in a neat, linear form. Sometimes, it's found in the beautiful mess of life, the tension between faith and doubt, between hope and worry. As we learn to be bread for others, we also learn to hold our doubts and our worries with grace, knowing that these struggles don't disqualify us from the abundance God offers.

In *A Beautiful Mess: Holding Doubt and Worry in the Same Hand*, we will explore the delicate balance between faith and uncertainty. Just as the journey we've walked has been marked by both light and shadow, so too is our experience of doubt and worry. These are not signs of spiritual failure, but parts of our shared humanity that God meets with compassion and understanding. In the messiness of our questions and concerns, we find that God's presence is often the most real, the most intimate.

This next chapter invites us to embrace our doubts without fear, to bring our worries into the light, and to trust that God is at work in both our faith and our questions. In doing so, we discover that doubt does not have to be an obstacle to peace; instead, it can be a bridge to deeper trust in the One who holds us, even in the midst of the mess.

Declarations

I declare and decree that I will not be anxious about anything, refusing to carry the burden of fear and anxiety, and rejecting the lies of the enemy.

I declare that I will stand firmly on the Word of God, choosing to walk in supernatural faith.

I declare that the peace of God, which transcends all understanding, will guard my heart and mind, keeping me safe and secure.

I declare that my thoughts will be anchored in gratitude, as written in Philippians 4:6-7, and I will seek to pour out my life for others, empowered and guided by the Holy Spirit.

Prayer

Pray the following poem as a prayer…

I worried a lot. Will the garden grow, will the rivers
flow in the right direction, will the earth turn
as it was taught, and if not how shall
I correct it?
Was I right, was I wrong, will I be forgiven,
can I do better?
Will I ever be able to sing, even the sparrows
can do it and I am, well,
hopeless.
Is my eyesight fading or am I just imagining it,
am I going to get rheumatism,
lockjaw, dementia?
Finally, I saw that worrying had come to nothing.
And gave it up. And took my old body
and went out into the morning,
and sang.
(Mary Oliver, I Worried)

Reflection Questions

When I think of anxiety, what comes to mind is...

1. If it were a colour, it would be...
2. If I could taste it, it would taste like...
3. If I could smell it, it would smell like...
4. If I could touch it, it would feel like…
5. If I were to locate it in my body, it would be...
6. If I no longer struggled with anxiety, the ways I imagine my life might be different are...

Journal Prompt

Reflect on a moment when you felt broken yet chosen to offer something of yourself to others. What did that act of giving reveal about your own healing journey? Without judging or fixing, gently name what was present in that moment.

CHAPTER 9

Holding My Fear

"A part of you was left behind very early in your life: the part that never felt completely received. It is full of fears. Meanwhile, you grew up with many survival skills. But you want yourself to be one… Try to keep your small, fearful self close to you… Let it teach you its wisdom; let it tell you that you can live instead of just surviving. Gradually you will become one, and you will find that Jesus is living in your heart and offering you all you need."
~ *Henri Nouwen, The Inner Voice of Love*

"I sought the Lord, and he answered me; he delivered me from all my fears." ~ *Psalm 34:4*

"So do not worry, saying, 'What shall we eat?' or 'What shall we drink?' or 'What shall we wear?' For the pagans run after all these things, and your heavenly Father knows that you need them. But seek first his kingdom and his righteousness, and all these things will be given to you as well. Therefore do not worry about tomorrow, for tomorrow will worry about itself. Each day has enough trouble of its own." ~ *Matthew 6:31-33*

When Worry and Doubt Shadows Faith

Fear doesn't always shout. Sometimes it slips in quietly, tightening the chest, clouding the mind, or circling the edges of belief with whispered doubts: *What if God doesn't come through this time? What if I'm not enough? What if it all falls apart?* I've known these thoughts. I've sat with them in the quiet hours of the night and felt their weight in seasons of uncertainty.

There was a time I believed that fear and faith were opposites, that one cancelled the other out. But over the years, I've learned they often live side by side in the same heart. Even as I've ministered to others, spoken of God's goodness, and witnessed His healing touch, I've also wrestled with deep internal questions. My worry and fear didn't mean I lacked faith, it meant I was human, and I was learning to bring my whole self, doubts and all, before a gracious God.

This chapter is about learning to hold worry and fear gently, not to feed it, but to face it without shame. It's about recognizing how fear can distort truth and paralyse hope yet also become a place of honest encounter with God. For it is often in our trembling, not our certainty, that God meets us most tenderly.

Our Takeaway

In one of our endless conversations, Barry and I try to distil all those trips to developing countries into a simple takeaway, what we want to carry forward and what we're ready to leave behind. One moment always comes to mind: an early morning drive to Delhi airport, the only time India seems to pause and breathe. The sky is just starting to blush pink as the sun rises through the haze, and for a brief moment, the chaos feels muted.

As we drive, thoughts drift toward home, and I turn to Barry, exhaling, *"I feel really happy."* It's a quiet, content moment. But within a minute, the car slows, and we pass a dead body sprawled on the road, the victim of a motorbike accident with a truck. There's no covering, no sign of dignity, just stark, raw reality. Rilke's words echo in my mind:

Let everything happen to you
Beauty and terror
Just keep going.
And so, we keep going (Rilke's (1934/2001, p. 35).

That moment captures the essence of India, the extremes, the paradoxes, the breathtaking beauty tangled up with heartache. It's such a beautiful mess. In many ways, it mirrors the human experience: we hold joy and sorrow, hope and despair, clarity and confusion in the same hand. India teaches you to breathe amid contradictions. It forces you to hold the chaos and the calm together, to find peace in disarray, and to move forward regardless.

Doubt as a Doorway

Doubt and uncertainty make fine bedfellows with worry and anxiety, all rooted in the same soil, fear. But as John Patrick Shanley (2005) reminds us in *Doubt: A Parable*, doubt isn't just weakness; it's a doorway to growth: Doubt requires more courage than conviction does. Conviction is a closed door. Doubt is an open one, leaving us vulnerable.

Often mistaken for failure or faithlessness, doubt may be the very ground where transformation begins. When our hard-won beliefs seem to slip away and nothing feels certain, it can feel like a wrong turn. But that sense of being lost is often the soul's cry for renewal, the Spirit breaking through the rigid patterns of our mind.

This unravelling may simply be our emotional longing for the familiar. But transformation is often born of disorientation. Doubt doesn't just call us back to the present, it invites us to surrender. And in surrender, the cracks of uncertainty become spaces where light breaks in.

Three Questions Under the Surface

Perhaps we wrestle so much with doubt and uncertainty because they force us to confront deep, spiritual questions about pain and suffering, questions often left unspoken. Philip Yancey, in *Where Is God When It Hurts*, identifies three timeless questions that haunt human suffering:

1. Is God unfair?
2. Is God silent?
3. Is God hidden?

An old Chinese proverb reminds us: *"Deep doubts, deep wisdom; small doubts, little wisdom."* Doubt demands honesty. It strips away our pretence and forces faith down to bedrock. We wrestle with the contradictions between what we believe and what we experience. Why isn't life unfolding as we expected? Why do our prayers seem to vanish into silence? Yet, mature faith doesn't bypass doubt, it leans into it.

Walter Ciszek, a Jesuit missionary imprisoned in Soviet Russia for over twenty years, offered profound insight into this spiritual terrain. Accused of being a Vatican spy, he endured isolation, interrogations, and hard labour in the Gulag. At first, he prayed fervently for release, for purpose, for signs of God's intervention. But over time, something shifted. He stopped demanding answers and began asking different questions.

In his memoir *He Leadeth Me*, Ciszek (Ciszek & Flaherty, 1973) describes the transformation of his faith. *"It was I who had to change,"* he wrote, *"not God. I had to learn to see life not as I wanted it to be, but as it was, and find* God there." He learned to narrow his focus to the present moment, surrendering control and the need for understanding. His faith deepened, not because he escaped suffering, but because he encountered God in the very heart of it. Doubt became his crucible of trust.

The Way Out is In

Sheldon Kopp (2013, p. 11) once wrote, *"In dealing with fear, the way out is in."* We don't overcome doubt and uncertainty by avoiding them, but by facing them with courage and grace. Francis Bacon (Bacon, cited by Wormald, 1993, p. 39) observed: *"If we begin with certainties, we shall end in doubts; but if we begin with doubts, we shall end in certainties."*

During COVID-19, doubt and uncertainty pushed me into deeper soul work. I had to confront what couldn't be explained or reasoned away. I brought it all to God, raw and unanswered, asking for something tangible, like bread in my hand. A simple gift of hope to sustain me for tomorrow.

Against Pleasure: The Ache of Worry

Jesus came to set us free from worry, to release us into the fullness of life with free minds, open hearts, and willing obedience. Our thoughts shape our inner reality. And one of the most universal forms of torment? Worry. Robin Becker's (2006) poem *Against Pleasure* captures this relentless ache:

Worry stole the kayaks and soured the milk...
In the dark, Worry wraps her long legs around me,
promises to be mine forever.

Worry calcifies our joy. It robs us of presence. It wraps itself around our lives, whispering, *"You belong to me."*

Jesus offers a different way, *"Do not worry about your life... Look at the birds of the air; they do not sow or reap... and yet your heavenly Father feeds them. Are you not much more valuable than they?"* (Matthew 6:25–26).

The Paper Exercise: A Visual of Joy Lost

Here's a simple exercise to visualize the impact of worry:

1. Take a blank piece of paper and write the word **JOY** in bold across the centre.
2. Write a specific worry in one corner. Tear it off. Throw it away.
3. Repeat, each time with another worry, until nothing remains.

This mirrors how worry works. Bit by bit, it erodes joy, until there's nothing left. We don't even recognize it as harmful anymore. It becomes socially acceptable. Even worse, we rarely consider how it grieves God.

Naming Our Worries

What kinds of things do we worry about? Take time to write a few down. Some examples:

- Do I worry about whether others like me?
- Do I worry about being found out for a mistake?
- Do I worry about how I look or whether I measure up?
- Do I worry that I'll never be enough

Research suggests that women, in particular, tend to worry in four key areas:

1. Job
2. Money
3. Spouse (or lack thereof)
4. Themselves

When we allow worry, fear, and anxiety to dominate our lives, they rob us of the joy that comes from truly living. The tragedy is that many of us are addicted to worry. It feels familiar, even necessary. But Jesus invites us to live differently. A life without worry may seem impossible, but that's exactly the freedom He offers.

How Worry, Doubt, and Uncertainty Affect Wellbeing

Physical Health

During my children's teen years, worry took a toll on my body. My immune system weakened. I began medication for high blood pressure and migraines. Prolonged worry affected my neurotransmitters and worsened my osteoarthritis. It became a cycle, worry fed illness, and illness increased anxiety.

Mental Health

Worry depleted the chemicals that elevate well-being, serotonin and endorphins, leaving me drained and fearful. I lost confidence. Conversations with my children became fraught with tension. Over time, negativity became my default setting (see Figure 1. *Cycle of Negativity*).

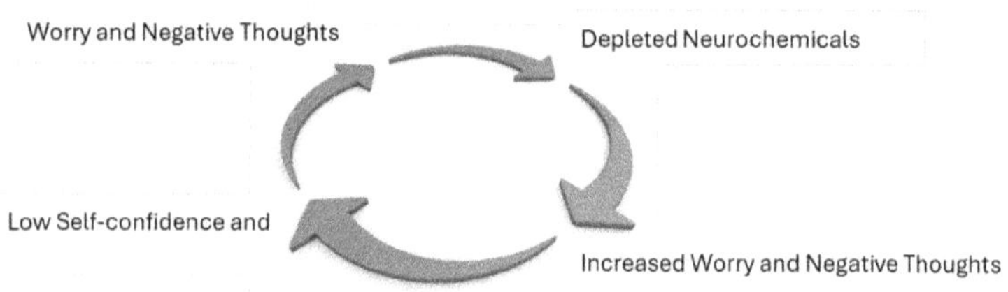

Figure 1. *Cycle of Negativity*

As Shakespeare said, *"There is nothing either good or bad, but thinking makes it so."* Milton (1667; 2003) took this further: *"The mind is its own place, and in itself can make a heaven of hell, a hell of heaven."* What we think truly shapes how we live. But even more profoundly, what we surrender to shapes who we become.

Emotional Health, and the Prison of the Mind

The **amygdala**, a key structure in the limbic brain, plays a vital role in processing emotion. It's often called the brain's emotional alarm system. Worry and negative thinking, then, are more than fleeting moods; they are physiological and spiritual assaults, on the heart, the brain, and ultimately, the soul.

Worry, in essence, is negativity expressed through self-disclosure. When I repeatedly said things like *"I'm so stressed," or "I'm overwhelmed,"* I was engaging in a subtle but potent form of self-abuse. My ears heard the words, and my limbic system absorbed them. The amygdala listened and responded, reinforcing the emotional states that my language predicted. In these moments, I wasn't just speaking to others, I was programming my own internal world, layering lies and half-truths into the very structure of my brain.

As Karen Horney (2010) insightfully observed, these cycles often begin in childhood. When emotional needs are dismissed, shamed, or unmet, worry becomes a coping strategy, a hypervigilant attempt to pre-empt rejection or punishment. Over time, I mimicked the emotional atmosphere that once rejected my needs, turning that same rejection inward. As mentioned in an earlier chapter, I told myself: *"You're too needy," "You're too much," "You're never enough."* In doing so, I internalized the voice of contempt, dressed it in my own tone, and called it truth.

This inner narrative became a kind of *mental incarceration*. I began to live, as **Walter Ciszek** described during his years in Soviet prison camps, with the gnawing sense of *"being cut off not only from the world but from God Himself"* (Ciszek & Flaherty, 1973). But like Ciszek, who discovered God's sustaining presence not in escape from suffering but in surrender to it, I, too, had to learn that healing doesn't begin by fighting my thoughts, but by surrendering them. I had to let go of the belief that I was unworthy of compassion and begin to speak to myself the way God speaks to His beloved.

Replacing these internalized toxins begins with **awareness**, recognizing the negative inner dialogue for what it is: a distortion. A form of spiritual and emotional self-harm. And then, with deliberate, Spirit-led effort, we replace them with words of grace, truth, and compassion. This is the work of transformation.

Worry and Spiritual Health

In the Sermon on the Mount, Jesus directly addresses the burden of worry, not once, but **five times** (Matthew 6:25–34). He speaks to our anxious striving, our future-focused fear, and our attempts to secure control in a world of uncertainty. His invitation is gentle but firm: *Do not worry.* Trust the Father who knows your needs.

The Oxford English Dictionary (Simpson & Weiner, 1989) defines worry as *"the state of being anxious and troubled over actual or potential problems."* Interestingly, the Old English root of the word *worry* means *"to strangle."* And indeed, worry can feel like a constriction, an invisible force choking out peace, suffocating joy, and draining our energy.

Jesus' teaching dismantles worry on both practical and theological grounds:

> *"Therefore I tell you, do not worry about your life, what you will eat or drink; or about your body, what you will wear... Look at the birds of the air; they do not sow or reap... yet your heavenly Father feeds them. Are you not much more valuable than they?" (Matthew 6:25–26, NIV).*

In this passage, Jesus highlights four ways that worry spiritually disorients us:

1. **Our values get distorted.**

   Worry shifts our focus from what truly matters. *"Is not life more than food, and the body more than clothing?"* Jesus asks. Our fixation on survival eclipses the deeper meaning of life.

2. **We become self-focused.**

   When worry reigns, our thoughts revolve around our needs: *What shall we eat? What shall we wear?* But Jesus reminds us that the Father already knows what we need.

3. **Our beliefs become distorted.**

   Worry lures us into thinking like those who don't know God. *"The pagans run after all these things,"* Jesus says, highlighting how worry causes us to forget the reality of divine care.

4. **We dread the future.**

   Worry fixates on tomorrow, a realm we cannot control. *"Each day has enough trouble of its own,"* Jesus says. We're not meant to carry the burdens of imagined futures.

From Worry and Anxiety to Trust

In moments of worry and deep anxiety, I've often felt God's silence more acutely. But like Ciszek, I've also found that *"God does not abandon us in our suffering; He accompanies us through it"* (Ciszek & Flaherty, 1973). Worry thrives in a vacuum of trust. When I fix my eyes on my own fears, I lose sight of the Father's face. But Scripture calls us back:

"Cast all your anxiety on him because he cares for you" (1 Peter 5:7, NIV).

"Do not be anxious about anything... but in everything, by prayer and petition, with thanksgiving, present your requests to God. And the peace of God... will guard your hearts and your minds" (Philippians 4:6–7, NIV).

"In all these things we are more than conquerors through him who loved us" (Romans 8:37).

This is more than religious advice. It is emotional rewiring. When we practice trusting God, we are forming new neurological pathways of peace and connection. The amygdala listens. And slowly, through prayer, presence, and truth, the fear-driven loops lose their grip.

Healing from worry is not instant. It is a process of unlearning fear and re-learning trust. And often, it begins with one small, whispered surrender: *"Father, into your hands I commit this fear."*

Closing Thoughts

As we return home, we carry more than memories; we carry transformation. We have seen that healing often comes in the breaking, and that abundance is not found in what we cling to, but in what we release. Like bread, our lives are meant to be taken, blessed, broken, and given. In that giving, we discover joy, peace, and a life that transcends the wounds we've known.

But even as we return with hope, we also return with questions. With worry. With the quiet ache of uncertainty about what lies ahead.

Worry is not only an addiction; it is, as difficult as it is to admit, also a sin. It may seem harmless, even virtuous, especially when cloaked in the name of responsibility. But beneath its surface lies something deeper: a fracture in trust. A doubt in the goodness and nearness of God. And yet, how gently Jesus meets us there. *"Do not worry,"* Jesus says, not as a harsh command, but as a tender invitation. An invitation to live differently. To trust.

Worry often begins as a whisper in the mind, but if left unchallenged, it becomes a persistent voice that shapes how we see everything, ourselves, others, even God. It is more than a mood. It is a signal. A warning light on the dashboard of the soul, reminding us that we are carrying burdens we were never meant to bear alone.

Physiologically, worry exacts a heavy toll, disrupting sleep, tightening muscles, draining vitality. Emotionally, it is rooted in early rejection and unmet needs, whispering lies that we are too much or not enough. Spiritually, it strangles trust and distances us from God's presence. The word worry, from the Old English *wyrgan*, means *"to strangle"*, and that's exactly what it does to joy, peace, and hope.

But there is another way. The path forward begins not with striving, but with surrender. With naming our worry, not hiding it, and placing it in the hands of the One who holds all things. It invites us to trace our anxiety back to its source, to unearth the lies we've internalised, and to receive the healing truth that we are deeply loved, fully known, and never alone. When Jesus says, *"Do not worry,"* He is not scolding. He is welcoming us into rest. Into a place of being held. Into freedom.

So perhaps the invitation is this: To become curious about our worry rather than ashamed of it. To grieve what has been lost or unmet. To name the hidden beliefs beneath it. And to turn, again and again, toward the One who speaks peace over our chaos.

In the next chapter, *Lies We Live By: Core Beliefs Underlying Anxiety*, we'll begin the courageous work of unearthing those silent scripts, those deep, often unconscious beliefs that drive our anxiety and distort how we see ourselves and God. This is more than psychology. It is the beginning of a spiritual awakening. Because to confront the lies we live by is to take the first step toward the truth that sets us free.

Declarations

I declare that I am casting all my cares on God, because He cares for me (1 Peter 5:7).

I declare that I will not fear, for God is with me; I will not be dismayed, for God is my God.

I declare that God strengthens me and helps me and upholds me with His righteous right hand (Isaiah 41:10).

I declare that I will take up the shield of faith that is able to quench all the fiery darts of the wicked (Ephesians 6:16).

Prayer

Pray David's prayer of gratitude to God from Psalm 18:16-19 (TPT):

[You] *then reached down from heaven, all the way from the sky to the sea.*
[You] *reached down into my darkness to rescue me!*
[You] *took me out of my calamity and chaos and drew me to* [Yourself], *taking me from the depths of my despair!*

Even though I was helpless in the hands of my hateful, strong enemy,
[You] *were good to deliver me.*
When I was at my weakest, my enemies attacked - but [You] *Lord held on to me.*
[Your] *love broke open the way and* [You] *brought me into a beautiful broad place.*
[You] *rescued me - because* [Your] *delight is in me!* [Parenthesis mine].

Reflection Questions

1. When I think of worry, what comes to mind is...
2. If it were a colour, it would be...
3. If I could taste it, it would taste like...
4. If I could smell it, it would smell like...
5. If I could touch it, it would feel like…
6. If I were to locate it in my body, it would be...
7. If I no longer struggled with worry, the ways I imagine my life might be different are...

Journal Prompt

Where do doubt and worry show up in your life and what would it look like to see them not as enemies, but as invitations to deeper faith? Without judging or fixing, gently name what was present in that moment.

CHAPTER 10

What is Anxiety Trying to Tell Me?

"Our anxiety does not come from thinking about the future, but from wanting to control it." ~ Samantha Gluck

"Anxiety is suffering that is yet to find its meaning." ~ Carl Jung

"I sought the Lord, and he heard me; he delivered me from all my fears." ~ Psalm 34:4

Exposing the Hidden Narratives That Keep Us Afraid

Anxiety doesn't always come from what's happening around us, it often rises from what's been planted deep within us. Over the years, I've come to see that beneath the shallow surface of tension and fear lie hidden narratives, unspoken beliefs I didn't know I had. *"I have to hold everything together." "If I let go, everything will collapse." "I'm not safe unless I'm in control."* These lies, often shaped by trauma or early experiences, create an inner world that feels constantly under threat.

Even when life is relatively stable, my body can remain on high alert, responding not just to present stress but to old messages etched into my nervous system. These lies don't shout, they whisper. They disguise themselves as responsibility, caution, or strength. But underneath, they keep me striving, guarded, and weary.

This chapter is about naming those hidden beliefs that fuel anxiety and hold us hostage. It's about learning to recognize the mental scripts that have shaped us and allowing God's truth to rewrite them. The turning point comes not by suppressing anxiety, but by gently uncovering what it's trying to protect. And in that uncovering, there is grace: the invitation to live no longer driven by fear but anchored in love.

Attempting to Control the Uncontrollable

The sunlight pours through my window on this beautiful Spring morning, and the Jacarandas stand in their breathtaking, almost heart-wrenching beauty. God's presence is woven into everything around me. Yet, I wake up trapped in my usual state of fear, reflecting on the ways I hurt others emotionally in my attempts to control life.

The weight of this realization makes me want to retreat into my cave, where I lose sight of who I truly am, a beloved child of the King, with all of His boundless resources available to me. My willpower feels futile. At the core of it all is my fear of rejection and abandonment that keeps me chained to old wounds, preventing me from stepping into the purpose God has designed for me.

As a young wife and mother, fear consumed me. The pain and struggles in my marriage, coupled with my disbelief that God could or would intervene, left me nearly paralysed. Over time, this same fear spilled over into my relationship with my children. Anxiety became a deep, aching longing for something I wasn't sure would ever be fulfilled. In my desperation to protect myself, I made an inner vow: *"To need hurts, so I will never need anyone again."*

That vow, meant to shield me, instead drained the life out of me. It hardened my heart and played right into the enemy's hands, leaving me cold and unfeeling. Rather than resting in God's perfect and unwavering love, love that casts out all fear of rejection and abandonment, I turned away. I chose to rely on myself, building my foundation on the most unstable platform imaginable. Unsurprisingly, this choice only deepened my anxiety and robbed me of peace.

As I look back, I see how anxiety often feels like an attempt to control the uncontrollable. It's not just fear of the future; it's a fear of being unprepared for what might come. It's a longing to manage every aspect of life, and in that desperation, I become overwhelmed, drowning in the very thing I sought to avoid.

But God, in His grace, is always there, inviting me to rest in Him, to trust in His unshakable promise: *"Never will I leave you; never will I forsake you."* And it's in these moments of surrender, of relinquishing control, that we begin to see anxiety for what it is: a symptom of deeper spiritual struggles, an invitation to trust where control is impossible.

Keeper of the Universe

For many who wrestle with anxiety, there comes a pivotal moment when we must relinquish our self-imposed role as the *"keepers of the universe."* We must learn to sit with the discomfort of uncertainty, trusting in something greater than ourselves. It is in this surrender that our hearts can awaken to their deepest longing for God and the abundant life He freely offers. Yet this trust can only be taken when we rest in the belief that God's promise is true: He will never leave us, nor abandon us.

Epictetus (2008) wisely observed, *"People are disturbed not by things, but by the views they take of them."* This insight resonates deeply with the Christian struggle with worry and anxiety. Many believers live under the weight of ignorance and shame, unable to explain how anxiety arises or how to address it. Often, they hesitate to seek help, fearing their struggles are a sign of weakness or moral failure. They dread being judged by a church culture that may view anxiety as purely a spiritual issue, suggesting it stems from a lack of faith. This perspective is as unhelpful as telling someone with a broken leg to throw away their cast and simply *"trust."*

Worry and anxiety are particularly challenging for Christians because they are explicitly denounced in scripture. Jesus taught that anxiety ultimately stems from a lack of faith. Both Jesus and Paul command us not to be anxious, leading to the difficult conclusion that anxiety is a form of sin. This can be hard to accept, as no one is immune to anxiety or the imperfect faith that accompanies it. Anxiety is a natural human response to new dangers, difficulties, or threats. Yet, scripture offers us a lifeline: *"When I am afraid, I put my trust in you"* (Psalm 56:3).

But here's the crux: how do we navigate this tension? How do we learn to trust God fully in the midst of our fears? The answer is not merely a matter of willpower or discipline. Trust is built through a deeper relationship with God, one rooted in His promises and His unchanging character. It grows as we experience God's faithfulness, even when our circumstances scream otherwise. And perhaps it is in the very struggle with anxiety that we encounter God's grace, His presence, and His healing most profoundly.

Janet's Story

Janet's story reveals the profound impact of unresolved trauma and the lies that anxiety weaves into the fabric of our lives. Her severe, high-functioning anxiety stems from a deep wound of abandonment and fear, rooted in the early and unexpected loss of her mother. The circumstances surrounding her mother's death were life-defining. Janet was forbidden to enter her mother's room while she was ill and dying. Returning home from school one day, she was told that her mother had passed away. Her mother was never mentioned again; it was as if she never existed. Janet was excluded from the funeral, and her father emotionally withdrew, leaving her to navigate grief and abandonment alone.

For Janet, the sudden and uncontrollable nature of her mother's death became a defining moment. It taught her that life is unpredictable and that she must always be on guard. The enemy capitalized on this wound, feeding her the lie that she was abandoned, unprotected, and must now carry the weight of fear alone. This fear manifests in her spiritual doubts, where she questions her salvation and fears committing the unpardonable sin, reflecting a deep-seated anxiety about being abandoned by God, just as she was by her parents.

Janet's Core Beliefs and Anxiety

At the heart of Janet's anxiety lies a belief that her survival depends on controlling her environment. *"My survival depends on certain events not happening, so I must be vigilant to remain safe."* This belief, deeply rooted in the trauma of her mother's death, perpetuates a cycle of hypervigilance and fear. She is constantly seeking ways to manage the chaos she feels around her, yet the very need to control everything only fuels her anxiety.

Her secondary belief: *"If I can remove myself from any situation where the threat occurs, I will not have to face the threat"* manifests in her attempts to control her relationships, particularly her marriage and her children. Yet, these efforts often result in emotional isolation and relational damage, furthering her anxiety and preventing her from finding the peace she desperately longs for. In the midst of these beliefs, the enemy whispers lies, promising safety through control, but leaving Janet trapped in a prison of fear and isolation.

This story of Janet reminds us that the roots of anxiety are deeply tied to past wounds, lies we have believed, and the attempt to control that which we cannot. But there is another truth: *God is not distant in our struggle.* He walks with us, offering healing and restoration even in the deepest parts of our fears. When we stop trying to control everything and rest in His promise: *"Never will I leave you; never will I forsake you,"* we can begin to break free from the lies that fuel anxiety and find true peace in His presence.

Barry's Story

Rigid, Demanding, Unrealistic Beliefs and Expectations

Perfectionism was Barry's defence mechanism. His story illustrates how perfectionism can become a way to cope with deep-seated insecurities and fears about one's worth. As a response to early messages of inadequacy, perfectionism often takes root in childhood and manifests in adulthood as an overwhelming need to control outcomes and avoid failure at all costs. The need to appear flawless becomes a way to suppress the pain of feeling *"not good enough,"* but it also creates a cycle of anxiety, self-criticism, and disconnection from others.

The Roots of Perfectionism

Perfectionism typically arises from early experiences where one's value was either conditional or unacknowledged. In Barry's case, the message that he was *"not good enough"* became internalized, fuelling his desire to prove his worth through flawless performance. The anxiety associated with perfectionism stems from the constant fear of failure, exposure, or rejection. Barry's belief that he must always meet high standards to be accepted led him to overextend himself, suppress his true needs, and isolate himself emotionally. The fear of being exposed as *"not good enough"* kept him trapped in a cycle of people-pleasing and self-criticism, distancing him from authentic connections with others

Deep Longing for Approval

Barry's narrative reveals the profound impact of unrealistic expectations and the deep longing for acceptance in relationships, both personal and professional. His need for perfectionism and approval, as well as the expectations placed on his family and workplace team, reveal how such internalized beliefs can drive destructive patterns of behaviour. His need to control outcomes and secure others' love to avoid being hurt led to an endless cycle of trying to please everyone, without ever feeling secure in his own identity.

This core belief fuelled his movement into becoming an approval addict. Even though he realized it is impossible for everyone to like and approve of him, he could not stop rescuing people and removing their responsibility. He tried hard to please everyone, but in doing so, he lost his identity and had no idea what he legitimately needed. He became so dependent on the approval of others that he never felt secure in their responses. His internal agreement was: *"If I can make you love me, you will not hurt me."* This self-protective strategy constituted a flight from desire, a deep longing to be accepted without the compulsion to earn it.

The Root of the Problem: Fear and Unmet Longings

At the heart of Barry's struggle is a deep, unmet longing to be accepted for who he truly is, not for what he can do or how perfectly he performs. This longing for unconditional acceptance is a common human need, but when it becomes distorted through perfectionism and approval-seeking, it turns into an insatiable desire that never brings true peace. The belief, *"If I can make you love me, you will not hurt me,"* reflects a desire for control over others' affections, which ultimately leads to a loss of self and a lack of authentic connection.

A similar pattern played out in my story. The unrealistic expectations I placed on Barry and my children were fuelled by the belief that my worth was dependent on their behaviour, moods, and opinions. I was caught in a cycle of trying to get my needs for esteem, security, and closeness met through others, rather than finding those needs fulfilled through my relationship with God. Instead of being life-affirming, this reliance on others for validation led to spiritual sterility, loss of authenticity, and the absence of intimacy, because I could never receive enough.

The problem with relying on a source outside of ourselves to meet our needs is that it is highly unreliable. My unrealistic expectations could not be sustained no matter how much I loved Barry and my children, who felt responsible to give the impossible. Eventually, the intense demands crushed life and spontaneity from my relationships, leaving only obligation and resentment.

The Destructive Pattern: Control, Obligation, and Resentment

The dynamic of controlling others and seeking validation creates spiritual sterility, where intimacy and authenticity are lost. When relationships are based on meeting unrealistic expectations or fulfilling personal needs for approval, they become transactional rather than life-giving. Instead of nurturing mutual love and care, they become driven by obligation, resentment, and disappointment.

This is a form of relational bondage. As Nancy Groom (2019) points out, if we let others be themselves, they might disappoint us. If we love them for who they truly are, they might not become the people we want them to be for our own gain. Instead of loving others, we are determined to make them love us back. Our goal becomes not to give, but to take, and the relationship becomes more and more restrictive as time goes on. The focus shifts from loving others to trying to obligate them to love us in return. The more we try to get our needs met through controlling others, the more constrictive and draining the relationship becomes. This cycle not only harms our relationships but also prevents us from truly experiencing the freedom and peace that come from loving others without strings attached.

Linda's Story

The Root of Linda's Struggle: Fear of Vulnerability

Linda's story highlights another facet of anxiety and its destructive impact on relationships. Her struggle with ruminations and nightmares reflects a deep-seated fear of vulnerability and a belief that exposing her true self would lead to devastation. While this belief seems protective in her mind, it creates a barrier between her and her husband, who longs for her openness and connection.

Linda's anxiety stems from the belief: *"What I long for may never happen. Therefore, I must try to get what I need from myself."* This belief fosters isolation and self-reliance, as she assumes others cannot be trusted with her deepest emotions and desires. Her agreement with the enemy is: *"If I am vulnerable, I will be destroyed. If I withdraw, nothing and no one can hurt me."* These defence mechanisms are rooted in fear.

Linda's chosen shame shield, withdrawal and hiding, is a strategy to avoid the perceived danger of rejection or betrayal. However, this approach not only isolates her but also leaves her husband feeling shut out and disconnected, creating a cycle of unmet needs and growing distance in their relationship. It also prevents her from experiencing the intimacy and acceptance she deeply desires. Her inability to express softer emotions such as sadness, longing, or fear creates a relational void that leaves both her and her husband aching for connection.

Her ruminations, while offering a false sense of control, rob her of peace and joy. The energy spent worrying about possible scenarios prevents her from being present and engaged in the moments that matter most. Over time, this pattern leads to feelings of despair and hopelessness, as the very strategies she uses to protect herself reinforce her sense of isolation and fear.

At the heart of Linda's struggle is a deep longing to be known and accepted, but her fear of vulnerability has convinced her that this desire is unattainable. By withdrawing, she protects herself from the risk of rejection, but she also closes herself off from the possibility of love and connection. Her husband's longing for her vulnerability is not just about emotional intimacy; it's an invitation for her to step into a space of trust and authenticity. Vulnerability, while risky, is the key to breaking free from the cycle of fear and isolation that has trapped her.

John's Story

The Root of John's Struggle: Fear of Failure

John's story illustrates a different manifestation of anxiety and its coping mechanisms. His shame shield is rooted in a need to assert control and avoid vulnerability by moving aggressively toward others' needs and opinions. This outward display of strength and dominance masks an inner fear of failure and powerlessness. John's belief: *"If I have power, no one can hurt me,"* reflects a deep-seated fear of being powerless and failing. This agreement with the enemy drives his need to dominate and control situations and people around him. His strategies of domination, blame, and manipulation are protective mechanisms that allow him to maintain the illusion of control and avoid confronting his fear of inadequacy.

Yet, beneath this façade lies a profound longing to be seen and understood for who he truly is, not for the power he wields or the victories he achieves. His aggressive approach to relationships and life is not about genuine connection but about protecting himself from perceived threats to his identity and worth.

Shame is a powerful force that keeps us locked in a cycle of fear, self-protection, and isolation. Remember how Brené Brown defines it? Shame is *"the intensely painful feeling or experience of believing that we are flawed and therefore unworthy of love and belonging."* This belief often drives us to hide, whether from others, from God, or even from ourselves. Yet, as Dan Allender and Tremper Longman III emphasize, we can't be healed of the wounds we won't acknowledge (Miller, 1990).

The Flight from Desire and the Illusion of Control

The need to control is often a reaction to unacknowledged wounds and unfulfilled desires. Janet, Barry, Linda, John, and I all illustrate how the flight from desire manifests as a desperate attempt to control the uncontrollable. Whether through perfectionism, withdrawal, or aggression, the underlying motivation is the same: to avoid vulnerability and protect us from further pain. Yet this strategy backfires, creating a prison of shame and anxiety.

Ultimately, the healing comes not through our own control, but through the vulnerability that allows us to trust God with our deepest desires. By surrendering the need to protect ourselves, we open ourselves to the possibility of true connection, both with God and with others. Only in vulnerability can we experience the freedom and love that are not contingent on our performance, approval, or control.

Closing Thoughts

Anxiety is never just about the future; it's about the past echoing into our present, whispering lies that we are still alone, unprotected, or powerless. But as children of God, we are not doomed to live imprisoned by fear or shaped by the false narratives that once kept us safe. When we begin to unearth the core beliefs buried beneath our anxiety, we start to see where our hearts have made agreements with fear instead of with truth.

God invites us to bring these beliefs into the light, not with shame, but with compassion. He is not angry at our anxiety. He sees the small child within us who was once abandoned, betrayed, overwhelmed, or left to fend for themselves. And He longs to meet us there. He calls us out of the cave, not to condemn us, but to remind us of who we truly are: Loved, held, secure, never forsaken.

Healing doesn't come by silencing every fearful thought. It comes by listening for the Voice that speaks a better word: *Peace, be still.* As we surrender the need to control what lies ahead, we grow in our capacity to rest in God's presence, here and now. And in that holy rest, our minds and hearts begin to renew.

If you find yourself caught in fear today, take heart. You are not alone. God is nearer than your next breath. He is not asking for perfect faith, only a willingness to trust Him, one trembling step at a time. Even there,

He walks beside you, holding your story, speaking truth into your deepest wounds, and gently leading you toward freedom.

But freedom isn't just about what we are released from. It's also about what we are called into. Because beneath the anxiety, beneath the shame and self-protection, something else begins to stir, a quiet ache, a holy longing. A flicker of hope that maybe, just maybe, we were made for more than survival. More than coping. More than numbing, striving, or managing fear. We were made for connection. For joy. For rest. For love. This longing isn't weakness. It's the imprint of heaven on our souls.

In the next chapter, *Wakening Desire: From Longing to Rest*, we'll begin to listen for the voice of desire, sometimes buried, sometimes burning, that calls us home. We'll explore how trauma can mute desire, how false beliefs can distort it, and how God gently awakens our hearts again, not with demands, but with invitation. Because healing isn't just about settling anxious minds. It's about stirring longing hearts. And it is in our longing that we find our way to rest.

Declarations

I declare that worry and anxiety is not of God, for His Word says He has not given me a spirit of fear, but of power, love, and a sound mind (2 Timothy 1:7). I renounce the lies and images planted by the enemy and release the weight of unhealthy, irrational thoughts. They have no authority over me.

I declare refusal to carry the burden of worry, fear and anxiety any longer, for I am not alone - my God is with me. I choose to stand on His Word, which is unshakable, and walk in supernatural faith, knowing that He is faithful to fulfill His promises.

I declare that the peace of God, which surpasses all understanding, guards my heart and mind in Christ Jesus. I am kept safe in His loving care (Philippians 4:6-7). I will not be anxious about anything but will bring all my concerns to God in prayer, with thanksgiving, trusting in His perfect plan for my life.

I declare that I am free, loved, and secure in Christ. Worry and anxiety have no hold on me, for I am a child of God, and His peace reigns in my heart. Amen.

Prayer

Heavenly Father, I come before You with a humble heart, casting all my cares, burdens, responsibilities, worries, and anxieties onto You, for Your Word assures me that You love and care for me deeply (1 Peter 5:7). Thank You for being my refuge and strength, an ever-present help in times of trouble. I trust You as my Good Shepherd, knowing that You will lead me along paths of righteousness and restore my soul.

Lord, You are the keeper of my mind and my heart. I ask You to surround me with Your perfect, supernatural peace that surpasses all understanding. Let it guard my thoughts and emotions, calming every storm within me. I declare that I will fix my mind on You, for Your Word promises that You will keep in perfect peace those whose minds are steadfast because they trust in You (Isaiah 26:3).

Today, I choose to embrace Your truth over the lies of worry, fear and anxiety. I surrender control and trust in Your unfailing love and wisdom. I know You hold my future, and Your plans for me are good, plans to give me hope and a future (Jeremiah 29:11).

Thank You for Your constant presence and for being my rock, my fortress, and my deliverer. I rest in Your promises and trust that You will lead me well. In Jesus' name, I pray. Amen.

Reflection Questions

1. What primary belief underlies your secondary belief (see list above)? For example, "If I can remove myself from any situation where……………………...occurs (name the threat), I will not have to face the threat."
2. What secondary belief is your focus that keeps you anxious? For example, "My survival depends on………………………..not happening (name the situations/events). Therefore, in my close relationships I must remain safe and hidden."
3. What deep longing underlies these beliefs? For example, "I long to be loved and accepted for who I am and not what I do."

Journal Prompt

What fear or anxious thought might be masking a deeper belief about myself, God, or the world? What truth is God inviting me to receive instead? Without judging or fixing, gently name what is present in this moment.

CHAPTER 11

Awakening Desire

"A flea can trouble a lion more than the lion can harm a flea." ~ Kenyan proverb

"Anxiety in a man's heart weighs him down..." ~ Proverbs 12:25

"Cast all your anxiety on him because he cares for you." ~ 1 Peter 5:7

Seeing Anxiety as a Signal of the Soul's Longing

We often speak of anxiety as something to overcome or eliminate, as if it were a sign of spiritual failure or emotional weakness. But what if, instead, anxiety is pointing us to something deeper? Over the years, I've come to see that beneath the racing thoughts and tight chest, beneath the urge to fix or control, there is often something holy stirring: a longing. A desire.

Worry and anxiety, though distressing, are often symptoms of something sacred within us reaching for security, meaning, love, or belonging. From a faith perspective, these emotions aren't just problems to be solved, they are invitations to listen. What is my soul longing for? What am I afraid to lose? What am I struggling to trust God with?

In this chapter, I explore the possibility that our anxious thoughts may be messengers, not of doom, but of desire. Desire for safety, for control, for love, for God. And rather than shutting down these feelings or trying to silence them, perhaps we are called to follow them, to let them awaken in us a deeper dependence on the One who holds all things.

What Heals?

In the early morning, as sunlight flickers through the trees, I sit outside, immersed in nature's beauty. The air resonates with birdsong, a living symphony that lifts my spirit. I smile as Barry valiantly battles the cockatoos, determined to save our mandarin tree. The cockatoos, however, are decidedly winning! My heart feels soothed and full of praise as I bask in God's creation, finding solace in its simplicity and wonder.

This peaceful moment is a gentle reminder of what can soothe anxiety, not just the natural world, but also the presence of God in the ordinary. Worry and anxiety may arise from biological, psychological, or spiritual sources, often a complex mixture of all three. In my own journey, counselling has been an essential support, not only for myself but for those I've walked alongside through anxious seasons. Sitting in the stillness of this morning, I'm reminded again of the healing power of creation, prayer, and compassionate presence.

Facing the Storm

How do we understand worry and anxiety from a faith perspective? In Matthew 8:23-27, we read how easily we, like the disciples, are overwhelmed by fear:

> *"Then [Jesus] got into the boat and his disciples followed him. Suddenly a furious storm came up on the lake, so that the waves swept over the boat. But Jesus was sleeping. The disciples went and woke him, saying, 'Lord, save us! We're going to drown!*

He replied, 'You of little faith, why are you so afraid?' Then he got up and rebuked the winds and the waves, and it was completely calm."

Jesus' question still pierces: *"Why are you so afraid?"* The Message translation is even more confronting: *"Why are you such cowards, such faint-hearts?"* His words compel us to examine the roots of our fear and where we have placed our trust.

The Flea and the Lion

A Kenyan proverb offers unexpected insight: *"A flea can trouble a lion more than the lion can harm a flea."* Worry and anxiety are like fleas, small, persistent parasites that sap our energy and steal our peace. They may seem minor at first, but they multiply quickly, taking over if left unaddressed. And yet, like fleas, they can be dealt with. There is a way to cleanse ourselves, not through sheer willpower, but through God's grace and wisdom.

Desire awakens in us when we begin to remember what we were made for. It stirs when we dare to believe there's more to life than anxiety and self-preservation, that we were created for peace, joy, and intimate connection with God. This awakening begins with honest questions: *What am I truly longing for? What lies beneath my anxiety?* Courageously facing these questions can open the door to a life lived in God's freedom, not fear.

Peace for Anxious Hearts

John Calvin (cited in Watterson, 1990) taught that anxiety is conquered through implicit trust in God. Jesus, in John 3:16, makes our salvation clear, reminding us that peace flows from grasping God's unmerited, steadfast love. One old hymn puts it beautifully (Rippon, 1787):

Fear not, I am with you, O be not dismayed
For I am your God and will still give you aid
I'll strengthen you, help you, and cause you to stand
Upheld by My righteous, omnipotent hand.

This hymn affirms the unwavering love of a God who never abandons us. Imagine if the opposite were true, that God could turn away from us. Spurgeon once reflected that such a thought would plunge the heavens into darkness. To be forsaken by God would be more unbearable than never having existed at all. Yet this is exactly the lie anxiety often whispers: *God's love has limits. His patience will run out. You're alone.*

But the truth is far different: God's love is eternal, His presence unwavering. During anxious seasons, it's vital to confront these lies with the unshakable truths of Scripture. When we reject fear's narrative and choose instead to dwell on God's promises, we begin to reclaim our peace. Psalm 91 (MSG) offers a vivid picture of God's protective presence:

"You who sit down in the High God's presence,
spend the night in Shaddai's shadow,
Say this: "God, you're my refuge.
I trust in you and I'm safe!"
That's right, he rescues you from hidden traps,
shields you from deadly hazards...
His huge outstretched arms protect you,
under them you're perfectly safe..."

In times of worry, these words offer not just comfort but truth. God's arms are always outstretched, His angels always at work, His presence always near. We are not alone.

Trusting the One Who Cares

God designed us with deep desires and longings that reflect His own heart. But anxiety often grows when we cling too tightly to control. When we push God to the margins, He doesn't withdraw. He remains, faithful, patient, always working behind the scenes.

David's prayer in Psalm 56:3 offers a simple but powerful practice: *"When I am afraid, I put my trust in you."* This is the bridge from anxiety to peace. When we cast our cares on Him (1 Peter 5:7), we're not just letting go, we're placing our burdens into the hands of the One who deeply loves us. It's not a one-time event but a daily rhythm of surrender.

Relinquishing Attachment to Attachments

It's often in the areas we care most deeply about that we suffer the most. Our attachments, to people, outcomes, identities, can become sources of anxiety. Yet God invites us to anchor our hearts in Him, where fear loses its grip. Philippians 4:4-7 offers a pathway:

> *"Rejoice in the Lord always. I will say it again: Rejoice!... The Lord is near. Do not be anxious about anything, but in every situation... present your requests to God. And the peace of God... will guard your hearts and your minds in Christ Jesus."*

This peace is not just an emotion, it's a shield. It guards our hearts and minds when we lean into God's nearness.

Like a Child in the Park

Picture a mother with her toddler at the park. The child's courage to explore the world depends on her nearness. If he stumbles or feels afraid, he looks to her. Her face, her presence, her voice, these anchor him. He knows where safety is.

We are that child. God is that loving parent. When we know He is near, we can navigate life with confidence. If we forget, anxiety creeps in. But when we remember, we rest.

The Nearness of God

Philippians 4 reminds us that our Lord is near, approachable, attentive, compassionate. To internalize this truth in a noisy, fast-paced world is no small task. Fears bombard us from every side. The media stirs our anxiety. Advertisements promise relief in all the wrong places. And yet, the answer remains simple, powerful, and life-changing: *the Lord is near.*

How will Changing Habits Help?

Philippians 4:4-7 invites us into a life shaped not by worry, but by prayer, thanksgiving, and trust. For those of us who wrestle with anxiety or a restless mind, this passage offers a simple yet profound path toward peace. We are encouraged to form new habits, habits of rejoicing, relaxing, and resting, that gently reshape our inner life. These aren't quick fixes but practices that, over time, renew our hearts and minds.

1. The Habit of Rejoicing

Worry often arises from fear, fear that God's love won't be enough, that He won't come through, or that our hearts will be disappointed again. Rejoicing helps us reframe our focus. It's a spiritual practice of choosing joy even in the midst of pain, trusting that God's love endures beyond our circumstances.

Try This:

Begin each morning by naming one thing you're grateful for. Say it aloud. Write it down. Let it be small, a warm shower, a good night's sleep, a kind word. Let that gratitude anchor your day in God's goodness.

Philippians 4:4 commands, *"Rejoice in the Lord always. I will say it again: Rejoice!"* Like a muscle, joy grows stronger with practice. Research shows gratitude reduces stress, builds resilience, and increases happiness (Emmons & McCullough, 2003). It even reshapes neural pathways, rewiring the brain away from fear and toward hope.

Try This:

In the evening, ask yourself or someone close to you, "What was your gift today?" Reflect on one life-giving moment. If it helps, keep a gratitude journal, or take photos throughout the day of things that move your heart. Let these become your testimony of God's ongoing faithfulness.

The Ignatian practice of the Examen is another powerful tool for cultivating gratitude and awareness of God's presence. It's a simple five-step reflection:

1. Become aware of God's presence
2. Review the day with gratitude
3. Pay attention to your emotions
4. Choose one feature of the day and pray from it
5. Look forward to tomorrow

Try This:

Before bed, take five minutes in silence. Ask God to help you see where He was present. What lifted your spirit? What drained it? Gently notice, without judgment. Over time, rejoicing shifts our emotional centre. Instead of being driven by fear or what's missing, we begin to live from a place of abundance and hope.

2. The Habit of Relaxation

Philippians 4:5 says, *"Let your gentleness be evident to all. The Lord is near."* The word *"gentleness"* here can also be translated as *moderation, reasonableness, or sweet forbearance*. In essence, it invites us to loosen our grip, to stop striving to control outcomes and trust in God's nearness.

Try This:

Ask yourself, "What am I holding too tightly right now?"

Breathe deeply. Imagine placing that person, outcome, or concern in God's hands.

Say aloud: *"God, I entrust this to you."*

Relaxation doesn't mean apathy; it means surrender. It's allowing ourselves to exhale, to soften, and to trust that God sees what we cannot.

Nature can also be a doorway into relaxation. Research into forest bathing (Shinrin-yoku) shows that time in green spaces lowers cortisol, heart rate, and anxiety (Park et al., 2007). Nature offers what anxiety cannot: stillness, beauty, and perspective.

Try This:

Spend 10 - 15 minutes outside today. Notice the breeze, the colours, the sounds. No phone. No podcast. Just presence. Even a moment near a tree, garden, or sky can ground you again in the now.

Try This with Loved Ones:

Share a calming moment with someone, sit in the sun with tea, take a slow walk, or simply gaze at the ocean or stars together. Beauty is even more healing when shared. Wendell Berry's (2022) poem reminds us that in stillness, fear dissipates. We don't have to chase healing; it finds us when we slow down.

I go among trees and sit still.
All my stirring becomes quiet
around me like circles on water.
My tasks lie in their places
where I left them, asleep like cattle.

Then what is afraid of me comes
and lives a while in my sight.
What it fears in me leaves me,
and the fear of me leaves it.
It sings, and I hear its song.

Then what I am afraid of comes.
I live for a while in its sight.
What I fear in it leaves it,
and the fear of it leaves me.
It sings, and I hear its song.

After days of labor,
mute in my consternations,
I hear my song at last,
and I sing it. As we sing,
the day turns, the trees move.

3. The Habit of Rest

Paul ends this passage with a promise: *"The peace of God... will guard your hearts and your minds in Christ Jesus."* This peace is not passive, it is strong, like a sentry standing guard over our most vulnerable places. But peace comes only when we let go, and rest in the presence of Christ.

Try This:

Build in small moments of Sabbath throughout your week. A 20-minute nap. Turning off your phone. Sitting in silence with a lit candle. Listening to worship music while lying on the floor. Rest doesn't have to be long, but it does need to be intentional.

Rest reminds us that we are not God. We are held, not driven. As Psalm 62:5 says, "*Yes, my soul, find rest in God; my hope comes from him.*"

In 1941, Brother Lawrence (2017), a 17th-century Carmelite monk, shared his journey of cultivating peace in *The Practice of the Presence of God*. He worked in a monastery kitchen, and discovered deep rest not through escape, but through presence. His secret? Turning every ordinary moment into a conversation with God.

Try This:

While washing dishes or folding laundry, whisper, "Lord, I'm here. You're here. Let's do this together." This gentle attentiveness, practicing the presence of God, can turn even mundane moments into sacred rest.

The Impact of Anxiety on Sleep and Practical Steps Toward Rest

Anxiety is not just a mental burden; it affects every part of our being, including our sleep. Both anxiety and depression can profoundly disrupt our sleep patterns, leading to the vicious cycle of restlessness, emotional exhaustion, and further distress. In the Bible, the line *"I sleep, but my heart waketh"* from Song of Songs 5:2 (also in Shakespeare's *Hamlet*) reflects the restlessness caused by anxiety that robs us of peace. When we are anxious, our bodies and minds are in a state of heightened alertness, preventing us from entering true rest.

Sleep difficulties are a common manifestation of anxiety, and this impact on sleep often worsens the cycle of emotional pain. Anxiety leads to fragmented, restless sleep, while depression often causes people to wake up early in the morning, unable to fall back asleep due to overwhelming worry or sadness. Those who battle anxiety frequently describe vivid, unsettling dreams or nightmares that further disrupt their rest. Interestingly, as anxiety and depression improve, the content of dreams tends to shift toward a more peaceful and positive direction. In fact, better sleep is one of the most effective antidotes to the emotional and psychological strain of anxiety and depression.

Our bodies and minds are interconnected in ways that science is only beginning to fully understand. One powerful example of this is the role of serotonin, a neurotransmitter in the brain that affects mood and sleep. Serotonin is essential for healthy sleep cycles, and its deficiency is often linked to both insomnia and emotional distress. For instance, people with depression often report waking up at 3 a.m., a sign of serotonin imbalance, while anxiety creates a cycle of restless nights and constant worry. These disrupted sleep patterns further contribute to emotional instability, making it harder to heal and find peace.

But it's not just our thoughts and emotions that play a role in this cycle; our anger, whether directed at others, ourselves, or even at God, can deeply influence our sleep and emotional health. Repressed anger often manifests as sleeplessness, agitation, and chronic worry. Negative emotions like anger stir up anxiety, which in turn creates a ripple effect of emotional and physical stress. The powerful connection between body and mind underscores the importance of managing our emotional states to improve both mental well-being and physical health.

In Proverbs 2:21-26, we are reminded of the importance of *"clear thinking and common sense,"* which are essential for our mental and emotional well-being. The passage beautifully highlights that when we guard our thoughts and minds, we are able to *"travel safely"* and sleep soundly without fear. The deep peace that comes from surrendering our worries to God allows us to rest, not just in body, but in soul.

To support this healing process, there are practical ways to improve the quality of our sleep and ease the weight of anxiety. Below are simple yet effective strategies that may help break the cycle of insomnia and anxiety.

Try This:

1. **Stick to a Sleep Schedule:** Going to bed and waking up at the same time each day supports the body's natural circadian rhythms and helps regulate sleep patterns.

2. **Dim the Lights in the Evening:** Exposure to darkness in the evening encourages the production of melatonin, the hormone responsible for sleep regulation.

3. **Avoid Stimulating Activities Before Bed:** Keep your evening calm and peaceful for at least two hours before sleep. Avoid intense discussions or emotional stressors, though sex can be a natural tranquilizer that aids rest.

4. **Skip Alcohol as a Sleep Aid:** While alcohol may initially help you fall asleep, it disrupts the deeper stages of sleep, leading to restlessness later in the night.

5. **Limit Caffeine After 2 p.m.:** Avoid caffeine or stimulants that could interfere with your ability to wind down in the evening.

6. **Exercise in the Late Afternoon:** Physical activity helps release excess adrenaline and calms the body, making it easier to relax at night.

7. **Minimize Noise:** Consider using earplugs or a white noise machine to create a peaceful sleep environment.

8. **Watch Your Evening Meals:** Eating large or heavy meals too close to bedtime can disrupt sleep. Choose lighter snacks and avoid foods that can cause indigestion.

9. **Try Tryptophan-Rich Snacks:** Foods like bananas, turkey, and milk are rich in tryptophan, which promotes sleep. Pair them with carbohydrates like toast for better absorption.

10. **Avoid Sleeping Pills:** While they may offer temporary relief, sleeping pills disrupt the natural sleep cycle and are not a long-term solution.

11. **Laugh More:** Laughter has been shown to reduce stress and promote a sense of calm, which can improve sleep quality.

12. **Cultivate Optimism:** A positive outlook can reduce anxiety and stress. Cultivating gratitude and focusing on the positive aspects of life can encourage mental peace.

13. **Ask God for Purpose and Rest:** Focusing on a kingdom-centred purpose and asking God for peace can bring emotional clarity and restfulness to the mind and spirit.

14. **Practice Christian Meditation:** Meditation, as practiced in the Christian tradition, offers a powerful tool for rest. Reflecting on Scripture and the presence of God can provide both mental and emotional healing, bringing peace to both body and spirit.

Incorporating these practices alongside surrendering our anxieties to God can lead to the kind of peace that surpasses all understanding, allowing us to experience true rest and renewal.

Final Encouragement

Changing habits isn't about pressure, it's about permission. Permission to stop striving. Permission to be human. Permission to practice peace in small ways that form us over time.

If you begin to cultivate just one of these habits, rejoicing, relaxing, or resting, start where your heart feels most drawn. Let the Spirit lead you gently. Transformation doesn't happen all at once; it happens through repeated grace. And as Paul promised, when we do this, *"the peace of God, which transcends all understanding, will guard your hearts and your minds in Christ Jesus."*

Closing Thoughts

The most effective antidote to worry and anxiety is simple yet profound: *Worry about nothing, and pray about everything,* with a heart of gratitude. This invitation to prayer brings us closer to God, where true rest and peace become possible. Philippians 4:6–7 (MSG) expresses it with such clarity and beauty:

> *"Don't fret or worry. Instead of worrying, pray. Let petitions and praises shape your worries into prayers, letting God know your concerns. Before you know it, a sense of God's wholeness, everything coming together for good, will come and settle you down. It's wonderful what happens when Christ displaces worry at the centre of your life."*

For me, learning to surrender has been a slow, sacred journey, marked not by perfection, but by daily return. The sweet peace that comes from laying down my plans and placing my confidence in God's faithfulness is like water to my soul. Jeremiah 17:7-8 paints the image so vividly:

> *"But blessed is the one who trusts in the Lord, whose confidence is in Him. They will be like a tree planted by the water that sends out its roots by the stream. It does not fear when heat comes; its leaves are always green. It has no worries in a year of drought and never fails to bear fruit."*

Now, before I even get dressed in the morning, I pause to surrender. I invite the Holy Spirit, my ever-present Helper, to lead me into the day. He steadies me when I feel uncertain, strengthens me when I'm weary, and never leaves me to walk alone.

But even with trust, surrender, and daily grounding in God's presence, there are emotions that still rise, emotions that don't always bow easily to peace. One of the hardest for me has been anger. Sometimes anger comes in a flash, sharp, hot, protective. Other times it simmers just beneath the surface, masking deeper wounds of grief, fear, or betrayal. For many of us, especially those who've experienced trauma, anger can feel like both a shield and a prison.

In the next chapter, *The Monster Who Was Sorry: Loosening the Grip of Anger*, we'll begin to explore this powerful emotion. We'll reflect on the ways anger can distort our relationships, shut down our vulnerability, and keep us trapped in cycles of shame or defensiveness.

But we'll also uncover the deeper truths beneath it, the hurts that need tending, the boundaries that need rebuilding, and the God who invites us to bring even our rage to Him. Because healing doesn't mean pretending that we're not angry. It means letting God transform our anger into something redemptive, something that leads not to destruction, but to restoration. Let's go there together.

Declarations

I declare that the stronghold of worry and anxiety is broken. Through prayer and petition, with a heart full of gratitude, I cast all my cares on Jesus, who keeps me in His perfect peace.

I declare that I choose not to carry the weight of worry, fear, or anxiety, and I reject the lies of the enemy. Instead, I stand firmly on the truth of God's Word.

I declare that God's peace guards my heart and mind, surrounding me with His safety. The Lord is my stronghold, my refuge, and He loves me with an unrelenting, steadfast love. I am never alone, for God has promised to be with me wherever I go.

Today, I choose to be still and let God fight for me.

Prayer

Spirit of worry and anxiety, I bind you in the powerful name of Jesus and by the authority of His shed blood on the cross. I command you to release your hold on me right now and leave my life completely. You have no place here. From this moment forward, I refuse to listen to your voice. No longer will I cower under your influence. Worry and anxiety are no longer welcome in my life.

Today, I choose faith in God and His Word over worry. I choose faith in God and His Word over fear. I choose faith in God and His Word over anxiety.

Jesus, I ask for Your forgiveness for the times I've listened to the enemy's lies instead of Your truth. Heal me, Lord, and seal the entry points the enemy has used to gain access to my heart and mind. Replace my worry and anxiety with Your peace, love, power, and a sound mind.

Hide me, Lord, in the secret place of the Most High, under the shadow of Your wings. Be my refuge and my fortress. Help me to trust You fully in every area of my life.

I pray this in the mighty name of Jesus, Amen.

Reflection Questions

When I think of desire, what comes to mind is...

1. If it were a colour, it would be...
2. If I could taste it, it would taste like...
3. If I could smell it, it would smell like...
4. If I could touch it, it would feel like...

5. If I were to locate it in my body, it would be...
6. If I embraced desire, the ways I imagine my life might be different are...

Journal Prompt

In the Appendix, you'll find the *Devotional & Prayer Guide: Rejoice. Relax. Rest.* Take some time to read through it and reflect on how you can incorporate these practices into your daily routine. Record your thoughts, experiences, and any insights you gain as you begin to embrace these rhythms.

CHAPTER 12

The Monster Who Was Sorry

"We love or hate our enemies to the same degree that we love or hate ourselves. In the image of the enemy, we will find the mirror in which we may see our own face most clearly." ~ Sam Kean

"Anger is an acid that can do more harm to the vessel in which it is stored than to anything on which it is poured." ~ Mark Twain

"Speak when you are angry and you will make the best speech you will ever regret." ~ Ambrose Bierce

"It is not the mountain we conquer but ourselves." - Edmund Hillary

Facing the Shame Behind Our Anger

Anger has many faces. Sometimes it explodes outward; other times it simmers quietly beneath the surface. It can feel like strength, or shame, or a desperate cry for something we've lost. In the aftermath of trauma or long-buried pain, anger often becomes the voice of what was never spoken, the protest of a heart that didn't feel seen, safe, or heard. But when we've been taught to fear or suppress anger, especially as people of faith, we often bury it, only to have it leak out sideways or turn inward as self-contempt.

This chapter is an invitation to approach anger not as a monster to banish, but as a messenger worth listening to. What is it trying to tell us? What story does it carry? And how can we bring it, in all its rawness, into the compassionate presence of God, the One who is neither threatened by our fury nor ashamed of our need?

Letting Go of a Mother's Rage

For years, I wrestled with the anger I carried from my mother's destructive rage. When she lay dying, I sat by her bedside, reading Psalms aloud in an attempt to soothe her evident anxiety. She had lost the ability to speak, but the look in her eyes, dark, menacing, and filled with silent rage, spoke volumes. Even in her weakened state, she flailed her arms, as if trying to strike me one last time.

The night she died, my husband, brother, and I gathered around the kitchen table, reflecting on our childhood. Barry, in his gentle way, tried to steer the conversation toward something positive. *"What's one memory of your mother's kindness?"* he asked. Stunned, neither my brother nor I could recall a single moment. Deep down, I had already known this to be true, but hearing it aloud struck a different chord. My brother, in particular, reeled at the realization. It plunged him into three days of profound grief, numbed only by drugs.

Choosing not to attend my mother's funeral was a decision that hurt some family members, but I simply couldn't bring myself to sit there and hear people speak kindly of her when I knew, in my heart, it wasn't true.

Later, we had to empty her home for the new owners. Tragically, Barry's brother passed away the night before we were set to clear it out. Overwhelmed with grief, we sifted through her meagre belongings, giving what we could to neighbours and tossing the rest into a large bin. I didn't want to keep anything that would remind me of her, except for a few photo albums and letters. I promised myself I'd look at them once my emotions settled.

The months following her death were deeply challenging. Eventually, I found the courage to open one of her folders filled with papers. I knew what I might find, but I wasn't fully prepared for the flood of bitterness and hatred that poured out from the letters she had left behind. Her words were venomous, filled with disdain for me, my family, and humanity. The pain in my heart was so sharp, it felt physical. It was clear to me, I had to find a way to let her go, to release her suffocating grip on my life.

The Monster Who Was Sorry: Anger in Our Marriage

Closer to home, the unspoken anger in our marriage nearly tore it apart. Kathleen Norris (1998, pp. 4-5), in her book *Amazing Grace*, recounts the story of teaching children to write poetry inspired by the Psalms. One small boy wrote a poem titled *The Monster Who Was Sorry*. It begins with his honest confession about hating how his father yelled at him. His reaction? Throwing his sister down the stairs, trashing his room, and eventually destroying the entire town. The poem ends with him sitting in his messy house, saying to himself, "I shouldn't have done all that."Norris reflects on the boy's words:

> *"My messy house says it all. With more honesty than most adults could have mustered, the boy made a metaphor for himself that admitted the depth of his rage and gave him a way out...he was well on his way toward repentance, not a monster after all, but only human. If the house is messy, why not clean it up? Why not make it into a place where God might wish to dwell?"*

My marriage, too, was like that messy house, cluttered with unspoken anger, unresolved pain, and a longing for intimacy that remained unfulfilled. For me, that mess was also the ache of depression, a swirling mix of love, hate, and a suffocating need for Barry to meet impossible expectations I placed on him. When I couldn't find the words to express my feelings, I turned to manipulation, trying to force him into becoming something he was never meant to be.

The Inferno of Anger

Anger is undeniably powerful. Carl Jung wisely observed that an individual who has not experienced the intense emotional turmoil of their passions will never be able to effectively overcome them. Often, our anger is deeply rooted in our past, directed toward those who shaped our earliest understanding of God, parents, caregivers, or authority figures who may have been unkind, abusive, legalistic, or manipulative. Sometimes, this anger is misdirected at God Himself, as we project onto Him the traits of those who caused us pain.

This unresolved anger can act as a barrier, drowning out the gentle voice of the Holy Spirit and spilling over into our relationships with those we love. Paul Simon's (1973) lyrics in *Something So Right* capture the bittersweet ache of anger and its impact on our hearts:

> *"They've got a wall in China / It's a thousand miles long / To keep out the foreigners they made it strong / And I've got a wall around me / That you can't even see / It took a little time / To get next to me."*

The song reminds us of the disconnect anger can create, how it blinds us to love and grace, even when they are right in front of us.

The Nature of Anger

Ephesians 4:26-27 (MSG) offers this guidance:

> *"Go ahead and be angry. You do well to be angry, but don't use your anger as fuel for revenge. And don't stay angry. Don't go to bed angry. Don't give the Devil that kind of foothold in your life."*

So, how do we be angry without staying angry? What kind of anger gives the enemy a foothold?

In the West, we have a wide vocabulary for anger, reflecting its many shades. We might say we're mad, bitter, frustrated, seething, or furious. But in African proverbs, anger is often described in vivid imagery that conveys its destructive power. For example, one proverb states: *"When your mouth stumbles, it's worse than feet."*

This highlights how angry words can do far more harm than actions. Another African proverb says: *"Even a goat can bite when conditions become unbearable."* This reminds us that even the meekest among us can lash out when pushed to their limits.

Anger's Destructive Impact

Unresolved anger can lead to destructive behaviours, hurting others, tarnishing relationships, and breaking trust. Words like *hate, wound, despise, scorn, loathe, vilify*, and many others, illustrate how unchecked anger can escalate into harmful actions.

Reflect for a moment: *What makes you angry?* Anger is a God-given emotion, meant to serve as a signal, a response to hurt, injustice, or unmet needs. Though it's often feared, anger can be constructive when expressed wisely. It can be a catalyst for justice, healing, and change. But when misused, it becomes destructive, damaging relationships and deepening wounds.

Two Kinds of Anger

1. **Truthful, Legitimate, and Authentic Anger**

   This type of anger arises when we witness genuine injustice or wrongdoing. It is a healthy, constructive emotion that can motivate us to seek justice and change. For example, anger over exploitation can lead to advocacy and positive action.

2. **Lie-Based and Destructive Anger**

   This type of anger is rooted in unresolved pain and misconceptions. It becomes a protective mechanism, shielding the heart from further hurt while punishing the offender, whether the wrongdoing is real or perceived. Though it offers a temporary sense of control, this kind of anger corrodes the soul and relationships.

The Anger Continuum

Understanding anger involves recognizing its varying forms and intensities, from mild irritation to uncontrollable rage. Each stage reflects a different emotional response. Being aware of these distinctions helps us manage and address anger more effectively (see Figures 2 and 3: *Anger Scale* and *Anger Continuum*).

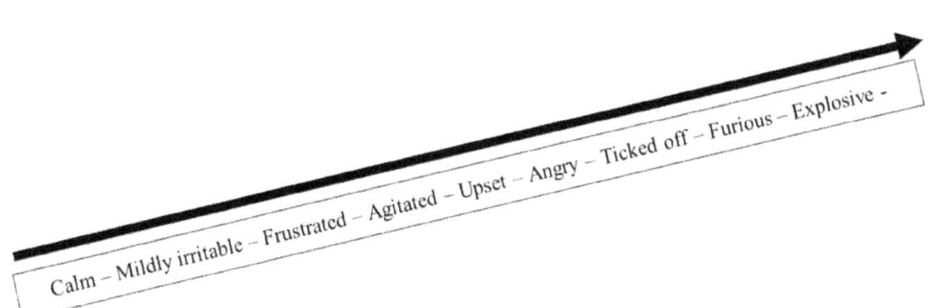

Figure 2. *Anger Scale*

Another way of depicting an anger continuum is:

ANGER CONTINUUM

Displeasure Annoyance	Irritability	Anger	Rage Violence	Fury Frenzy	Wrath
Grudge Grumble	Fume Cross	Seethe Temper Outburst	Feud Revenge	Roar Storm Injure	Annihilate Destroy

Figure 3. *Anger Continuum*

Recognising the Different Shades of Anger

Learning to recognise the different shades of anger helps us process and express our emotions in healthier ways. Instead of allowing anger to silently build until it explodes or erupts in destructive behaviour, we can grow in our emotional awareness and learn to name what we're feeling. Naming our emotions gives us the power to work with them. Language enables us to move beyond reactivity and towards understanding, both within ourselves and in our relationships. A *Feeling Word List* can be a helpful tool in this process, offering clarity and helping us express more accurately what's going on beneath the surface.

Anger Myths

Many of the myths we've absorbed about anger and conflict come from misguided attempts to protect ourselves from discomfort. But they rarely protect us, they often keep us stuck. These myths distort how we see conflict, leading us to avoid, repress, or mishandle it in ways that ultimately cause more harm than healing.

Here are some common myths about anger and conflict, why they fall short, and what a healthier approach might look like:

1. **Ignore It**
   Myth: If I ignore it, it will go away.
   Reality: Suppressing conflict doesn't resolve it, it just buries it. Unspoken hurt tends to fester, eventually surfacing in resentment or emotional shutdown.
   Healthy Approach: Gently address the issue when both people are ready. Bring it into the light rather than burying it in the dark.

2. **Soldier On**
   Myth: This is just my lot in life. I'll put up with it.
   Reality: Resignation doesn't bring peace; it often breeds bitterness and burnout.
   Healthy Approach: Your feelings and needs are valid. Seeking change is not selfish, it's part of growth and healing.

3. **Blame**
   Myth: It's their fault. Let them fix it.
   Reality: Blame creates walls, not bridges. It shuts down vulnerability and triggers defensiveness.
   Healthy Approach: Use "I" statements to express how you feel and what you need. It fosters openness instead of accusation.

4. **Deal with It Indirectly**
   Myth: If I talk to others about the problem, maybe they'll pass the message along.
   Reality: Triangulating through others creates confusion and mistrust. It can make the other person feel ganged up on or excluded.
   Healthy Approach: Speak directly and respectfully to the person involved. Honest, kind communication is the foundation of trust.

5. **Express and Dominate**
   Myth: If I come out strong, I'll win.
   Reality: In relationships, "winning" often comes at the cost of intimacy and connection.
   Healthy Approach: View conflict not as a fight to win, but a problem to solve together.

6. **Repress and Withhold (Silent Treatment)**
   Myth: Withdrawing will teach them a lesson.
   Reality: The silent treatment doesn't resolve anything, it just deepens emotional distance.
   Healthy Approach: If emotions are running high, take a short break, but always return to the conversation with a willingness to listen and understand.

Why Confrontation Is Necessary for Growth

We often associate conflict with division, but in healthy relationships, conflict can be an invitation to deeper connection. Confronting what's wrong, honestly and lovingly, is a pathway to growth. Love doesn't avoid tension; it leans in with care and courage. Conflict often arises *because* we care. There's something important at stake, respect, closeness, shared values. And when we face conflict with openness, we give ourselves the chance to heal old wounds and build new trust.

Anger Affects Our Health

Unresolved anger doesn't just affect our relationships - it takes a toll on our bodies and minds. When we stay in a state of chronic anger, our nervous system gets stuck in fight-or-flight mode, releasing a constant stream of stress hormones like cortisol and adrenaline. This can have long-term consequences.

According to the Department of Health & Human Services in Victoria, Australia (2018), chronic anger can lead to:

- **Anxiety and Depression** - Prolonged anger can increase emotional distress, preventing calm and emotional regulation.
- **High Blood Pressure** - The body's stress response raises blood pressure, increasing risk of heart disease.
- **Digestive Issues** - Anger can aggravate conditions like ulcers, acid reflux, and IBS.
- **Skin Problems** - Stress hormones can trigger acne, eczema, or psoriasis.
- **Headaches** - Chronic tension from suppressed anger can lead to migraines or daily headaches.
- **Heart Attack and Stroke** - Persistent anger can damage blood vessels and raise the risk of serious cardiovascular issues.

Clearly, how we handle anger matters, not just for our relationships, but for our well-being.

When Anger Turns to Conflict

Anger is often a signal emotion, a flare that something deeper needs attention. Conflict, on the other hand, is what happens when those underlying needs and emotions go unaddressed. Over time, unspoken pain, resentment, and unmet needs can build a wall between two people, even in loving relationships.

In close relationships like marriage, it's easy to fall into the trap of avoiding conflict to maintain surface harmony. But unacknowledged anger doesn't disappear, it hardens into bitterness. As the writer of Hebrews warns, bitterness *"defiles many"* (Hebrews 12:15). It spreads beyond the initial issue and begins to affect every interaction.

Take John's example. When someone cuts him off in traffic, he erupts in anger, but the rage is disproportionate to the situation. His emotional reaction hints at something deeper. Often, what looks like simple irritation is actually a shield for more vulnerable feelings: fear, anxiety, powerlessness. These emotions may stem from childhood wounds or present-day struggles that haven't been named or processed. Anger becomes a quick-release valve, but it's only a temporary illusion of control.

In John and Mandy's marriage, this pattern becomes a dance: his eruptions lead to her withdrawal, and her withdrawal fuels his resentment. The same dynamic plays out in countless relationships, a cycle of anger, hurt, silence, and disconnection. That's where the *Volcano Metaphor* helps make sense of what's really going on.

The Volcano Metaphor

Imagine a volcano: at the top is visible anger, yelling, blaming, sarcasm, withdrawal, or defensiveness. But beneath the surface are the more vulnerable emotions we often don't express - fear of rejection, pain from past wounds, helplessness, or shame. These are the primary emotions. They build pressure inside us when unacknowledged, eventually erupting as secondary emotions like rage or silent contempt (see Figure 4. *Our Volcano*).

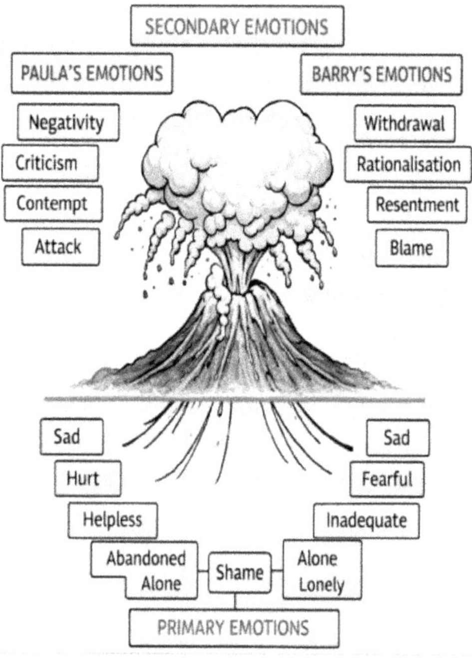

Figure 4. *Our Volcano*

We've used this metaphor around the world because it resonates deeply with peoples lived experience. At the top of the volcano is anger, loud, hot, explosive. But underneath the eruption are primary emotions, feelings like fear, sadness, shame, and helplessness. These emotions build pressure beneath the surface. If we ignore them, the volcano eventually erupts, and usually not in helpful ways.This simple but powerful image helps people see that anger isn't always what it seems. It's often a signal that something deeper needs attention.

In our own marriage, Barry and I recognised how we were each acting out of these secondary emotions. My anger came out through criticism and defensiveness. Barrys came out through rationalising, pulling away, and blame. These patterns kept us trapped in a cycle of disconnection.

But the real turning point came when we realised that underneath all this were the *primary* emotions, painful and tender ones we had buried. I discovered that my own anger was often a mask for deep feelings of abandonment, helplessness, and shame. I feared not being seen, not being enough. When I sensed judgment from Barry, even when it was unintentional, I would lash out to protect myself from the deeper fear that I was somehow unlovable.

Shame is a heavy burden. For me, it was rooted in childhood wounds, especially from my mother, and reinforced by years of perfectionism and self-doubt. My anger became a way of shielding myself from the vulnerability of shame. But unless I was willing to face those hidden emotions, my anger would only grow stronger, feeding the cycle of pain. It was the *volcano*, in our marriage, in ourselves.

Shifting the Story

To change, we had to challenge the stories we were telling ourselves, about each other, and about ourselves. Our assumptions, interpretations, and unspoken expectations shaped how we saw conflict. As we began to unearth those deeper stories, we were able to extend more compassion to each other. Anger no longer felt like the enemy, it became a messenger pointing us to our deeper needs and fears.

John Gottman (2007; 2015), a leading marriage researcher, offers sobering insight. After decades of studying thousands of couples, he claims he can predict with 91% accuracy whether a couple will divorce, simply by observing how they argue. What matters most isn't *whether* couples argue, but *how* they do it. Gottman found that healthy couples maintain a ratio of 5 positive interactions for every negative one. When negativity outweighs positivity, disconnection takes root.

He identified six warning signs that predict divorce (Lisitsa, 2013):

1. **Harsh Start-up** - How a conversation begins often determines how it ends.
2. **The Four Horsemen of the Apocalypse** –
    - Criticism
    - Contempt
    - Defensiveness
    - Stonewalling
3. **Emotional Flooding** - Feeling overwhelmed and emotionally hijacked.
4. **Distancing Body Language** - Nonverbal cues that signal withdrawal or tension.
5. **Failed Repair Attempts** - When efforts to de-escalate conflict fall flat.
6. **Negative Memories** —When bad memories eclipse the good.

What's striking is that these *"Horsemen"* all erupt from the top of the volcano, criticism, contempt, defensiveness, and stonewalling are classic signs of secondary emotions in action. Beneath them lie deeper wounds that haven't been named, validated, or healed.

But there's hope. When we begin to recognise what's underneath our anger and dare to bring those vulnerable emotions into the light, we open the door to a different kind of connection, one built on compassion, courage, and truth.

Releasing a Mother's Hold on My Soul

The enemy's tactics are subtle. He doesn't come with obvious weapons but with whispering lies, sowing division at our most vulnerable points. One of the enemy's favourite doorways is shame. Not the healthy shame that pricks our conscience and leads us to repentance, but toxic shame, the kind that seeps into our identity and tells us we are fundamentally flawed.

This kind of shame begins early, often before we can even name it. It grows in the hidden spaces of a parent's disapproval, emotional abandonment, or even in the well-meaning religious messages that taught us to perform in order to be loved.

In my life, shame didn't initially look like sorrow. It looked like anger. I didn't realise it at the time, but my rage toward my mother was fuelled not just by her actions, but by a deep and unnamed shame. I had buried the grief of never being truly seen, nurtured, or held. And in its place grew a festering anger that leaked into other parts of my life, into my parenting, my marriage, my sense of self.

One day, a caption under a photo of my sad-looking grandmother stopped me in my tracks:

> *Mum [my grandmother] in main street of Katoomba, where she and I lived for 6 months after she had a nervous breakdown in 1932. I was enrolled at school there and Dad used to come up on weekends. We boarded at a guesthouse in Cascade St and I got lost in the heavy winter mists on the way home from school.*

Something cracked open in my angry heart that day. For the first and only time in my life, I felt a connection to my mother. Through the eyes of my heart, I saw her not as the woman who had caused me pain, but as a frightened little girl. Her world had been shattered; her sense of safety destroyed. She was a desperate only child who had lost her own mother to the depths of depression, left utterly alone. I began to understand. Her survival had depended on shutting down all emotions except the blazing rage of abandonment. And maybe that's why she had passed it on to me.

In response, I wandered through a toy shop until I found a small, fluffy bear. I returned to her grave and placed the toy there. I told her how I grieved for the helpless little girl she had once been. In that moment, I was also grieving for my own inner child.

The third time I visited her grave, something deeper shifted. My teenage daughter was struggling. We were invited to a weekend of family counselling, where I asked her for forgiveness. But something the facilitator said struck a nerve. Her comments felt intrusive, too familiar. Later, it hit me: she reminded me of my mother's intrusive presence in my life. That's when I saw it clearly. My mother's deep wounds had left such a mark on me that I was now relating to others from that place of brokenness.

It broke me all over again. I asked God for forgiveness and found myself standing outside a florist, tears streaming down my face. I bought the most beautiful bunch of white roses I could find, hoping to spare the florist from the awkwardness of my grief.

At the cemetery, I found her grave again, marked by a dead rose bush. I placed the roses there and said aloud: she would no longer come between my daughter and me. She would no longer steal the beauty God had placed in me to share. As my tears fell, they watered her grave, and I walked away feeling like a prisoner set free.

The Enemy's Lies and the Path to Release

The enemy loves to sneak in right at the point of offense, planting lies that can derail us and keep us stuck. I've heard them in my own mind:

- *"If I let go of this anger, they'll get away with it."*
- *"Letting go means I'll get hurt again."*
- *"Forgiveness makes them right."*
- *"If I let go, I'm weak."*

But the most seductive lie was this: *"I must keep punishing those who've hurt me, sometimes for years, maybe even a lifetime."*

We may feel powerful in our anger, but it often imprisons us more than those we're angry at.

Gottlieb (1999) offers a powerful analogy:

> *"Try to ride [anger] and you most likely will end up eating dust. Probably you will break something that would better be left whole. Get back on the horse and the 'buckin' bronc' will throw you again. You can keep trying, or you can get smart and have someone show you how to tame the animal. Once you have learned to tame a wild horse, you will discover a magical relationship between you and the horse. The animal you tamed will become a good friend."*

Morgan Harper Nichols (2020) captures this journey so well in her poem: "You have picked petals":

without regard for their stems,
leaving them stripped of their color,
and when you saw what you had done,
you ran
and ran
and ran
eastbound
through the deserts
to hide
never to return to flowers again.

A new day is calling you
to stumble into the sunlight,
where the old ways
of thinking
are made right
so you can be at peace
to roam through the flowery fields again.

For mercy is always
louder than sharp cries of shame.
It knows where you have been
but still calls you by your name
inviting you to step forward
with the boldness to begin
a way of living that gives freedom
and to sow new seeds
into the earth again.

The journey out of shame is rarely linear. It takes time, tenderness, and grace. But each moment of awareness, every act of forgiveness, towards others and ourselves, is a step toward freedom.

God is not ashamed of us. He draws near to the brokenhearted. He calls us beloved even when we feel unlovable. And He never stops inviting us to sow new seeds of life, even when all we've known is barrenness.

Closing Thoughts

Anger is such a powerful emotion, and it exists on a broad spectrum, from quiet resentment to fiery outbursts. Often, it rises not as a first emotion, but as a shield, protecting us from what lies beneath. Hurt. Disappointment. Fear. Grief. In many ways, anger can be a mask we learned to wear when vulnerability didn't feel safe.

These self-protective strategies often trace back to the environments we grew up in, homes where emotions were confusing, overwhelming, or even forbidden. In those spaces, anger may have felt like the only way to be heard… or the only option to survive. But what if we began to get curious about our anger instead of ashamed? What if, rather than silencing it, we learned to listen?

In the next chapter, *What Is Anger Trying to Tell Me?* we'll explore the many faces of anger, its purpose, its messages, and its roots. Rather than offering a *"one size fits all"* solution, I'll offer a variety of perspectives to help us understand anger's complexity and uncover what might be hiding beneath its heat. Because sometimes, it's in the fire that we begin to find our way back to truth, healing, and even love.

Declarations

I declare that I choose, with all my heart, to forgive (insert the person's name here) for what they did. The specific issue is (state the issue clearly). I release them and place them fully in God's hands, trusting that He will handle them with both justice and mercy.

I declare that I let go of any desire for vengeance, bitterness, or resentment toward them. I cancel their debt to me; they owe me nothing. They don't need to apologise, change their behaviour, or even value me to be forgiven. My worth is set by God, and He values me completely.

I declare them free, and in doing so, I declare myself free from the anger, bitterness, or resentment that has tied me to them.

I declare Your forgiveness over the bitterness and resentment I've held toward (insert the person's name). Please heal my heart, take away the pain, and reveal Your truth about this situation.

(Take a moment to listen for God's response, a word, picture, or feeling, and write it down.)

(Adapted from *Biblical Foundations of Freedom* by Mathias, 2010, p. 111).

Prayer

I so much want to be in control.
I want to be the master of my own destiny.
Still I know that You are saying:
'Let me take you by the hand and lead you.
Accept My love
and trust that where I will bring you,
the deepest desires of your heart will be fulfilled.'
Lord, open my hands to receive Your gift of love.
Amen.

(Henri Nouwen, 2023, A Prayer)

Reflection Questions

When I think of anger, what comes to mind is...

1. If it were a colour, it would be...
2. If I could taste it, it would taste like...
3. If I could smell it, it would smell like...
4. If I could touch it, it would feel like…
5. If I were to locate it in my body, it would be...
6. If I no longer struggled with anger, the ways I imagine my life might be different are...

Journal Prompt

How might releasing my anger or unforgiveness open the door for healing and freedom in my heart today? Without judging or fixing, gently name what is present in this moment.

CHAPTER 13

What is Anger Trying to Tell Me?

"When you get married, your spouse is a big truck driving right through your heart. Marriage brings out the worst in you. It doesn't create your weaknesses (though you may blame your spouse for your blow-ups), it reveals them."
~ Timothy Keller, The Meaning of Marriage

"He who angers you conquers you." ~ Elizabeth Kenny

"Fools give full vent to their rage, but the wise bring calm in the end." ~ Proverbs 29:11

When Victimhood Becomes a Refuge and a Trap

Several years ago, I had a painful encounter with a family member that left me emotionally torn. I felt pulled in two directions: one toward resentment, the other toward understanding. As was my default pattern, I withdrew, not only from others but from my own life. I slipped into a familiar fog of helplessness, guilt, shame, and emotional numbness. I felt like a small boat tossed about in a stormy sea. A Victim mentality quietly crept in and took the helm.

Living as if I was perpetually at the mercy of others' actions was utterly exhausting. But this mindset wasn't new, it had been silently shaping my reality for years. It's a common survival strategy for those of us who grew up in emotionally unpredictable or unsafe environments.

Unlike a martyr complex, where one suffers for love or duty, a Victim mentality is rooted in helplessness and tends to avoid accountability. It doesn't just ask others to hear our pain; it silently demands agreement with our narrative. After all, if I'm a Victim, then I'm powerless, and someone else must be to blame. Victimhood, however, thrives on disempowerment. And disempowerment triggers anger.

The Complexity of Anger

In the previous chapter, we used the volcano metaphor to explore how anger often masks deeper emotions like fear, shame, helplessness, or grief. Anger becomes our shield, offering a sense of control or power when we feel exposed or unseen. As one therapist once told me, *"Anger is pain's bodyguard."*

Psychologist Jennifer Freyd (2002) described how, after traumatic events such as terrorist attacks, feelings of hatred and rage often emerge as a cover for grief and fear. When people are overwhelmed and feel unsafe, anger offers a quick, if temporary, sense of clarity and power. After the 9/11 attacks, for example, frightened shoppers chased Middle Eastern women and children out of a store, assuming they were terrorists. When fear can't flee, it fights.

But anger is complex. It's never just one thing. As Henry Wadsworth Longfellow (1857) reflected, *"If we could read the secret history of our enemies, we should find in each man's life sorrow and suffering enough to disarm all hostility."* When we peel back the layers, we often find that persistent anger is grief in disguise, an ache for love, justice, and safety that never came.

Anger, when explored with curiosity, can become a powerful messenger. It asks us to look deeper. *What am I protecting? What fear am I avoiding? What grief have I buried?*

In this chapter, we'll examine anger through two lenses: the Drama Triangle and righteous anger that aligns with God's heart.

The Drama Triangle

Someone once said, *"Maturity begins when drama ends."* That's a fitting segue into the concept of the Drama Triangle, a relational pattern many of us unknowingly adopt early in life. Originally developed by Stephen Karpman (1968) and later expanded upon by authors like Carmen Berry (2003), the Drama Triangle includes three main roles (Johnson, 2018):

1. Victim
2. Persecutor
3. Rescuer (or "Messiah")

Each role is a distorted way of coping with pain and shame. We slip into these roles not because we're flawed, but because we're wounded. They form a triad of emotional survival, keeping us trapped in cycles of blame, resentment, and emotional disconnection (see Figure 5. *The Drama Triangle*).

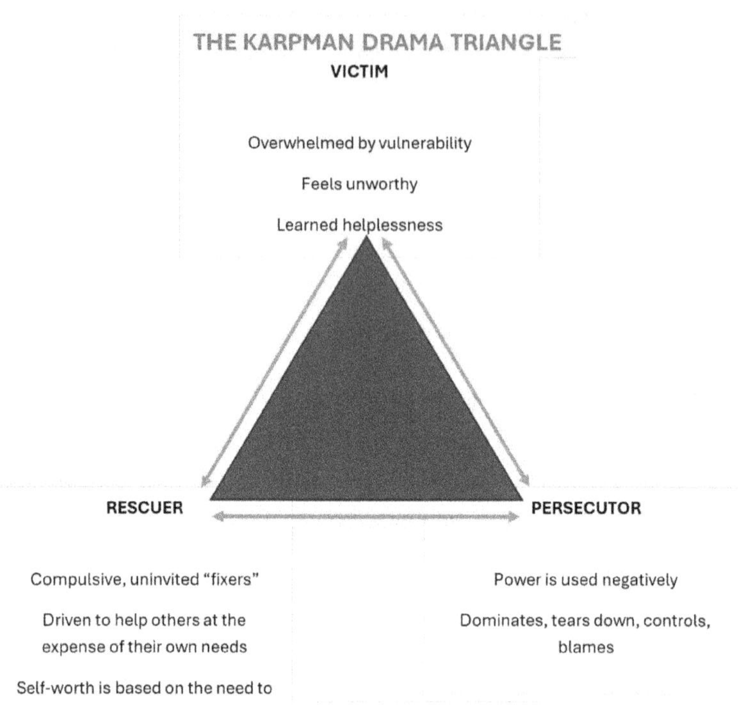

Figure 5. *The Drama Triangle*

It's not uncommon to move between the three roles in the Drama Triangle, Victim, Persecutor, and Rescuer. However, most of us tend to gravitate toward one role as a default, often using it as a defence against shame. For example, in my own childhood, which was far from ideal, I unconsciously slipped into the Victim role. It became my shield for protecting my fragile sense of self-esteem and managing the anxiety triggered by people, situations, and events around me.

My parents didn't encourage me to take on age-appropriate responsibility for myself. As a result, I grew into an adult who felt entitled to care and attention but resented others when I didn't receive it. The role I chose for self-protection as a child, Victim, now distorts my sense of power and responsibility as an adult.

This pattern is all too common for those raised in abusive or manipulative homes. It can leave us trapped in the destructive cycle of the Drama Triangle, where we adopt one of the roles, Victim, Persecutor, or Rescuer (Berry, 2003). Each role keeps us stuck in unhealthy dynamics, often mirroring the behaviours and unresolved issues that are symbolized by the eruption at the top of the volcano. Ultimately, these roles all violate the boundaries of others. But here's the crucial point: all three roles are driven by deep pain and a fear of vulnerability.

Now, let me break down how each role plays out in these dynamics.

The Victim

In my childhood home, the Victim role offered me a place to hide. I wasn't required to take responsibility for my emotions, and I grew into an adult who unconsciously blamed others for not giving me what I didn't know how to ask for. The message that settled deep in my bones was this: *"If I'm hurting, someone else must be the cause."*

As a child, I believed I was the reason for the chaos around me, that I was unlovable and the cause of others' disappointment. As an adult, that belief translated into feelings of shame, helplessness, and quiet resentment. The inner monologue sounded like this:

1. "Poor me. Nothing ever goes right."
2. "If people valued me, I would feel valuable."
3. "No one sees me. No one cares."
4. "Others seem to have it all together. Why can't I?"
5. "Even God feels distant. He'll disappoint me too."

Martin Seligman's (1991) concept of *learned helplessness* helped me understand this more deeply. Victims assume they are powerless, interpret setbacks as personal and permanent, and often give up trying. They withdraw, blame, and isolate. Over time, they may become passive, depressed, or quietly seething with unexpressed anger.

My own journey was marked by that pattern. As mentioned previously, I internalised my mother's voice: *"You're the cause of all the problems around here."* And so, I wore the name I gave myself: *Ruiner of Relationships.* This was the lie that shaped my anger, not just at others, but at myself and, at times, even at God.

Reflect...

1. Do you recognise any aspects of the Victim role in your own life?
2. What false beliefs or internal messages have shaped your responses?
3. What names or labels have you given yourself?
4. Are they rooted in truth, or deception?

The Rescuer

A Victim inevitably seeks a Rescuer, and I found mine in my husband. The Rescuer, or "Messiah", operates under the belief: *"If I take care of others long enough, maybe they'll care for me someday."* Sadly, this rarely happens because their "help" is usually directed toward Victims, who are often unable or unwilling to care for themselves.

The Rescuer's Cycle

Rescuers take control by sacrificing their own needs in what appears, on the surface, to be an act of care for others. Socially, they are often praised for their selflessness. However, the driving force behind their actions is a compulsive sense of responsibility, a need to rescue their Victims from pain and solve their problems. This behaviour helps Rescuers escape their own feelings of guilt or inadequacy. In this way, we fit together like a hand in a glove.

The Rescuer's Trap

Rescuers often sacrifice their own well-being by attaching themselves to people they believe desperately need saving. My husband, as a Rescuer, found purpose, and a sense of identity, in being needed by me. On the surface, his care looked selfless. But beneath it, his attempts to *"fix"* me were a way of vicariously addressing his own unresolved pain: the deep ache of not being loved or accepted simply for who he was, but only for what he could do.

Though his intentions were often caring, they sometimes crossed boundaries. During one particularly fragile season for me, he insisted I see a doctor who specialised in dietary solutions for emotional issues. He was convinced this would help. But in truth, his need to fix me overshadowed my autonomy. It left me feeling unseen, unheard, and even more helpless. Ironically, his rescuing reinforced my Victim role, keeping me dependent and, on some level, giving me unspoken permission to fail. By pouring himself into my problems, he avoided facing his own.

Years later, when his efforts weren't reciprocated in the way he'd hoped, he was left feeling disappointed and directionless. That's the turning point for many Rescuers: when their help goes unacknowledged or unreturned, they often shift into the Victim role themselves, feeling betrayed, used, and unappreciated. Their unspoken cry becomes: *"After all I've done for you, it's never enough."* And over time, unaddressed resentment builds. It simmers until it erupts, emerging as anger at the top of the volcano.

For years, our marriage see-sawed precariously around that volcano's rim. My husband, convinced he could heal me and our relationship by fixing me, took on a subtly superior role. When I resisted his help or failed to improve, his care turned to frustration, then to bitter resentment. I, in turn, ensured his efforts failed, by refusing to take responsibility for my behaviour, and by lacking the motivation to truly change.

Looking back now, it's clear: neither of us recognised the destructive cycle we were caught in. We didn’t yet see how much harm we were doing, to ourselves and to each other. We were both playing roles that kept us from the healing and intimacy we longed for.

Reflect...

1. Do you identify with the Rescuer role? In what ways?
2. What needs are you trying to meet by “fixing” others?

The Persecutor

The Persecutor uses anger as armour by controlling, criticizing, shaming, or domination. Their power lies in aggression, whether loud and volatile or quiet and cold. The anger of a Persecutor can be biting, sarcastic, sharp, or silent. But it’s rarely about the person they’re targeting. Like all roles in the Drama Triangle, it’s about pain.

Persecutors often grew up in homes where vulnerability was dangerous, where showing fear or sadness made them targets. Somewhere along the way, many made an inner vow: *“No one will ever make me feel that small again.”* Control became their shield. Contempt became a weapon. And anger became a fortress. But beneath the armour is often a deeply wounded child, ching to be seen, terrified of being shamed, and profoundly lonely.

Daniel is a textbook example of a Persecutor. Like many in this role, he lives by the belief: *“I feel safe when I hurt or intimidate others.”* His identity is built around the deception that others are to blame for his unhappiness. He often perceives himself as the true Victim, which fuels his anger and justifies his harsh and punishing responses.

For Daniel, anger isn't just an emotion, it's an addiction. He chases the adrenaline rush that comes with rage and confrontation. The emotional high of lashing out momentarily numbs the deeper wounds he refuses to face. This pattern keeps him stuck at the top of the volcano, constantly simmering, always one provocation away from erupting.

In Daniel's world, frustration justifies fury. Rather than sit with his own distress, he projects it outward. He sees others as weak or stupid, reinforcing his distorted view of the world and propping up a fragile sense of superiority. Feeling *less than* is intolerable, so he overcompensates by becoming *better than*. His superiority shows up in judgment, sarcasm, and biting contempt. You can hear it in phrases like:

1. *"See what you made me do..."*
2. *"If it weren't for you..."*
3. *"If only others would... the world would work."*

Anger becomes Daniel's way of staying in control. He believes that by dominating others, he can keep his anxiety and depression at bay. But his strategy is built on a lie: that power protects him from pain. In truth, his refusal to feel powerlessness drives him deeper into it.

Like many Persecutors, Daniel doesn't feel safe enough to admit pain. His anger says: *"I don't need you. You're the problem. You don't get to hurt me."* But beneath that anger lies exiled grief, buried shame, and a desperate longing for connection.

You Owe Me

I know this dynamic all too well, not just as a therapist or teacher, but as a human being. I remember a morning when I felt raw and misunderstood by my husband. He tried to explain his point of view, but I was too hurt to hear it. Instead, I cut him off mid-sentence and walked away. My silence was loud. I didn't raise my voice, but I made him pay. That was Persecutor energy, disguised as *"protecting my boundaries."* In the moment, I felt justified. But afterward, shame settled over me like a fog. I hadn't spoken from truth; I'd spoken from a wound.

Sometimes we slip into the Persecutor role in subtle ways: sarcasm, eye rolls, silent treatment, passive-aggressive behaviour. Other times, it's more overt: yelling, criticizing, controlling. Either way, the root is often the same, unprocessed pain masked by power.

Persecutors are often former Victims who never found a safe way to feel their pain. Now, they channel it outward, hoping to avoid the vulnerability they once feared would destroy them. But in doing so, they push away the very intimacy they long for. Daniel, like so many others, craves connection, but denies his need for it. He attacks instead of reaching out. He punishes instead of asking for help. He feels entitled, *"You owe me"* but beneath that entitlement is deep, aching need. To admit fault would mean confronting the shame he's spent a lifetime avoiding. And that shame is more terrifying to him than the damage his anger causes.

The Consequences

Daniel's rage perpetuates the very cycle he fears. Though he denies it, his greatest fear is powerlessness. Beneath the bravado lies a crippling fear of failure. As the Department of Health & Human Services (State Government of Victoria, Australia, 2018) notes: *"Those who fly into rages often have low self-esteem and use their anger as a way to manipulate others and feel powerful."*

But the end result is always the same. Persecutors like Daniel are left feeling isolated, unloved, and unlovable. Their anger, meant to protect them, becomes a prison. It cuts them off from the connection, care, and understanding they so desperately need.

Reflect...

1. Have you ever shifted into the Persecutor role, even subtly?
2. What emotional need were you trying to protect in that moment?

Trapped: Breaking Free from the Drama Triangle

The Drama Triangle, with its three roles, Victim, Rescuer, and Persecutor, keeps us locked in a cycle of dysfunction and conflict, especially in our relationships with others, including our spouse. Beneath the roles we play, there is often a hidden, wounded part of ourselves: an isolated, sad, or defensive side. Sometimes, we are not even aware of it, or we choose to ignore it. However, the first step toward transformation is acknowledging and understanding the origins of these roles.

What's profound is that the very role we adopt for self-protection can be the source of emotional abundance and vitality once we confront and embrace it. This journey begins with acknowledging the deeper, often unconscious wounds we've carried and how they manifest in our relationships.

When we reflect on the Drama Triangle, we don't just uncover harmful patterns; we also come face to face with the sources of our anger. Anger, especially when it arises in the context of these roles, often signals deeper unmet needs, violated boundaries, unhealed wounds, and distorted stories we tell ourselves. These stories may not align with God's truth. But here's the hope: Anger, when brought into God's light, can lead us to healing and authenticity.

What Is Anger Trying to Tell Me?

Anger is often more than just an emotional reaction, it's a signal. It doesn't appear out of nowhere. It rises up to draw our attention to something beneath the surface:

1. A **need** that has gone unmet
2. A **boundary** that's been crossed
3. A **wound** that still aches
4. A **lie** we've been believing

Rather than suppress or shame our anger, Scripture invites us to bring it into the light. The Psalmist models this kind of courageous honesty, *"Search me, O God, and know my heart... see if there is any offensive way in me and lead me in the way everlasting"* (Psalm 139:23-24).

God isn't asking us to judge ourselves for feeling angry. He's inviting us to bring our anger to Him, not to be punished, but to be *understood*. In His presence, anger becomes a doorway to healing. He gently uncovers the pain beneath it and leads us into freedom and restoration.

What is Healthy Anger?

Anger that has been carried into adulthood often stems from old wounds that are buried deep. As Nancie Carmichael (2011) points out, wounds heal, but sometimes, we need the Great Physician to perform the necessary work to allow that healing to happen properly. Psalm 139:23 invites God to do this work, to investigate and cross-examine our hearts, exposing the underlying causes of our anger.

The origin of anger can be traced back to the fall in Genesis 3, where Adam and Eve ate the forbidden fruit and immediately sought to hide, experiencing shame and separation from God. This was the beginning of the defensive mechanisms we use today, anger being one of them, to shield ourselves from vulnerability and pain.

When we experience anger, it's important to ask ourselves: *"What goal has been blocked, and who or what blocked it*?" "Is this anger connected to something from my past? Is it tied to an unhealed wound?" Digging deeper into these questions allows us to begin the process of healing and repentance. We can ask those closest to us how they experience our anger and whether unresolved issues may be fuelling it. In this way, anger can become a bridge toward transformation.

Repentance and Renewal

Repentance is a vital part of this process. It's the decision to turn away from the false sources of security we've clung to, and to return to God, the Source of Living Water. This renewal is often precipitated by a failure or a painful experience, times when our attempts to control life and relationships have fallen short, or when suffering shakes us. The choice to walk in the Spirit becomes one of trusting God's perfect love to sustain us.

Facing our anger head-on, acknowledging the past wounds, and asking God to show us the truths He desires for us to understand is not an easy process. It requires courage, perseverance, and a willingness to do deep internal work. This is where a trained counsellor or trusted guide can be invaluable in supporting us through this journey. The path to healthy anger involves surrendering our defences, allowing God to lead us toward healing.

Anger That Honors God

Ephesians 4:26 instructs us to *"be angry, but do not sin."* But how do we differentiate between righteous anger and destructive anger? The metaphor of God's "long nose" in the Bible offers insight into this. In the Old Testament, God is described as having a "flared nose" when anger arises at injustice. But the Bible also describes God as "slow to anger" (Exodus 34:6), which invites us to cultivate patience and discernment in how we respond to anger.

Righteous anger is rooted in grief over injustice rather than personal offense. It is "slow to anger" and centred on God's will, not our own desires. The sin does not lie in feeling anger, but in nurturing it and allowing it to turn into bitterness. Ephesians 4:29-32 warns us about the dangers of unaddressed anger, which can lead to harmful words that bring lasting harm. In these moments, we must learn to control our reactions and allow God to guide us toward healthy expressions of anger, anger that leads to healing, not destruction.

Redeeming the Drama Triangle

God offers us a way out of the Drama Triangle. We do not have to stay stuck in the roles we adopted in childhood or during times of emotional pain. Through God's transforming power, we can experience redemption and healing. Here's how in Table 1. *Redeeming the Drama Triangle*:

DRAMA ROLE	EMPOWERED IDENTITY	SPIRITUAL INVITATION
Victim	Empowered Overcomer	Take responsibility. Let God meet you in your pain. Reclaim your agency.
Rescuer	Compassionate Companion	Care without control. Trust God with the outcome. Set boundaries with love.
Persecutor	Courageous Truth-Teller	Speak truth with grace. Own your anger. Stay connected with tenderness.

Table 1. *Redeeming the Drama Triangle*

Transformation requires courage. It asks us to examine the deeper questions: What are we really angry about? What part of us is still grieving? What truth do we need to hear from God in this place of pain?

God's Invitation

God is not afraid of our anger. In fact, Scripture is filled with raw, honest emotion. The Psalms cry out in fury and grief. The prophets rage against injustice. Even Jesus expressed His anger when He flipped the tables in the temple.

God invites us to bring our anger to Him, not to push it down, but to listen to what it's trying to reveal. Anger often speaks to places where we feel abandoned, unsafe, rejected, or ashamed. These are the areas where God wants to meet us, offering healing and the opportunity to let go of old patterns and embrace His truth.

Closing Thoughts

The Drama Triangle sheds light on the deeply ingrained survival strategies we often adopt: The Victim, the Rescuer, and the Persecutor. These roles can keep us trapped in unhealthy patterns of relating, often fuelled by unresolved anger, pain, or a deep sense of powerlessness. But thankfully, the story doesn't have to end there.

God, in His mercy, not only reveals these patterns to us, He invites us to step out of them. Scripture offers a path toward healing and freedom, even from the most destructive forms of anger. Through His presence and truth, we are no longer bound to the roles we learned in pain or the strongholds we built to survive.

In Part Four, *Breaking Free: From Strangleholds to Strength*, we begin the journey of loosening the grip of the lies, patterns, and emotional strongholds that have kept us stuck. The first chapter, *Breaking the Power of Strongholds*, explores how these deeply rooted mindsets take shape, and how God leads us, step by step, into wholeness, truth, and strength.

Declarations

I declare that in the name of Jesus Christ, I renounce and rebuke the spirit of anger that has sought to take root in my life.

I declare that I will no longer give in to outbursts of anger, harsh words, or any other ungodly manifestation of its influence. Holy Spirit, I ask You to expose the root causes of my anger and help me address them at their source.

I declare that the Holy Spirit will empower me to respond to difficult situations with patience, kindness, and self-control.

I declare that You, God, will fill me with Your perfect love that casts out all fear and anger. I choose to walk in the fruits of the Spirit - love, joy, peace, patience, kindness, goodness, faithfulness, gentleness, and self-control.

I declare that destructive anger will leave me now, in Jesus' name. I will no longer tolerate its presence or influence.

Prayer

O God of such truth as sweeps away all lies,
of such grace as shrivels all excuses,
come now to find us
for we have lost our selves
in a shuffle of disguises
and in the rattle of empty words.

We have been careless
of our days,
our loves,
our gifts,
chances…
Our prayer is to change, O God,
not out of despair of self
but for love of you,
and for the selves we long to become
before we simply scuttle away.

Let your mercy move in and through us now…
Amen.

(Ted Loder, 2013, *My heart in my mouth: Prayers for our lives*)

Reflection Questions

1. How do you recognise the patterns of the Drama Triangle (Victim, Rescuer, Persecutor) in your own life?
2. How do they influence your relationships and reactions?
3. In what ways has God provided guidance in Scripture for dealing with anger?
4. How can you apply this wisdom to experience freedom from destructive anger?
5. How might you break free from the cycles of the Drama Triangle and find healing through God's peace?
6. What steps can you take to replace the ingrained survival strategies of the Victim, Rescuer, and Persecutor with healthier, more Christ-centred responses?
7. How can you invite God's peace into your life to heal the pain caused by anger, and how might that transformation impact your emotional and spiritual well-being?

Journal Prompt

Take a moment. Breathe.

- When was the last time you felt intense anger?
- What was beneath it?
- Which role in the Drama Triangle do you most often play?
- What might it look like to let God meet you there, not with condemnation, but with compassion?

Your anger is not your enemy. It's a doorway.

Let it guide you, not into blame or bitterness, but into truth, healing, and the God who welcomes you, even in your fury.

CHAPTER 14

When My Strongholds Began to Crumble

"We all leave childhood with wounds. In time we may transform our liabilities into gifts. The faults that pockmark the psyche may become the source of a man's or woman's beauty. The injuries we have suffered invite us to assume the most human of all vocations- to heal ourselves and others." ~ Sam Keen (1992, p. 61)

"Every source of blessing is a source of attack."
~ David McGee

Tearing Down the Lies That Once Felt Like Truth

There was a time when the lies I believed felt like solid ground. They gave me structure, predictability, even a sense of control, like emotional strongholds carefully constructed to keep me safe. "I am on my own. I must handle things myself." *"I must protect others from my feelings." "I'm the Ruiner of relationships."* These messages, shaped in the shadows of pain and reinforced by trauma, took deep root in my thinking. And for a while, they helped me survive.

But strongholds built on lies are prisons disguised as fortresses. What once protected me began to confine me. I saw it in my relationships, in my inability to rest, in the way shame crept in at the edges of joy. And slowly, through the loving presence of God and the piercing truth of His Word, the walls began to crack. Not all at once, but moment by moment, memory by memory, belief by belief.

This chapter traces that unravelling. It's about the painful but liberating process of naming the lies, confronting the fear beneath them, and allowing God's truth to seep in like light through broken stone. It's a story of crumbling strongholds, but even more, it's a story of a gentler foundation being laid, one built not on fear, but on love.

When Rage Becomes Your Mirror

My mother was a *rager*. Without warning, her anger could escalate from zero to nuclear in seconds. As I mentioned earlier, I learned quickly to stay out of her way. She wielded my vulnerabilities as weapons, using them to overpower and erase any sense of self I had. It made her feel powerful.

Gary Larson's cartoon says it all (see Figure 6. *My Mother, The Rager*). As I've mentioned before, her unspoken message was clear: *"You are the cause of all the problems around here, and we'd all be better off without you."* Those words, whether uttered directly or implied through her actions, cut me to the core. And the enemy seized upon them. It's not just what we remember that wounds us, but how we *perceive* what happened, and my perception was crystal clear: I was the problem. The enemy whispered names into my soul: *Ruiner. Damager.* I believed him

Figure 6. *My Mother, the Rager*

Lies That Take Root

There's an infamous principle of propaganda often attributed to Nazi minister Joseph Goebbels (1941): *"Repeat a lie often enough, and it becomes the truth."* That's what happened to me. The enemy repeated his lie until I accepted it as reality. And once I did, he built a stronghold in my life that followed me into adulthood.

Ironically, the strategies I used to prove him wrong only reinforced his lie. I vowed to be the best wife and mother I could be. I devoured books, adopted a *"cookbook"* approach to relationships, and modelled myself after my seemingly put-together mother-in-law. I believed if I followed the right steps, I'd get the right results. But of course, I eventually failed, because self-worth isn't built by *doing*. It emerges from *being*.

I feared that my outward actions reflected my inner brokenness. If people looked too closely, they'd see the truth: I was a ruiner of relationships, leaving damage in my wake. So, I hid behind a polished mask of competence, unwilling to let anyone see the real me.

D.H. Lawrence once wrote:

> *"And dimly she realised one of the great laws of the human soul: that when the emotional soul receives a wounding shock, which does not kill the body, the soul seems to recover as the body recovers. But this is only appearance... when we think we have recovered and forgotten, it is then that the terrible after effects have to be encountered at their worst"* (cited in Krockel, 2016, p. 152).

The Breaking Point

At twenty-eight years old, long after I believed I had moved on, I fell apart. I was consumed by the thought that my mother was right: I *did* ruin everything. Maybe everyone really would be better off without me. The self-loathing was so intense I could barely survive each day. I went numb just to keep going. My life dissolved into years of persistent depression. I felt trapped: in a failing marriage, in emotional paralysis, and in shame over my mothering. Failing even at suicide, remember how I made an inner vow, *"I'll never need anyone again. Needing hurts too much."*

That vow became another foothold for the enemy. It fortified the stronghold already built in my wounds. And I carried the crushing shame of believing I had damaged my children's lives, shame that was unbearable and unforgiving.

The Enemy's Hidden Work

I didn't know it then, but the enemy was working beneath the surface. After years of hearing the stories of others in pain, I came to see that emotional abuse is like cancer, it creeps in silently and spreads if left untreated (Vachss, 1994). Only when I began to see the enemy's schemes clearly did I recognise how he had kept me in bondage for so long, hidden behind lies and fortified walls of shame.

The day came when I confronted the enemy. I renounced the names he had branded into my soul and repented for believing his lies instead of God's truth about who I was. I invited Jesus into every memory, every broken place, and every painful wound. I asked Him to heal what was shattered and redeem what the enemy meant for harm.

That was the beginning of deliverance.

A New Name

In prayer, I asked Jesus: *"Who do You say I am?"* He brought Isaiah 43:2 to mind,

> *"Don't be afraid, I've redeemed you. I've called your name. You are mine."*

Then, Song of Songs 1:15-16 echoed in my spirit:

> *"I love you. I delight in you. You fill me with such pleasure. Listen to me, my child, I call you Lovely. You are my Beloved."*

Then Revelation 2:17:

> *"To the one who is victorious, I will give a white stone with a new name written on it, known only to the one who receives it."*

I asked the Holy Spirit, "What is my new name?" And He answered, faithfully:

> *My Healer. My Restorer. My Life-Giver.*

I sensed His smile:

> *"Did you notice these names are the opposite of the ones your mother called you?"*

Psalm 23 says, *"He restores my soul."* That restoration continues. Every broken part of me is being gathered into His love, transforming me from the inside out. No longer condemned but embraced in Christ (Romans 8:1). My heart is no longer blocked. And from this restored heart flows deep gratitude, for His love, His sacrifice, and His power to set me free.

What Is a Stronghold?

A stronghold, in biblical Greek (*ochurōma*), is a *"hard place"*. It's a fortress or bastion set up in a field of battle (Strong, 1995). Spiritually, a stronghold is anything that opposes the knowledge of God. It can be a mental block, distorted thinking, emotional patterns, or rigid beliefs that keep us stuck in darkness.

Strongholds can take many forms: worry, fear, insecurity, resentment, bitterness, self-loathing, guilt, or rage. These lies infiltrate our minds, shape our emotions, and eventually affect our choices and relationships.

For me, the stronghold was a deep-rooted belief: *"I am unlovable. I don't matter. No one will come for me."* The enemy used my wound as a doorway to whisper lies that shaped how I saw myself and others. Over time, it was like soul cancer, spreading, strangling, leading to a kind of emotional death.

But God's truth? *I am loved beyond measure. I matter. He has come for me, and He will never leave me.*

The Battle for the Mind

Thoughts have power. Mahatma Gandhi claims, *"You can chain me, you can torture me, you can even destroy this body, but you will never imprison my mind."* That's true, to a point. But Scripture reminds us that our thoughts are also a battleground. Paul writes, *"We take captive every thought to make it obedient to Christ"* (2 Corinthians 10:5). This implies our thoughts, left unchecked, can become unruly and destructive.

Dr. Caroline Leaf (2013) writes:

> *"75% to 95% of the illnesses that plague us today are a direct result of our thought life... We create the conditions for illness; we make ourselves sick! Fear alone can trigger more than 1,400 known physical and chemical responses and activate over 30 different hormones."*

As a therapist, I've learned that when a person hits a roadblock, when healing seems stalled, it's often due to a stronghold that needs to be torn down.

Paul himself understood this war. In *Romans 7:15–20 (MSG)*, he confesses:

> *"What I don't understand about myself is that I decide one way, but then I act another, doing things I absolutely despise... I can will it, but I can't do it... My decisions, such as they are, don't result in actions. Something has gone wrong deep within me and gets the better of me every time."*

The battle for the mind is real, and fierce.

Countering Lies with the Truth

So how do we win this battle? How do we *take every thought captive*? First, by recognizing that we are in a spiritual war, *"a life-or-death fight to the finish against the Devil and all his angels"* (Ephesians 6:12 MSG). Paul teaches that we do not fight this war with worldly weapons, but with divine ones, powerful enough to demolish strongholds.

> *"For though we live in the world, we do not wage war as the world does. The weapons we fight with are not the weapons of the world. On the contrary, they have divine power to demolish strongholds. We demolish arguments and every pretension that sets itself up against the knowledge of God, and we take captive every thought to make it obedient to Christ"* (2 Corinthians 10:3–5 NIV).

The Greek word for *"captive"* in this passage is *aichmalōtizō*, which literally means to take a prisoner of war at spearpoint (Strong, 1995). In other words, we are called to confront lies, the enemy's accusations and deceptions, with our weapon: the Word of God. We don't coddle these thoughts; we confront them. We don't manage them; we make them bow.

The Aramaic translation of this passage offers a vivid image (TPT, 2017). It speaks of demolishing *"rebellious castles"* - fortified strongholds of thought that resist the light of the gospel. These are not just mental habits; they are spiritual strongholds that must be brought under the rule of Christ.

Paul uses the word *hupakoē* for "obedient," which means *"to bring under control,"* or *"to listen under"* (Strong, 1995). This invites us to ask: *Are my thoughts listening to Christ?* Because if I don't take a thought captive, it will take me captive.

Strongholds That Sound Familiar

Remember how Barry, my husband, believed, *"Nothing I ever do is enough; I'll never be good enough?"* This wasn't just a passing thought, it was a deeply entrenched belief, a lie that shaped his identity and actions. But as a child of God, this was simply not true. Scripture counters that belief:

> *"Not that we are competent in ourselves to claim anything for ourselves, but our competence comes from God"* (2 Corinthians 3:5).
>
> *"There is now no condemnation for those who are in Christ Jesus"* (Romans 8:1).

Barry eventually learned to replace his old narrative, *"I'm not good enough"* with *"Jesus is enough, and I am enough in Him."* He began to declare, *"My grace is enough; it's all you need. My strength comes into its own in your weakness"* (2 Corinthians 12:9 MSG).

The only way to replace a lie is with truth. A thought must be *displaced,* not just dismissed. That's why Scripture becomes our sword. That's how we demolish strongholds and begin to walk in freedom.

Knowing the Enemy's Weapons

Paul reminds us that *"our struggle is not against flesh and blood, but against the rulers, against the authorities, against the powers of this dark world and against the spiritual forces of evil in the heavenly realms"* (Ephesians 6:12). Then he adds, *"Be prepared. You're up against far more than you can handle on your own"* (Ephesians 6:13 MSG). In other words, we are not fighting people. We are engaged in a spiritual war that demands spiritual weapons and vigilant awareness of the enemy's strategies. Three of his most common weapons are deception, temptation, and accusation.

Deception

Deception is *"the act of causing someone to accept as true or valid what is false or invalid"* (Merriam-Webster.com, n.d.). It's the enemy's specialty, distorting truth until we no longer recognize the lie.

I fell into deception when I believed a deeply painful lie: *"I'm unlovable. I don't matter."* Over time, this lie became a stronghold in my thinking. Worse still, I attributed the lie to God, reasoning, *"He allowed me to be abused when He could have intervened."* That single seed of deception grew into a toxic root system, shaping how I viewed myself, others, and God.

But the Holy Spirit didn't leave me there. He equipped me with truth, spiritual weapons to fight the enemy's lies. Paul describes them in Ephesians 6: the **belt of truth** (v.14) and the **sword of the Spirit**, which is the **Word of God** (v.17). The belt of truth helps us discern what's real, the sword of the Spirit cuts through deception.

When the enemy whispered, *"God is not good,"* I learned to counter with the truth. Scripture teaches that evil exists because of the condition of the human heart: *"From within, out of a person's heart, come evil thoughts, sexual immorality, theft, murder..."* (Mark 7:21). Yet, God does not abandon us in our suffering. He promises, *"After you have suffered a little while, the God of all grace... will himself restore, confirm, strengthen, and establish you"* (1 Peter 5:10 ESV).

When the enemy told me I was unlovable, the Spirit led me to these powerful truths:

> *"Fear not, for I have redeemed you; I have called you by name, you are mine... when you walk through fire you shall not be burned, and the flame shall not consume you" (Isaiah 43:1-2 ESV). "I have loved you with an everlasting love; I have drawn you with unfailing kindness"* (Jeremiah 31:3 NIV).

Temptation

From the very beginning, Satan used temptation to plant doubt about God's goodness. In Eden, he tempted Eve by twisting God's words and suggesting God was withholding something good. He used the same strategy with Jesus. In the wilderness, he tempted Jesus to turn stones into bread, to gain power, and to test God. Each temptation was an attempt to lure Jesus into false attachment, meeting His own needs on His own terms.

Author Gerald May (2007, p. 138) writes that Satan tried to trick Jesus into believing He could *"handle it"* without the Father's help. But Jesus saw through the lies. He stood firm, resisted the devil, and drew near to God (James 4:7). He wielded Scripture like a sword, refuting every temptation with the truth of God's Word. Temptation often appeals to our unmet longings, love, identity, power, comfort. But when we stay rooted in God's truth and presence, the enemy's power to tempt us begins to unravel.

Accusation

Satan is called *"the accuser of the brethren"* (Revelation 12:10). He loves to stir up shame, guilt, and condemnation, especially through our unhealed wounds. Sometimes these accusations come as internal thoughts:

> *You're a failure.*
> *You're too damaged to be healed.*
> *You'll never be enough.*

Other times, they come through the words or actions of others, hitting tender places we've tried to protect. The enemy uses these fiery darts to keep us in emotional and spiritual bondage.

But Ephesians 6:16 tells us to *"take up the **shield of faith**, with which you can extinguish all the flaming arrows of the evil one."* This shield protects the whole body. Roman shields were designed to catch and snuff out flaming arrows before they could do any harm. Likewise, our faith can shield us from accusations that aim to ignite shame and self-hatred.

The other pieces of armour, like the belt of truth, breastplate of righteousness, and helmet of salvation, are described as already being worn. But the shield must be taken up. It's an intentional, daily choice to trust in God's love, truth, and goodness, especially when the lies feel more believable than the truth.

Countering the Lies: A Reflection Tool

Table 2. *Common Lies vs. God's Truth* is a list of common lies the enemy uses to deceive, tempt, and accuse us, along with truths from God's Word that dismantle them. Take a moment to identify which lies have targeted your mind. Then prayerfully reflect on the corresponding truths. God's Word is not just information, it's transformation.

LIES FROM THE ENEMY	TRUTH FROM GOD'S WORD
I'm a failure. I can't do anything right.	You may struggle, but you can do all things through Christ who gives you strength (Philippians 4:13).
I am a mistake.	You are fearfully and wonderfully made by Me (Psalm 139:14).
If God cared, why would He let this happen?	I cause everything to work together for My glory and your good. My grace is sufficient for you (Romans 8:28; 2 Corinthians 12:9).
I'll always be this way.	You are a new creation; the old has gone, the new is here (2 Corinthians 5:17).
I am not enough.	You are chosen, forgiven, and blessed by Me (1 Thessalonians 1:4; Ephesians 1:3-7).
I'm afraid.	I give you a spirit of power, love, and self-control (2 Timothy 1:7).
I am in bondage.	You know My truth and you are set free (John 8:31-32).
I'm alone.	I will never leave you or forsake you (Hebrews 13:5).
I'm dumb.	I give you My wisdom (1 Corinthians 1:30).
I have no purpose.	You are called by Me (2 Timothy 1:9).
I don't have enough faith.	I've given you a measure of faith (Romans 12:3).
I can't cope.	Cast all your cares on Me, for I care about you (1 Peter 5:7).
I can't forgive myself.	If you confess your sin, I forgive you. There is no condemnation (1 John 1:9; Romans 8:1).
Life is not worth it.	It will be worth it—I am making all things new (Revelation 21:5).
I can't do anything.	You can do all things through My strength (Philippians 4:13).
I can't figure it out.	I will direct your steps (Proverbs 3:5-6).
I'm too tired and weary.	Lean on Me and I will give you rest (Matthew 11:28-30).

Table 2. *Common Lies vs. God's Truth*

Let this table become a daily practice: Identify the lie, confront it with truth, and declare the Word of God aloud. This is how we *"take captive every thought to make it obedient to Christ."* Not by willpower alone, but by truth, empowered by the Spirit and anchored in the love of God.

Closing Thoughts

Strongholds don't fall in a day. They crumble slowly, as we take every thought captive, as we dare to challenge the lies we've carried for too long, and as we invite the light of God's truth into the hidden places of our hearts. Healing is often quiet and persistent. It's found in the steady, everyday defiance of despair. In choosing to trust God's voice, even when old fears echo louder.

Throughout this chapter, we've seen how trauma can create inner fortresses, structures that once protected us, but now imprison us. Shame, fear, and distorted beliefs may grip us tightly, but the Spirit gently leads us toward freedom, not with condemnation, but with love and truth.

Breaking strongholds is only the beginning. Once the walls fall, a new question arises: **Who will I listen to now?** The next chapter, *Whose Voice Am I Hearing?* invites us to become more attuned to the voices that shape our thoughts, choices, and identity. We'll explore how to discern truth from deception, God's whispers from the enemy's accusations, and how to anchor ourselves in the voice that speaks life, healing, and belonging. Because freedom isn't just about tearing things down. It's about learning to live as children of the Light, guided by the One who knows us, loves us, and calls us His own.

Declarations

Jesus, **I declare** that you, God, want me to live a life of freedom.

I declare that the enemy is the father of lies.

I declare that from today, I choose truth over darkness and that I will no longer believe the enemy's lies.

I declare that I am accepted, not abandoned, and I am worthy of love and belonging, not rejection and fatherlessness.

I declare that my fear and shame is clothed with the glory of Jesus, and I am free.

I declare your promise that no weapon formed against me shall prosper (Isaiah 54:17).

Prayer

Heavenly Father, I come before You today, acknowledging the fierce battle that rages within my mind. The enemy seeks to deceive me, tempt me, and accuse me, but I choose to stand firm in Your truth. I know that in this war, the victory begins with a right perception of who You are, who I am in You, and the truth that will set me free.

Lord, I thank You for the words in Philippians 4:8-9, which remind me to fill my mind with what is true, noble, reputable, and gracious. Help me to meditate on what is beautiful and praiseworthy, and to reject the lies and negativity that the enemy seeks to plant in my heart.

When the enemy brings accusations, temptations, or deception, may Your truth be my shield. Teach me to put into practice all that I've learned from Your Word, all that I've seen and realized in Your presence. I trust that as I align my thoughts with Your will, You will work everything together for my good, bringing my life into harmony with Your divine plan.

Father, in the quiet of Your presence, help me to experience victory, even in the solitude of the battle. I know that the greatest triumphs are the ones only You see—the moments when I lean on You and trust in Your strength. May every victory begin on my knees, surrendering my thoughts, my heart, and my will to You.

I pray that Your peace would guard my heart and mind in Christ Jesus, and that Your Spirit would continually renew my thoughts and perceptions, transforming them to align with Your truth.

Thank You for being my refuge, my strength, and my victorious King. In Your mighty name. Amen.

Reflection Questions

In Appendix 1 there's a *Guided Reflection and Prayer - Replacing Lies with Truth*. Set aside unhurried time to prayerfully engage with this guide for personal reflection, journaling, and renewal.

Journal Prompt

Take a moment to quiet your heart and ask God to gently reveal one lie you've believed about yourself, perhaps something spoken over you in childhood, or something that's lingered in your self-talk. Write it down honestly and without judgment.

Now ask:

1. *Where did this belief come from?*
2. *What did it cost me to carry it?*
3. *How has it shaped the way I see myself, others, or God?*

Then, prayerfully ask: *What does God say instead?*

Write out a truth that counters the lie, grounded in Scripture or in your sense of God's loving voice.

Let that truth settle. Write a short prayer, asking God to help you live from that truth instead.

CHAPTER 15

Whose Voice am I Hearing?

"If you do all the talking when you pray, how will you ever hear God's answers?" ~ Aiden Wilson Tozer

"Our failure to hear His voice when we want to is due to the fact that we do not in general want to hear it, that we want it only when we think we need it." ~ Dallas Willard

"For the word of God is alive and active. Sharper than any double-edged sword, it penetrates even to dividing soul and spirit, joints and marrow; it judges the thoughts and attitudes of the heart." ~ Hebrews 4:12

Discerning the Voices That Shape Our Identity

We are shaped by voices, some loud, some subtle, some so familiar we no longer notice them. The voice of a parent, a teacher, a bully, a friend. The voice of trauma. The voice of culture. And underneath them all, the quiet but persistent whisper of the enemy: *"You're not enough." "You're too much." "You'll never change."*

For years, I couldn't tell the difference. I assumed that critical inner commentary was just part of me, my conscience, my truth. But slowly, I began to recognize the voice of the Accuser, cleverly disguised in my thoughts. His lies often sounded like my own voice. That's what made them so convincing.

This chapter is about learning to discern. About tuning in to the voice of the Shepherd who calls us by name and leads us with kindness, not condemnation. It's about noticing which voice we follow when we're tired, afraid, or ashamed, and choosing to turn toward the One who speaks truth in love.

Underpinnings of Freedom

Jesus profoundly cares about freedom from strongholds and bids me to depend on him for sustenance. The Holy Spirit longs to heal me. But I must learn the underpinnings of freedom and tune my heart to listen for his voice above all other voices. I'm learning what it means to recognize when it is God himself speaking to me. He cares. He is near. He comes to help, even when I can't scream or explain my fear in words (Lawton, 2012). This chapter explores: How do I keep learning to listen for his voice?

Satan always exploits our vulnerability to whisper his lies. The crisis for many Christians is that we don't know our own voice, we confuse the whispers of the enemy with our own thoughts and desires. As Eldridge (2016, pp. 175–176) warns, many believers riskily assume that every thought and desire is their own. Discernment is essential. To hear God's voice clearly, three foundational truths must be brought into the light:

1. An accurate perception of who God is

As explored earlier, I need an accurate perception of who God truly is. How can I trust in God's goodness if I believe he's a punisher lurking in the shadows, waiting for me to slip up? This distorted image creates fear, not intimacy. Freedom begins with seeing God as He truly is, loving, gracious, and trustworthy.

2. An accurate perception of who I am in Christ

Likewise, my freedom depends on understanding my true identity in Christ. If I view myself as a failure or unworthy, how can I bring my mind into submission to Christ? My thoughts about God and myself shape my emotions, which in turn influence my actions. Paul, in Romans 7:15-20, began his journey of transformation with raw honesty: *"What a wretched man I am."* But *"wretched"* here doesn't mean self-loathing; it expresses deep desperation over the war within. Paul's cry, *"Who will rescue me?"* is a longing for help and healing. He knew that shame and self-condemnation could never set us free. In fact, they rob us of hope.

God never asks us to punish or belittle ourselves. Rather, He invites us to acknowledge our need for rescue. Where are you acutely aware of needing help? Bring that to Him.

3. A foundation of truth

Jesus defined truth as God's Word. Scripture is not just encouragement; it's legal ground for freedom. Revelation 12:11 declares, *"They triumphed over [the enemy] by the blood of the Lamb and by the word of their testimony."* When Jesus was tempted in the wilderness, he countered every lie with, *"It is written..."* (Matthew 4:3). God's Word is a sword, our offensive weapon to dismantle strongholds (Ephesians 6:17).

When the battle intensified for Paul, he remembered that he was deeply loved by God and that condemnation does not come from Him. If condemnation and shame could heal us, we would be whole by now. But the opposite is true. Only God's truth, grounded in His love, can restore us. So, where does the enemy still accuse you? And where do you continue to accuse yourself?

To demolish a stronghold, it must be exposed, opposed, illuminated, and displaced by the light of God's Word. Then it must be undergirded by prayer. Paul urges us in Ephesians 6:10–18 (MSG):

> *"Be prepared. You're up against far more than you can handle on your own... God's Word is an indispensable weapon. In the same way, prayer is essential in this ongoing warfare. Pray hard and long. Pray for your brothers and sisters. Keep your eyes open. Keep each other's spirits up so that no one falls behind or drops out."*

A Life Never Imagined

The life I live now is one I never imagined. After a week of exhausting yet beautiful ministry in India, I find myself searching for something I can't name. I feel both broken and more whole. A friend recently observed that I tend to see everyone as broken. I've thought long and hard about this and have come to believe that without an awareness of our own brokenness, we cannot come to God in dependence. Nor can we extend true mercy or offer real hope to a hurting world.

As I age, I'm learning to live with paradox: joy and sorrow, beauty and starkness, strength and fragility, abundance and poverty. I'm learning to carry others' brokenness without it crushing me. Perhaps I come closest to wholeheartedness when I am most aware of my fractures, because it's then I know how much I need God. And this week in India, I've needed Him desperately. He has not disappointed, and He never will.

To my friend I want to say: maybe we are all broken. But those who acknowledge it can embrace the mystery of a flawed humanity and speak that native language with fluency.

Parker Palmer (2018, pp. 149-150) tells a story:

> *"A disciple asks the Rabbi why the Torah instructs followers to place the words 'upon' their hearts. 'Why not in our hearts?' The Rabbi replies, 'As we are, our hearts are closed, so we place the words on top. And there they stay until one day the heart breaks, and the words fall in.'"*

There is comfort in journeying with those who wrestle, who walk with a limp like Jacob, who lean into God with honest questions. In this life I never imagined, I allow God's Word to fall into the cracks of my broken heart, and I know with certainty: as I hold the pain of the world, I too, am held.

The Residual of Complex Trauma

At some point, we all ask: *Am I enough? Am I too much? Do I belong? Will I still be loved if you see the real me?* In complex trauma, the answers often feel like a resounding no. The enemy establishes strongholds that distort our sense of self and damage our capacity to connect.

How I interpret my thoughts shapes my reality. My thoughts shape my emotions, which influence my behaviours. Remember how King Solomon, thousands of years ago, said, *"As he thinks in his heart, so is he"* (Proverbs 23:7). That's why I must ruthlessly eliminate toxic thoughts with truth. I can change my neural pathways. By intentionally choosing how I think, I can break free from lies and cultivate life-giving patterns (Leaf, 2015, p. 21).

Satan seizes on our wounds to whisper lies. But like Jesus, we can use God's Word to counterattack. When Satan says, *"You failed again, you are a failure,"* we reply: *"In Christ, I am a new creation. Sin has no dominion over me. There is no sin in Him, and I am in Him"* (1 John 3:5). The enemy does not want us to focus on God's gracious nature. But I declare with assurance: God has removed my sin, and I am free from its power. Jesus said, *"My grace is sufficient for you, for my power is made perfect in weakness."* Paul responded, *"Therefore I will boast all the more gladly about my weaknesses, so that Christ's power may rest on me"* (2 Corinthians 12:9-10).

The Word of God assures me: I can change my thoughts and feelings by taking them captive and fixing my gaze on Jesus. I have authority over the enemy. Jesus gave it to me: *"I have given you authority... to overcome all the power of the enemy"* (Luke 10:19). *"They overcame him by the blood of the Lamb and by the word of their testimony"* (Revelation 12:11). Matthew 7:24-27 reminds me that God's Word is not just for study, it's a foundation to build my life upon. When storms come, the house that stands is the one built on the rock.

My emotional wounds opened a door to the enemy's lies, but I can close that door with God's truth. As I continue in His Word, I discover true freedom, *"If you continue in My word, then you are truly disciples of mine; and you will know the truth, and the truth will set you free"* (John 8:31–32).

Closing Thoughts

Healing from shame is not a one-time event; it is a sacred, unfolding journey. And on this path, God is never in a hurry. He meets us in the shadows and in the stumbling, whispering through the noise of condemnation: *You are mine. You are beloved. You are redeemed.*

To walk in freedom, we must learn to trust the voice of Love over the voice of accusation. This takes courage. It means noticing when the old narratives resurface, pausing long enough to ask: *Whose voice is this?* And then choosing, sometimes with trembling hearts, to return to the truth that in Christ, we are already enough.

Though shame may have shaped parts of our past, it does not get to write the final chapter. As we root our identity in the One who carried our shame to the cross, even our most wounded places can become holy ground, places where grace takes hold, and the Spirit breathes over the dust.

But what about the moments when we're triggered before we can even think? When a look, a word, or a tone pulls us into emotional flashbacks and floods us with old pain? In the next chapter, *Roots That Still Bleed: Healing Emotional Triggers*, we'll explore how trauma lives in the body, how unhealed wounds can surface unexpectedly, and how the Spirit meets us there, not to shame us, but to lead us gently toward wholeness. Because healing isn't just about what we know. It's about what still hurts, and the love that enters in.

Declarations

I declare that I am no longer defined by shame, but by the truth of who I am in Christ, beloved, chosen, and redeemed.

I declare that every lie spoken over me is being dismantled by the power of God's Word, and I am being renewed day by day.

I declare that I have authority through Jesus to overcome the enemy's accusations, and I stand firm in the victory of the cross.

I declare that my heart is being healed, my mind is being transformed, and my soul is anchored in the unshakeable love of God.

Prayer

Lord, Jesus,
You see every wound, every hidden shame, and every silent cry.
Thank You that You do not condemn me, you rescue me.
Help me to recognize Your voice above all others.
Heal what is broken, and replace every lie with Your truth.
Teach me to walk in the freedom You died to give me.
I surrender my thoughts, my wounds, and my identity to You.
Let Your love be the loudest voice in my soul.
In Jesus name. Amen.

Reflection Questions

1. In what areas of my life do I still hear the voice of shame more loudly than the voice of truth?
2. How has my image of God been shaped by past wounds or distortions, and how is it being reshaped now?
3. What strongholds or lies about myself do I sense the Lord inviting me to dismantle with His Word?
4. Where have I experienced God's nearness in my weakness, and how has that changed me?
5. What would it look like today to live as someone who is already deeply loved and free?

Journal Prompt

Today, I will invite God to speak truth into the place where I feel most unworthy and listen for His voice. Without judging or fixing, gently name what is present in this moment.

CHAPTER 16

Roots That Still Bleed

"People get into this place of perceived powerlessness. They believe that they are bad and unworthy and there is nothing they can do to change. People stay in painful circumstances, jobs and relationships because they feel they do not deserve anything better."
~ Sharon Wegscheider-Cruise

"Triggers are like little psychic explosions that crash through avoidance and bring the dissociated, avoided trauma suddenly, unexpectedly, back into consciousness."
~ Carolyn Spring

The Hidden Wounds Behind Our Triggers

Some wounds don't fully heal the first time. They lie beneath the surface, quiet, buried, and easily forgotten, until something unexpected pulls them open again. A tone of voice. A look. A memory. And suddenly, we're flooded with emotion that feels too big for the moment.

That's the power of a trigger. It bypasses reason and awakens pain that's still rooted deep inside. For years, I didn't understand why certain situations could unravel me so completely. I thought I was over it. I thought I had forgiven. I thought I had moved on.

But the truth is, some roots still bleed. This chapter is an invitation to compassionately explore what lies beneath those sharp reactions, not to shame ourselves, but to seek the deeper healing God longs to bring. Because our triggers don't mean we've failed. They mean there's more restoration still to come.

When Regret Awakens Old Shame

A hard conversation with someone triggers me. I berate myself with deep regret for the wrong I perpetrated on this person, a wrong that led to their confrontation. It ignites the very core of my shame, and I'm unable to quiet my soul. Though I ask for forgiveness, it's refused. The person I hurt now becomes the one who wounds me. All this is still alive in me when we travel to New Zealand for a pre-arranged spiritual retreat.

Surrounded by Spring

The retreat is nestled in a lush, rural setting, bursting with brightly coloured spring flowers that spill over garden beds. Wildflowers pepper the grass. Three Shetland ponies graze peacefully beside a few black cows. It's as if the land itself breathes new life. Ironically, we're here to ask God what He wants us to do and where He wants us to go in this final season of life, while I carry the weight of inner chaos.

On the property stands a tiny cabin with brightly coloured stained-glass windows. The door is unlocked, inviting. Inside, I'm greeted by a treasure-trove of experiential materials, paper, crayons, books, stones, shells, small toys, even someone's story artwork on the coffee table. Like Goldilocks, I try out each chair until I find the one that feels just right. Under the table is a box of coloured cards, and I'm drawn to them immediately. I've always resonated with colour and its symbolism.

Exploring My Inner Landscape with Colour

The instructions on the box invite me to choose a card that represents a problem I can't seem to resolve. My hand is drawn to a murky green card, envy.

I pause.

My personality pattern, according to systems I've studied, is associated with envy. But I've never felt envious in the way most people understand it. I've sat with the pain of so many women, I know everyone's life has thorns. I don't crave what others have. In fact, many women have been envious of me. Yet here is this colour, asking me to look again.

Next, I'm to pick a colour that symbolizes what's blocking my progress. I choose red. The description suggests fear, of being trapped, of becoming too attached. It hits close to home. I gnaw on past pain like a dog with a bone.

> *"There is a Sufi story about an old dog that had been badly abused and was near starvation. One day, it found a bone and gnawed it clean, desperate for nourishment. A kind man began leaving food nearby, but the dog clung to the bone, and starved to death" (The Enneagram Institute, n.d.).*

This story pierces me. It captures my soul's entrapment. Months before the retreat, the conversation mentioned earlier sent me into soul-searching. I kept chewing on it, replaying it, unable to let it go. My old story reared up: *I am flawed. Something is missing in me that others have.* I see how disappointment, especially when expressed aggressively, reinforces this belief. I wonder: How much of my story is no longer true? And even more urgently: How do I let go of the bone and receive nourishment?

The Colours of Healing

The next step invites me to imagine myself under a waterfall, letting the problem wash away. I choose yellow, freedom from worry, from self-criticism. Yellow represents joy, confidence, and the sense that I have what I need. It feels far off. Still, I cling to the possibility.

I'm then asked to choose a colour that represents my new thoughts and feelings. I pick turquoise. Something about it feels light and playful. The description speaks of intuition, creativity, and being true to oneself. I smile. Maybe.

Finally, I choose a colour that embodies the new me. Magenta leaps out. I love it. The words that accompany it resonate deeply: *grateful and free*.

What began as a simple exercise now begins to stir something deeper. At first, it felt like a game. But meaning is percolating just beneath the surface.

The Story Before Sleep

Later that evening, I climb into bed with a novel, a nightly ritual to help quiet my mind. As I read, I come across a story that grabs me just before sleep overtakes me. When I wake, it's still with me. *Holland and Italy*. The story lingers, its simplicity and truth moving me.

I sit up and whisper a prayer: *"God, please show up for me on this retreat. I feel tired and disengaged. My body hurts. My soul feels disconnected."* And as He so often does, God responds gently, connecting the story in my novel with the colours I'd chosen earlier. The message is clear. He is near. He is weaving meaning.

Here's the story that connects the colours:

Welcome to Holland

> *When you're going to have a baby, it's like planning a fabulous vacation trip, to Italy. You buy a bunch of guidebooks and make your wonderful plans. The Coliseum. The Michelangelo David. The gondolas in Venice. You may learn some handy phrases in Italian. It's all very exciting.*

After months of eager anticipation, the day finally arrives. You pack your bags and off you go.

Several hours later, the plane lands. The flight attendant comes in and says, "Welcome to Holland." "Holland?!?" you say. "What do you mean Holland?? I signed up for Italy! I'm supposed to be in Italy. All my life I've dreamed of going to Italy."

But there's been a change in the flight plan. They've landed in Holland and there you must stay. The important thing is that they haven't taken you to a horrible, disgusting, filthy place, full of pestilence, famine, and disease. It's just a different place.

So, you must go out and buy new guidebooks. And you must learn a whole new language. And you will meet a whole new group of people you would never have met. It's just a different place. It's slower paced than Italy, less flashy than Italy. But after you've been there for a while and you catch your breath, you look around . . . and you begin to notice that Holland has windmills . . . and Holland has tulips. Holland even has Rembrandts. But everyone you know is busy coming and going from Italy . . . and they're all bragging

about what a wonderful time they had there. And for the rest of your life, you will say "Yes, that's where I was supposed to go. That's what I had planned." And the pain of that will never, ever, ever, ever go away . . . because the loss of that dream is a very, very significant loss. But . . . if you spend your life mourning the fact that you didn't get to Italy, you may never be free to enjoy the very special, the very lovely things . . . about Holland (Kingsley, 1987).

Insight explodes within: I'm mourning Italy.

Due to painful losses in childhood, my life has been shaped by a deep yearning, for beauty, for love, for something broken and lost that I cannot name (Heuertz, 2017). I long for Italy, for the day when beauty and love will redeem me.

And yet, I find myself in Holland.

I'm enveloped by grief and envy when I see seemingly happy families, ones that aren't chaotic, ones where trauma hasn't been passed down like heirlooms. They seem to live in Italy. But I live in Holland, among failed dreams and unspoken resentment. I never signed up for this. And the painful truth is, I feel stuck here.

Today, I feel old. Lifeless. Without beauty.

Holland feels one-dimensional, second-best. I cannot be my full self here. To survive, I've learned to maintain a secret self, one I privately nurture and hide.

Yes, there have been exquisite moments, times when I've actually *visited* Italy. Times when my heart felt at home. Italy, I love your lakes, your mountains, your coastlines. I love the freedom to simply *be*. I want to live in your joy, to feel proud, to know my mothering matters. I long to be free from judgment and expectation.

But I always return to Holland. Constantly triggered back into disappointment and grief.

I'm angry at myself for resenting Holland and craving Italy. I'm emotionally paralysed, fatigued, ashamed of who I've become, sometimes unable to function. I've grown so attached to unrequited longing and disappointment that it has become my identity. The unspoken agreement I've made, perhaps with the enemy, is that longing and disappointment define me. That they are unchangeable. That I am destined to suffer.

The image that expresses this grief is the *weeping angel* (see Figure 7. *Weeping Angel*).

Figure 7. *Weeping Angel*

The Spirit Whispers

Then, the Holy Spirit speaks.

> *"Welcome to Holland,"* he says gently. *"You can learn to find joy here, if you'll let me in. You can enjoy your family for who they are, not what they lack. You can live with people and challenges you can't change. Instead of sitting alone in your hotel room, you can step outside and see the countryside. There's much beauty here. I'll give you the eyes to see it, if you'll let me."*

So, I venture out, and there they are: the windmills, the tulips, the Rembrandts...

Pain Versus Suffering

It's day two of my retreat. Just as I begin to receive Holland for what it is, Jesus whispers something more, *"I want to give you Italy."*

Wait, what?

He continues: *"There's a difference between pain and suffering. You'll always feel the pain of your family, but you don't have to suffer. When you don't choose the pain, you choose to cling to the suffering. So, how's that working for you?"*

The question lands hard.

I've spent years judging my feelings harshly, trying to squash them. What would happen if I welcomed them instead, as a map pointing to the truth? Maybe I fear the truth. Maybe I'm still clinging to the fantasy of rewriting the past. Unable to fully forgive myself, I'm stuck in perpetual regret. But God doesn't want me to live there.

My greatest need is to become who I already *am* in Christ. Transformation means letting go of the false identity that says I'm more flawed than others, that I'm missing something essential others possess. God wants me to live from my *True Self*, rooted in the Spirit. He wants me to bear the fruits of love, joy, peace, patience… (Galatians 5:22–23). Fruits that grow from a heart centred, calm, and grounded (Riso & Hudson, pp. 203, 205).

So today, I repent. I repent of my attachment to suffering, to longing that never fulfills. I repent of not believing that my Redeemer offers me daily treasures, yes, even in Holland. I repent of clinging to my painful feelings, rather than to the reality of God's kingdom.

A Nagging Question

But still, one question won't leave me alone: *What am I supposed to do with wounds that won't go away?* (Rohr, 1987). Richard Rohr notes that much of church ministry operates on the assumption that *words* bring change. But for trauma survivors like me, that's not always true.

Often, my nervous system is so tense, so triggered, that words simply can't land. I hear truth, but I can't *absorb* it. Rohr observes that in Jesus' ministry, words were only part of the healing. Jesus *touched* people, physically, emotionally, spiritually, so they could *receive* the words. So, what would help *me* receive them?

A memory rises: I'm in Uganda, alone, teaching trauma recovery at a university. I'm invited to speak on marriage to a group of villagers. The meeting takes place in a building without windows, sunlight pouring in as children peek through the frames. The call to gather is made by drums that echo across the valley.

The moment stays with me, not for what I said, but for what I didn't do. A sick man, covered in sores, thrusts out his hand. I hesitate. The Ugandan woman next to me slaps my hand away. *Don't touch him.*

What would Jesus have done? I still grieve not touching him. What might have opened in his heart, if I had? Could my touch have helped him receive the words? Could it have healed his spirit?

Letting the Wound Heal Differently

Sometimes, I want a magic cure. I want the pain to vanish. But it rarely does. Most people go to the grave carrying their emotional wounds. What changes isn't the wound itself, but its *power*, its power to define me, to destroy me, or to hurt others (Rohr, 1987).

So how do I deal with my *constant* triggers? I don't have all the answers. But I'm beginning to believe that healing looks like this:

- Letting Christ into my Holland.
- Daring to touch others, even with my wounds.
- Learning to welcome the pain, without letting it turn into suffering.
- Discovering that tulips and windmills have their own beauty.

And, perhaps most deeply of all, trusting that even if I never make it back to Italy, my soul can still flourish in Holland.

What is a Trigger?

A trigger can be likened to an emotional allergy. Just as our body might misinterpret harmless particles like pollen as threats, the words or actions of someone important to us can be perceived as emotional threats. In essence, a trigger reveals a hypersensitivity to a previous emotional injury. Like physical allergies, emotional triggers can range from mild to severe and often intensify with repeated exposure. Triggers arise when we are reminded, consciously or unconsciously, of painful past events, provoking an outsized reaction in the present.

An emotional wound can be activated by remembered or even imagined stimuli, such as a death, disaster, home invasion, accident, childhood neglect, or abuse. Triggers can include visual images, sounds, smells, tastes, people, faces, words, tones of voice, opinions, places, physical sensations, specific events or dates, strong emotions, or even seemingly random experiences.

Listening to the Body

People with trauma histories (and HSP) are often highly sensitive to sensory input. This can include noise (like barking dogs or screaming children), bright or strobe lighting, strong smells or tastes, and even textures. Physical factors like hunger, fatigue, or being in a crowd can also be overwhelming. van der Kolk (1994) notes that any of these inputs can activate the body's stress response, releasing adrenaline, cortisol, and norepinephrine, and triggering the fight, flight, or freeze response.

van der Kolk (2006) further explains that trauma survivors often struggle to identify sensations, emotions, or physical states, which makes it difficult to attune to others' emotional needs. In this fog of dysregulation, people may shut down or lash out unexpectedly. Levine (cited by Sattin, 2016) observes that we often react to perceived threats, real or not, when we feel someone might take away something precious. We respond with fear or anger, then rationalise our reaction. Trust erodes.

A trigger is, at heart, a present experience that reawakens an old emotional memory, often accompanied by intense feelings like anger, fear, sadness, or shame (see Figure 8. *An Emotional Trigger*).

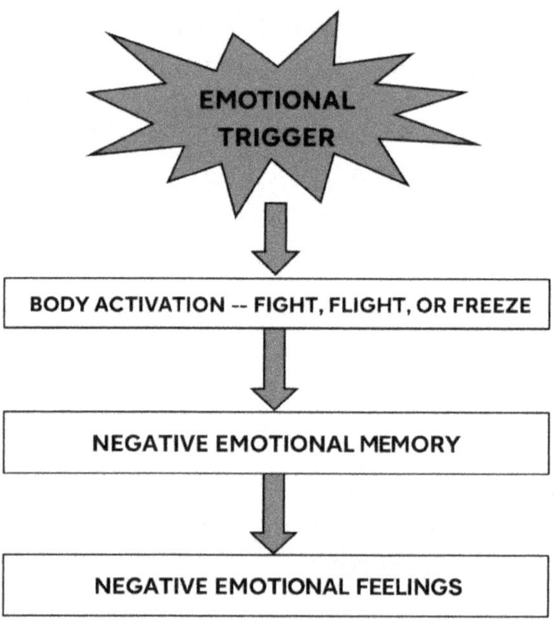

Figure 8. *An Emotional Trigger*

Listening to Emotions

Emotions matter. They are signals pointing to what we believe deep down. Larry Crabb once said emotions are like the warning lights on a car dashboard (1987, pp. 184-185). If ignored, the car, and our relationships, can break down. As Catherall (2004) aptly said, *"The most damaging feelings are those that are never discussed."*

Intense emotional reactions are typically tethered to memory. Our past always leaves its mark on the present. Sometimes we're unaware of just how much lives inside us: moments of abandonment, harsh words, abuse, neglect, misunderstanding, or suffering. These experiences shape us, leaving invisible traces in our bodies and minds. It's not a matter of whether they're still there, but how they shape us (Levine, cited by Sattin, 2016).

Listening to Memories

Memory lives in us in different forms. Implicit or procedural memories involve automatic actions, like riding a bike, and are usually emotion-free. Explicit memories, in contrast, are conscious recollections, like programming a GPS. Episodic memories carry emotional tones, like feeling peaceful while watching waves because of a childhood memory of the ocean.

But there are also emotionally charged body memories. The experience of terror imprints itself physically: our stomach flips, our heart races. Even when we understand our feelings, our body often reacts before we do. These procedural reactions, ingrained early and often unconsciously, shape our responses in ways that bypass our rational minds (Levine, cited by Sattin, 2016).

Listening for Old Wounds

Being triggered can feel like emotional survival. It's the psychological equivalent of a wound being ripped open. Someone pokes at the tender place inside us, and the pain feels raw and fresh, even if we don't consciously remember the original injury. Until that wound is healed, it will keep reopening.

Emotional wounds, especially from childhood, often live in our subconscious. As David Whyte (2002, p. 125) notes, children who have experienced trauma may remain emotionally stuck at the age when the injury occurred. We may push painful memories out of our awareness, but our body doesn't forget. When the present mirrors the past, the amygdala, our emotional alarm system, responds as though the threat is current. The thinking brain is bypassed. Fight, flight, or freeze takes over. The result: intense reactions to situations that aren't actually dangerous.

Like a gun going off after the trigger is pulled, the body's stress hormones rush in with no chance to hit pause. This can wreak havoc on our closest relationships, leaving both us and those we love confused or hurt. How can we be present for others if our inner child is still reacting to long-past injuries?

Complex Trauma and Triggers

In cases of complex trauma, like mine, triggers often stir up fear, leading to avoidance or collapse. An accusing tone can evoke memories of childhood scolding or shame. I freeze, or I shut down entirely in response to harsh words. The fear feeds on itself, trapping me in a never-ending horror film where I'm always trying to escape the monsters. I can't reach the remote. I learn to cope by soothing the monsters, hiding, or playing dead.

Eventually, I became so accustomed to running that it fused with my identity. I constructed a version of myself, the False Self, just to survive. Even when the actual danger passed, the running continued. It was like the girl in the Hound of Heaven YouTube video, endlessly fleeing from the One who could bring her peace.

Acceptable and Unacceptable Emotions

In an earlier chapter, we explored Horney's (1950) idea of basic evil, the absence of parental warmth and affection. When aspects of a child's emotional life are deemed unacceptable, those parts are pushed underground. In my husband's family, anger was the forbidden feeling. If he expressed it, he was shamed or rejected. Over time, he learned to suppress anger and express it passively, by withholding what I desired. If I said, *"You're angry,"* he'd deny it.

In other families, like Shaun's, no emotions were allowed at all. He heard messages like:

- "Don't cry."
- "It doesn't really hurt."
- "Stop crying or you'll get a belting."

As a boy, Shaun felt hurt and angry but learned quickly that expressing those feelings was unsafe. Even as his father lay dying, he was shamed for crying. The message? *"I'm not okay with your feelings. I'm not okay with you.*" Over time, Shaun stopped expressing emotion altogether. Eventually, he lost touch with his feelings, and with himself.

Children who grow up with these messages may completely disconnect from their emotions. Adult children of alcoholics often adopt an unspoken code: *"Don't talk. Don't trust. Don't feel."* As Brandon (2011, p. 152) puts it, when we hide our emotions, we hide ourselves. We become strangers to our own hearts. We feel lonely, not just for others, but for the depth and vitality of our inner lives.

Creating a False Self to Cope

Our needs as children were valid. Shaun needed to be able to grieve his dying father. But instead of blaming those who withheld comfort, he blamed himself. He condemned his own needs. He fashioned a solution to survive: a False Self that would be accepted by others.

This False Self may function well in the world, but it hides the real person. In rejecting his True Self, Shaun avoided the anxiety that came from being unseen. As an adult, he still doubts his needs are legitimate. He still feels unacceptable, not just to his parents, but to his wife. And so, he copes... by disappearing.

In the aftermath of complex childhood trauma, both feelings and needs must be repressed to survive. To protect the authentic self from the pain of deprivation, a false self is often formed. This false self creates a façade that may allow us to connect with others while shielding us from reliving past emotional wounds. However, the false self is not real, and the energy required to maintain it drains our presence and aliveness.

Shaun, for example, found significance in doing rather than simply being. He learned to meet the needs of others while neglecting his own. Unable to turn to God for comfort, he became driven to *"do",* often through his Christian work. Sometimes, Shaun would withdraw or shut down emotionally, but the unresolved wound remained. When his needs went unmet or were dismissed, they emerged as emotional triggers.

For instance, Shaun married someone who, like others in his past, struggled to meet his emotional needs. His wife, despite being in counselling and making efforts to be responsive, inadvertently aroused the pain of his early deprivation. Shaun's pattern led him to anticipate rejection, even when his wife's affection was genuine.

In this way, Shaun found himself caught in a cycle of simultaneously craving and rejecting his spouse's care. This double message, *"Come here, go away",* confused and frustrated her, especially when it triggered her own relational wounds. Conflict and emotional gridlock followed, as each partner reacted from their respective, learned childhood relational patterns. For Shaun and his wife, this led to persistent conflict and, in some cases, the threat of divorce.

Negative Emotions, Beliefs, and the Enemy's Lies

One of the enemy's most insidious tactics is exploiting our unresolved negative emotions. When we let anger, unforgiveness, or other negative emotions fester without addressing them, we allow Satan to gain a foothold in our lives. His aim is to undermine our well-being by sowing lies and distortions about God, ourselves, and others. He uses our unhealed wounds to access our hearts and minds, whispering deceitful messages that erode our sense of self and faith in God's love.

For example, long-term anger or unforgiveness provides a gateway for the enemy to accuse and slander both us and the people we harbor anger against, whether it's our parents, spouse, friends, or colleagues. The enemy's goal is to break us down emotionally and spiritually, to strip us of our hope, and to destroy the relationships we value. Often, we are unaware of how he subtly enters through our emotional wounds, particularly when we are most vulnerable, to plant lies that shape our thoughts and feelings.

The most important step in resisting the enemy's influence is recognizing how he operates in our emotional lives. He seeks to diminish our self-esteem, sabotage our relationships, and drain us of all joy. It is not simply the wound itself that causes the greatest pain, but the lie about who we are that attaches to it. When our legitimate needs were not met as children, we often form beliefs about ourselves, beliefs that the enemy uses to keep us bound in shame, fear, and self-rejection.

The false self, then, may appear to be a solution in childhood, helping us survive and function in a world that seems indifferent to our needs. But it is a lie, one that ultimately robs us of our authenticity. The value we place on ourselves becomes tied to what we have, what we do, or what others think of us, especially those who are significant in our lives (Pennington, 2000, p. 31). The greatest pain often lies not in the wound itself, but in the lies embedded within it. These lies, implanted by the enemy, serve to keep us in bondage.

Consider the beliefs you may have formed as a result of unmet needs or early emotional neglect. These beliefs, as depicted in Table 3. *Unhealthy Beliefs About Ourselves*, often reflect the lies that the enemy whispers into our hearts to keep us from experiencing the fullness of God's truth and freedom. Take a moment to reflect and check which of these beliefs resonate with your own experience.

UNHEALTHY BELIEFS	
❒ I am unimportant	❒ I don't belong
❒ I am unacceptable	❒ I don't count
❒ I am unsafe	❒ I am not enough
❒ I am invisible	❒ I am too much
❒ I am inadequate	❒ I am not good enough
❒ I am untrustworthy	❒ I am not organised enough
❒ I don't matter	❒ I am not qualified enough
❒ I do not deserve	❒ I am not compassionate enough
❒ I am unlovable	❒ I am not decisive enough
❒ I am inappropriate	❒ I am not thin enough
❒ I am insignificant	❒ I am not outgoing enough
❒ I am powerless	❒ I am not selfless enough
❒ I am unworthy	❒ I am not spiritual enough
❒ I am unworthy of support	❒ I am too disgusting

Table 3. *Unhealthy Beliefs About Ourselves*

The Bible refers to Satan as *"The Accuser"* (Revelation 12:10). A powerful example of his tactics is found in the story of Adam and Eve in the Garden of Eden. When the enemy tempted them, they sinned. Afterwards, in Genesis 3:9-11 (NIV), we read:

> *"But the Lord God called to [Adam], 'Where are you?' He answered, 'I heard you in the garden, and I was afraid because I was naked; so I hid.' And [God] said, 'Who told you that you were naked? Have you eaten from the tree that I commanded you not to eat from?'"*

Adam is hiding because he is now aware of his nakedness. But God asks Adam, "*Who told you that you were naked?"* It's likely that God did not need an answer. Instead, He was pointing out to Adam, *"I did not tell you that you were naked. I created both of you naked without shame. Someone has told you that there is something wrong with your nakedness, that you are now defective in some way."* The enemy's lie, planted in the pain of their disobedience, led to their shame and separation.

The real tragedy was not simply the sin, the wound, or the pain they felt, it was the lie within the pain that they believed. This lie has been destroying relationships ever since.

Just as with Adam and Eve, the Accuser uses our wounds to whisper his lies and keep our hearts bound. Known as *"the father of lies"* (John 8:44), Satan twists our childhood wounds.

For example, an abused child may believe the abuse was their fault and that they are now dirty or worthless. In my own life, my mother's message to me was that I was the cause of all the problems at home, and that everyone would be better off without me. As mentioned earlier, the enemy took these messages and turned them into accusations, calling me names like *"Ruiner"* and *"Damager."* Whenever I found myself in a negative situation as an adult, or when I grew close to someone, the enemy would whisper these lies, pulling me into self-loathing. This cycle grieves God, causes me to hurt myself, and damages my relationships.

When we leave our wounds open, we give the enemy access. But when we close the door on those wounds, we deny him the opportunity to speak his lies over us. Even though the names and accusations from Satan contradict the Word of God, *"There is therefore no condemnation for those who are in Christ Jesus, who do not walk according to the flesh, but according to the Spirit"* (Romans 8:1), I have often lived in the shadow of hopelessness, believing his lies.

The truth, however, is this: Because I have received Jesus, I have been delivered from the power of darkness and brought into the kingdom of His love. *"For he has rescued us from the dominion of darkness and brought us into the kingdom of the Son he loves..."* (Colossians 1:13). The only way to counter the enemy's lies is with God's truth. But in order to experience this transformation, I must be willing to step outside of my comfort zone and embrace the reality of God's love, mercy, and grace.

Closing Thoughts

In the journey of healing, we often find ourselves face to face with the painful truth that the wounds of our past continue to echo, especially through emotional triggers. These triggers can transport us back to moments of deep hurt, resurfacing memories and feelings that seem impossible to escape. Yet, the beauty of our story is that we are not meant to carry these burdens alone. Just as God once asked Adam, *"Who told you that you were naked?"* He continues to ask us today, *"Who told you that you are broken, unworthy, or unloved?"* The lies we've internalized, the whispers from the enemy that surface through our triggers, are not the truth. They are traps, designed to keep us stuck in patterns of shame, fear, and self-doubt, preventing us from embracing the fullness of God's love and purpose.

Healing occurs when we confront those triggers, those lies, with the truth of who God says we are. His Word is the antidote to the poison of shame and fear, especially when our emotional wounds seem to rise up unbidden. His truth has the power to break the chains of our past that continue to bind us. Through His grace, mercy, and love, God does not see us as victims of our past or prisoners of our emotional triggers. He sees us as His beloved children, redeemed, restored, and free.

But what happens when those triggers threaten to overwhelm us? When a single moment or a memory can shatter the calm that we've worked so hard to cultivate? When the weight of our past seems to break us open all over again? In the next chapter, *When Regret Breaks You Open*, we will explore how emotional triggers can awaken the deep wounds of regret and pain, and yet, how God uses these very moments to heal us. For it is in the breaking that we discover the fullness of His healing, and the truth that even in our vulnerability, He is making us whole.

Let us hold on to the truth that the enemy's voice, amplified by our triggers, does not have the final say. God's voice, full of love and truth, does. And as we lean into His love, allowing Him to speak into our deepest wounds, we are healed, restored, and empowered to walk in the freedom He has promised.

Declarations

I declare that I will close the door on open wounds and deny the enemy access. My triggers that hinder progress, maturity and fruitfulness are now broken and torn down through the power of Jesus - perfectionism, rejection, hopelessness, comparison, shame, guilt, and fear.

I declare that the arguments and agreements made with the enemy will no longer be the lens through which I see God, myself, others, and my circumstances.

I declare freedom.

Prayer

Someone I loved once gave me
a box full of darkness.
It took me years to understand
that this, too, was a gift.

(Mary Oliver, *The Uses of Sorrow*, 2007, p. 11)

Reflection Questions

1. How do your unhealed wounds provide a foothold for the enemy to establish strongholds in your life?
2. In what ways has the enemy whispered lies at the time of your wounding, and how do you unknowingly believe these lies?
3. How did the creation of a false self, become a survival mechanism in response to these wounds, and how does this affect your identity?

4. Why have unhealed wounds resurfaced later as emotional triggers, and what role do these triggers play in your emotional responses?
5. What is necessary to heal from these wounds, particularly in identifying the unexamined beliefs and lies the enemy has implanted, nurtured, and reinforced?
6. How can you resist the temptation to distract or numb yourself when dealing with emotional wounds, and what makes it important to instead embrace the pain and feelings associated with them?
7. How does refusing to believe that we are loved by Everlasting Love contribute to re-victimising yourself, and how does this prevent genuine healing?

Journal Prompt

Reflect on a past wound or lie you've believed about yourself. How does God's truth challenge or transform that belief? Without judging or fixing, gently name what is present in this moment.

CHAPTER 17

When Regret Broke Me Open

"If you attempt to act and do for others or for the world without deepening your own self-understanding, freedom, integrity and capacity to love, you will not have anything to give others. You will communicate to them nothing but the contagion of your own obsessions, your aggressivity, your ambitions, your delusions and ends and means..."
~ Thomas Merton

"When I stand before thee at the day's end, thou shalt see my scars and know that I had my wounds and also my healing." ~ Rabindranath Tagore

"Nobody escapes being wounded. We are all wounded people, whether physically, emotionally, mentally, or spiritually. The main question is not 'How can we hide our wounds?' so we don't have to be embarrassed but 'How can we put our roundedness in the service of others?' When our wounds cease to be a source of shame and become a source of healing, we have become wounded healers."
~ Henri Nouwen, The Wounded Healer

The Wound of Knowing I Caused Pain

Regret has a way of curling itself around the soul, tight, suffocating, relentless. It isn't the same as guilt, which can lead us to repentance. Regret lingers longer. It replays what we cannot undo and reopens the ache of knowing we've hurt someone we cared about.

For me, it came like a storm, swift and devastating. A hard conversation, a confrontation I hadn't expected, and suddenly I was swallowed by sorrow. Not just for what I had done, but for how deeply it echoed the shame I'd carried since childhood. I couldn't run from it. I couldn't fix it. Even my attempts at apology were refused.

This chapter is about that unravelling. The raw honesty of facing myself. The long silence of not being forgiven. And the surprising grace that can meet us, not in resolution, but in surrender, when regret breaks us open, and we allow God to begin something new.

Be Curious

Healing regret begins with curiosity. I search for the earliest memories of being triggered. Like an archaeologist excavating a tell (tĕl), a mound of ancient ruins, I begin with the most recent layer and dig deeper. I ask the Holy Spirit to guide me. As Matthew 7:7-8 promises: *"Ask and it will be given to you; seek and you will find..."* A recent difficult conversation with my child's spouse surfaces.

As I sit with it, I realise my anger isn't about him, it's about my daughter, and my hurt. I begin a conversation with Jesus, the *"Wonderful Counsellor"* (Isaiah 9:6):

> Me: *Lord, my internal critic, my weeping angel, is back, judging me. She belittles me. Is she helping or hurting me? I feel remorse, anger, and a compulsion to fix the pain I've caused my children.*
>
> Jesus: *What you did was wrong, and it has consequences. But I love you just as much today as I ever have.*

I dig deeper. I choose to enter the pain. A core memory surfaces. I'm driving my teenaged daughter to a flute lesson. Her words are hateful, and they pierce my heart. Instead of responding with understanding, I make it about me. My trauma response frightens everyone, especially her.

Now I understand: my brain had stored this fight/flight/freeze response. It had fused that moment with earlier pain, even if I wasn't conscious of it. When the situation with my son-in-law arose, it echoed that earlier moment and triggered panic, defensiveness, withdrawal, or tears.

A Deeper Wound

The root goes deeper - to my childhood. I remember my mother's brutal words, her curses. I ask the Holy Spirit to help me process the unresolved pain. Before I can own how I've hurt others, I must grieve the way I was hurt. What happened wasn't primarily about me, it was about her. I was a child. I was a victim.

So, I give myself permission to feel, to really grieve. If I deny the hurt, the wound festers. I'll live in fear of being triggered again. Relationships will remain fragile. But now, I honour my pain. I'm finally strong enough to cry.

Disarming the Trigger

To disarm the trigger, I name the core wound: I was powerless as destructive words were hurled at me. Though it wasn't my fault, I didn't run to God. I developed a coping style of shutting down. This bled into every part of life, relationships, work, wellbeing. Eventually, I slumped into a victim mentality, abdicating responsibility.

I think of a gifted musician whose breakdown led him into eccentric isolation. It seemed like a free pass. Because in similar circumstances, I had to wrestle with God, choose healthier strategies, make changes. No one handed me an escape card. I had to grit my teeth and do the work.

The shift came when I realised: I am responsible for how I respond to the past. I have the God-given power to choose differently. But the deepest transformation came when my heart broke over how my hurt had hurt others. I continued the conversation with Jesus:

> Jesus: *If your heart is broken, you'll find Me right there. If you're kicked in the gut, I'll help you catch your breath (Psalm 34:17-18 MSG). Remember the thief on the cross. His past was full of regret, yet I welcomed him.*
>
> Me: *The thief's story undoes me. In my heart, I've acted as if Your sacrifice isn't enough to cover my wrongs. I see now how empty I was, how little my early parenting reflected trust in You. Forgive me, Jesus. I come empty-handed. Thank You for covering all my regrets.*

True Contrition

Contrition comes from the Latin *contritus*, *"ground to pieces."* The Hebrew *dakah* means *"crushed, broken, sore"* (Strong, 1995). Psalm 51:17 reflects this: *"My sacrifice, O God, is a broken spirit; a broken and contrite heart you, God, will not despise."* Translations echo the depth of this: *"a shattered heart," "a humble heart," "a sorrowful heart," "a bruised heart."*

True contrition goes beyond apology. It says: *I repent of doing life my way. I surrender.*

It is a lifelong process, moving from self-sufficiency to trust. From a false self, built on survival to a true self anchored in God's love. It involves facing shame and pain with the humbling realisation that our coping strategies were self-protective but ultimately insufficient. What felt like legitimate distress may have carried the residue of self-protection.

But a contrite heart, broken, humble, surrendered, will never be overlooked by God. That's where Peace enters the ruins.

How Do People Change?

I always ask my supervisee counsellors what they believe changes people, because their beliefs shape the way they work. Martin Luther had a clear belief about change. When he sparked the Reformation, he nailed his *Ninety-Five Theses* to the door of Wittenberg Cathedral. The first thesis read, *"Our Lord and Master, Jesus Christ... willed the entire life of believers to be one of repentance"* (Mark, 2021). Luther was connecting repentance with spiritual change. But what did he mean? Was he suggesting that repentance is a deliberate part of God's process for transforming us, a reflection of our deep union with Him?

For me, repentance has always been a pivotal part of transformation. My own retreat experience led me to repentance. The Hebrew words for repentance, *shuv* (to return) and *nicham* (to feel sorrow), illustrate two parts of the process: returning to God and feeling the sorrow of separation (Strong, 1995). The psalmist, King David, echoed this in Psalm 38:18: *"I confess my iniquity; I am troubled by my sin."* Repentance, for me, is a turning back to God, admitting guilt, resolving to change, and seeking to make amends where possible.

In the New Testament, the Greek word *metanoeō* shifts the focus a bit (Strong, 1995). It's less about sorrow and more about *"undergoing a change in frame of mind and feeling"* (Bible Hub, 2024). Romans 2:4 (MSG) beautifully says, *"In kindness, he takes us firmly by the hand and leads us into a radical life-change."* God's kindness, not our sorrow, leads to transformation.

One of the most poignant expressions of repentance is the parable of the prodigal son. In Luke 15:21, the son says, *"Father, I have sinned against heaven and before you. I am no longer worthy to be called your son."* It wasn't about money, it was about a broken relationship, one healed by the father's love and forgiveness. That radical forgiveness is what restores us, too.

Repentance as a Pathway to Renewal

During my retreat, I experienced repentance with a contrite heart. It led to a deeper, renewed joy, one that flowed from union with Christ. This union with Him increasingly shapes my desires and makes me long to align my heart with His. God's invitation to repentance is a gift, *"If we confess our sins, he is faithful and just and will forgive us our sins and purify us from all unrighteousness"* (1 John 1:9). True change begins with repentance from a contrite heart.

God invites me into what's called liminal space, an in-between place where the old self is dying, and the new self is being born. This space can be messy, chaotic, and uncertain. It feels like dying, but it's also the space where hope rises from the ashes. In the process of dying to myself, I am renewed. I hold on with faith, knowing that even when everything feels out of control, God is enough. I'm reminded of the hymn *Rock of Ages (Toplady, 1976)*:

Nothing in my hand I bring,
Simply to Thy cross I cling;
Naked, come to Thee for dress;
Helpless, look to Thee for grace;
Foul, I to the fountain fly;
Wash me, Saviour, or I die.

The True Nature of Repentance

It's often easier for me to think about what repentance is not. I'm adept at practicing pseudo-repentance, and I suspect you might be too. It looks like:

1. A shallow "I'm sorry."
2. A lack of appreciation for who God is.
3. No real grief over the state of my heart.
4. A focus solely on obeying the rules rather than on God's love.

But true repentance is a deeper process. It involves a shift in mind, heart, and behaviour. Repentance requires a surrender of control. Wickedness, at its core, is about refusing to let God be God in our lives. Repentance, in contrast, is about allowing God to take control.

When I hold on to my regrets, I avoid facing the harm my actions caused. I remain in control but unhealed. Grace begins its gentle work when I surrender these regrets to God, allowing Him to take control. Healing also means repenting of believing the enemy's lies, especially the lies I've embraced in my hurt, instead of turning to God in faith and trust.

The Four Parts of True Repentance

1. **A True Admission of Hopelessness:**

   This admission is hard. It's realizing that what I ache for most, what I want to fix, I can't do on my own. I cannot control my child or make her love me. Spiritually, I am bankrupt; I have no claim on God's goodness. But Romans 2:4 reminds me that "the goodness of God leads to repentance." It's not even about how deeply contrite I am, but about His grace.

2. **Feeling Godly Sorrow:**

   Godly sorrow arises when I realize how my independent actions have gotten in the way of deep intimacy with God. When I try to make life work on my own, I always fall short. Repentance requires acknowledging this failure and feeling the grief of it. As 2 Corinthians 7:10 says, "Godly sorrow produces repentance that leads to salvation."

3. **Confessing to God:**

   I must confess my attempts to make life work apart from God. This includes confessing my tendency to hold on to the identity of a victim and acknowledging that Jesus' death on the cross saves me from my own brokenness.

4. **Receiving and Offering Forgiveness:**

   Once I confess, I receive God's forgiveness, knowing that through Him, I can have a whole and lasting life (John 3:16). I must also forgive myself and others. Hurt people hurt people, and forgiveness frees me from the burden of blame. I no longer carry the weight of my regrets; I am free to love and move forward in grace.

A Conversation with Jesus

Jesus: *Listen carefully: Unless a grain of wheat is buried in the ground, dead to the world, it is never any more than a grain of wheat. But if it is buried, it sprouts and reproduces itself many times over. In the same way, anyone who holds on to life just as it is destroys that life. But if you let it go, reckless in your love, you'll have it forever, real and eternal* (John 12:24).

Me: *What makes healing my regrets so painful is this purging process. I must repent of my survival strategies, turn to You with a contrite heart, and trust You to take care of me. I'm realizing that the only way to keep growing is to die to self and let go of the old.*

Replenishment and Renewal

Replenishment, for me, is about resupplying my soul with God's truth and grace. As we walk through life's painful purging process, I've come to realize that regrets don't define me. In fact, God uses them to deepen my gratitude for His grace.

Jesus: *Have you always been "bad" in the way your regret suggests? Does your regretted behaviour erase every previous act of kindness? Could your regret actually be a sign of how much you care about your family?*

Me: *Yes, I've done my best to show kindness, to repair the damage where I can. Even in my regrets, there is evidence of my love. I can offer my children and their families over to Your care. I can be gentle with my granddaughters and hold my children accountable with compassion.*

Jesus: *Regrets reflect a tender heart. Let them deepen your thankfulness for My grace. What can you still do, despite your regrets, that is consistent with who you want to be?*

Me: *I am grateful for how You've transformed me. My regrets no longer define me. I can love and be present, as You have taught me to love.*

Looking Behind and Ahead

The following quote passes across my screen, *"The past is like using your rear-view mirror in the car, it's good to glance back and see how far you've come but if you stare too long, you'll miss what's right in front of you"* (Author Unknown) (see Figure 9. *Looking Back*).

Figure 9. *Looking Back*

The conversation continues:

> Jesus: *Forget the former things; do not dwell on the past. See, I am doing a new thing! Now it springs up; do you not perceive it? I am making a way in the wilderness and streams in the wasteland" (Isaiah 43:18-19).*
>
> Me: *I want to cease dwelling on the past and close the door on my triggers. I've repented of choosing suffering over pain, but I want to let go of my deep regret. Please help me, Lord.*

Restoration and the New Self

I make a list of twenty regrets. We head out to a wooded reserve and walk the path toward the waterfall. Barry climbs down onto the rocks, selects twenty stones, and hands them up to me. He asks if I want him to stay. I hesitate, I've always grieved alone, but this time, I ask him to stay. As I voice each regret, I throw a stone into the pooling waterfall, my heart filled with contrition as I let it go (see Figure 10. *Letting Go*). We hold each other, overwhelmed by great, wracking sobs. Then, we walk back along the path to *"Italy."*

Figure 10. *Letting Go*

Restoration

As I cast my regrets into the waterfall, a gradual awareness of God's presence begins to break through. I sense new opportunities to restore relationships with those I've hurt, especially those closest to me. I will be weak and make many mistakes. I'll feel awkward, driven by a hunger for justice. I won't be perfect, but I will let God's love, love through me. This is the way forward (Arnold & Moltmann, 2014, p. 7).

In this process of repentance, I experience a new freedom and a deep conviction that nothing can separate me from the love of God. I discover my true self, loved, significant, secure, vital, and real. I am someone who cannot be destroyed, someone on a journey toward goodness, becoming more God-obsessed, loving Him above all else, and loving others for His sake, not mine (Crabb, 2006, p. 163).

I am finding my true self. C.S. Lewis (2001, pp. 196-198) expresses it beautifully:

> *"The Christian life is different: harder, and easier. Christ says, 'Give me all. I don't want so much of your time and so much of your money and so much of your work. I want You. I have not come to torment your natural self, but to kill it. No half-measures are any good. I don't want to cut off a branch here and a branch there, I want to have the whole tree down. Hand over the whole natural self, all the desires which you think innocent as well as the ones you think wicked - the whole outfit. I will give you a new self instead. In fact, I will give you Myself; my own will shall become yours.'"*

Finding Treasures in Italy

Italy, my symbol of healing, holds many treasures, ones that are only revealed through the eyes of a contrite and repentant heart. One of the greatest treasures I've found is that I'm no longer afraid of others' tough, confusing, or dark emotions. Having walked through my own pain, I've learned to face it with compassion rather than fear. I'm no longer shocked by "sin" in others; I've witnessed so much chaos, unpredictability, and pain (Rohr & Ebert, 2001). I now treasure the ability to hold paradoxes, light and dark, joy and sorrow, the blessings of the present and the longing for more (Rohr & Ebert, 2001).

My new agreement with God goes like this: *"The LORD is my shepherd; I shall not want"* (Psalm 23:1). The Holy Spirit helped me create this list of truths about who I am:

1. I am not inherently flawed.
2. There is nothing missing in me that others possess.
3. I can stop expressing my disappointments as aggression toward myself.
4. I see the good in myself rather than what's lost.

5. I am not isolated; no one needs to rescue me.
6. I can show up for myself.
7. I believe in my own lovability.
8. I can stop fabricating situations where I'm rejected or abandoned.
9. I can risk opening myself up to receive the love and understanding I long for.
10. My heart is centred, present, and non-reactive.
11. What is, is enough.
12. I surrender my plans and expectations to God.
13. I am at rest in my True Identity.

My past regrets may continue to trigger me, to some extent. Like Jacob in the Old Testament, I limp because my regrets remind me of my constant need for God's mercy and grace. But they no longer have the power to define me. I'm learning to master the unmanageability of life as it is and to trust that I am cared for in its uncertainty and uncontrollability (Rohr, 2013). Rohr (2019, pp. 24-25) beautifully articulates the transformative power of pain:

> *"Pain teaches a most counterintuitive thing, that we must go down before we even know what up is. It is first an ordinary wound before it can become a sacred wound. Suffering of some sort seems to be the only thing strong enough to destabilize our arrogance and our ignorance. I would define suffering very simply as 'whenever you are not in control.*
>
> *All healthy religion shows you what to do with your pain. If we do not transform our pain, we will most assuredly transmit it. If your religion is not showing you how to transform your pain, it is junk religion. It is no surprise that a crucified man became the central symbol of Christianity.*

> *If we cannot find a way to make our wounds into sacred wounds, we invariably become negative or bitter, because we will be wounded. That is a given. All suffering is potentially redemptive; all wounds are potentially sacred wounds. It depends on what you do with them. Can you find God in them or not?*
>
> *If there isn't some way to find deeper meaning in our suffering, to discover that God is somehow in it, and can even use it for good, we will normally close up and close down. The second half of our lives will, quite frankly, be small and silly."*

As painful as my regrets are, they no longer control me. Over time, they have transformed into scars, faint, reminders of what I've been through. On most days, I forget they're even there because I encountered God in them.

What Will It Look Like When My Triggers and Regret Are Healed?

Healing from triggers and regret over the past will look like an emotional wound that has ceased to be an open sore. It will heal over into scar tissue; a memory no longer tied to raw emotion. The wound is simply remembered, not relived. Over time, I've learned to accept that I am still in process, that healing is a long, winding road. I'm still learning how to ask for help, how not to be afraid to show vulnerability when I need it, and how to embrace dependence instead of striving for self-reliance (Peck, 2010, p. 58).

Sometimes, healing is immediate, but more often it takes time because some wounds run deep. As painful memories are uncovered and brought to God for healing, the Holy Spirit reveals the lies and messages implanted by the enemy. Jesus knows that I can only handle the unveiling of these profound hurts in stages. His timing is always perfect.

The enemy does not easily release his hold. He battles fiercely against my freedom, but I can continually renounce his lies, using the power of God's Word to defeat him. When he comes again (and he will), whispering negative messages to my heart, trying to knock me down once more, I turn to the Holy Spirit for protection and ask for a Scripture verse to counter the attack. Confessing God's Word is powerful enough to overcome the enemy's lies.

For example, Psalm 1:1-3 declares:

> *"Blessed is the man who walks not in the counsel of the ungodly,*
> *nor stands in the path of sinners,*
> *nor sits in the seat of the scornful;*
> *but his delight is in the law of the LORD,*
> *and in His law he meditates day and night.*
> *He shall be like a tree planted by the rivers of water,*
> *that brings forth its fruit in its season,*
> *whose leaf also shall not wither;*
> *and whatever he does shall prosper."*

Who doesn't long to be that fruitful tree?

There are many apps available to store favourite verses that can be easily accessed in times of need. The enemy knows he's defeated, and Scripture confirms that truth, to him and to us. Satan hates that Jesus came to set the brokenhearted, the captive, and the oppressed free to live abundant lives (Isaiah 61:1; Luke 4:18). Jesus triumphed over Satan by the blood of the Lamb (Revelation 12:11). So, when he tries to condemn or shame us, we can choose to respond with the Word of God, praising God for His grace toward us. Alternatively, when we're too worn down, we can listen to one of the many worship songs that lift our spirits.

Like David, we can cry out to God in our distress: *"Answer me when I call to You, my righteous God. Give me relief from my distress; have mercy on me and hear my prayer"* (Psalm 4:1). God faithfully answers in Isaiah 41:10 (MSG), declaring: *"Don't panic. I'm with you. There's no need to fear, for I'm your God. I'll give you strength. I'll help you. I'll hold you steady, keep a firm grip on you."*

I'm learning that God truly is good, and genuine spiritual growth is marked by repentance, trust, and the willingness to take increasingly deeper risks. When I take a risk and make it through, I realize the risk was worth it. And when the next risk comes, I'll be a little braver. This is how faith gradually turns into trust (May, 2007).

Closing Thoughts

A contrite heart is a heart willing to be healed, a heart that no longer clings to the false selves we've created to shield ourselves from the pain of unmet needs and longings. Healing is a journey of surrender, moving from self-sufficiency to a dependence on God's sufficiency. It is a path that winds through woundedness, shame, and pain, but it is also a path where we encounter God's grace, mercy, and love. As we heal, our emotional wounds, once open sores, slowly transform into scars, no longer hurting but bearing the marks of God's redeeming touch.

Healing looks like an emotional wound that no longer holds the sting. The memory may remain, but it is now seen through the lens of grace, a grace that teaches us to remember differently. I am learning that healing is not a quick fix; it is an ongoing process. It's a sacred rhythm of risk, trust, and surrender, where with each step forward, we find ourselves becoming stronger, braver, and more able to stand firm against the lies of the enemy.

And yet, the journey doesn't end with our own healing. As we experience God's healing in our lives, we are called to embrace the message that emerges from our mess. Our wounds, once places of pain, become sources of strength and compassion. They prepare us not just for personal wholeness but for a redemptive calling that reaches beyond ourselves. Our scars are no longer signs of shame, but of grace, and through them, God writes a message of hope, healing, and restoration.

In the next chapter, *From Mess to Message: Embracing Healing and Change*, we will explore how our healing becomes part of a greater purpose. God invites us to share the story of our transformation with others, to let our mess become a message of His power to heal, restore, and renew. Healing is never just for us; it overflows, touching others with the hope we have received. Let's step into this new chapter together, where our scars become the very fabric of God's redemptive story. As Jane Hirshfield so beautifully writes in *Of Gravity and Angels*:

There are names for what binds us:
strong forces, weak forces.
Look around, you can see them:
the skin that forms in a half-empty cup,
nails rusting into the places they join,
joints dovetailed on their own weight.

The way things stay so solidly
wherever they've been set down-
and gravity, scientists say, is weak.

And see how the flesh grows back
across a wound, with a great vehemence,
more strong
than the simple, untested surface before.

There's a name for it on horses,
when it comes back darker and raised: proud flesh,
as all flesh,
is proud of its wounds, wears them
as honors given out after battle,
small triumphs pinned to the chest-

And when two people have loved each other
see how it is like a
scar between their bodies,
stronger, darker, and proud
how the black cord makes of them a single fabric
that nothing can tear or mend.

This is the paradox of grace: Our wounds, once places of deepest pain, become places of deepest strength. We carry our healing not in perfection but in our scars, testimonies to the mercy of God, the power of His truth, and the gentleness of His presence. We are not who we were. We are being made new.

Our wounds don't disqualify us, they prepare us. They shape our compassion, deepen our empathy, and open us to others' pain. As we surrender the false self and embrace the healing love of God, something extraordinary happens: our mess becomes the very place God writes His message. Scars that once marked our shame become signposts of grace.

In the next chapter, we'll explore how God not only heals but invites us into a redemptive calling. Healing is never just for us. It spills over. It multiplies. It becomes the very testimony others need to hear. It's time to embrace the sacred truth: your healing story is also your message.

Let's step into that together.

Declarations

I declare that every negative name or word spoken over me by myself or others, is now renounced and made null and void because of Jesus.

I declare repentance, healing, and forgiveness over myself because of what Jesus did on the cross for me.

I declare that I will no longer live as a captive to sin, and I claim the freedom that is mine in Jesus Christ.

Prayer

God Save me from coping
God help me to join, not separate
Help me to be with and in, not apart from
Show me the way of savoring, not controlling
Dear God,
Hear my prayer
Make me forever cope-less

(Gerald May, 2007, *The Wisdom of Wilderness*)

Reflection Questions

1. When have I, like the dog with the bone, clung to an old wound or regret so tightly that it prevented me from receiving nourishment or joy?
2. What dreams or expectations (my 'Italy') have I grieved, and how might I begin to see the beauty of the 'Holland' I'm actually living in?
3. What false identities or internal agreements have I made (for example, "I'm destined to suffer") that God may be inviting me to surrender?
4. In what ways am I still emotionally triggered by unresolved pain, and how can I begin to welcome those triggers as maps toward deeper healing?
5. What does it look like for me to distinguish between pain (which is inevitable) and suffering (which I may be choosing by holding on to the past)?

Journal Prompt

Today, I choose to notice the tulips and windmills in my life, even as I grieve the Italy I hoped for. Without judging or fixing, gently name what is present in this moment.

CHAPTER 18

From Mess to Message: How My Pain Became Purpose

"My old self has been crucified with Christ. It is no longer I who live, but Christ lives in me. So, I now live in this earthly body by faith in the Son of God, who loved me and gave Himself for me." ~ Galatians 2:20 (NLT)

"If the water kills you, what can you do to the water? You make soup with the water and eat it."
~ East African Workshop Participant on Grief

"Nothing is ever too far gone for hope to come find you."
~ Unknown

Transforming Wounds into a Source of Healing

There are seasons when life feels like nothing but a mess, a tangled knot of pain, confusion, and loss. When I look back, I can see how the mess of my past became a story I never wanted to tell. But what I didn't know then was that God doesn't waste pain. He doesn't dismiss our suffering or look past our brokenness. He redeems it.

Through the darkest moments, I began to see a glimmer of light, how the very wounds that once threatened to define me could, in time, become a message of hope. Pain transformed into purpose. Brokenness turned into healing for others. It wasn't easy, nor did it happen overnight. But God has a way of turning our messes into messages when we let Him.

This chapter is about how God rewrote my story, turning my pain into a source of purpose, showing me that even in the hardest seasons, He is working behind the scenes to bring beauty from ashes.

A Wounded Healer

These days, I see myself as a wounded healer. In many ways, I believe this is the deepest kind of healing, because in tending to my own wounds, God is shaping me into a source of life that leads others to Jesus, the ultimate Wounded Healer (Nouwen, 2010). For a long time, I avoided pain. But now, I long to bring the darker parts of my soul into the Light for His healing, because it's through my wounds that I become small, needy, and completely dependent on God's goodness (Rohr, 1987). It's a paradox: my brokenness actually drives me to seek God's presence.

I used to wonder why Jesus still carried His wounds after the resurrection. But now I find deep comfort in it. Perhaps it's those very wounds that invite me to bring my own before the Father, knowing He won't turn me away. His promise rings true: *"No one who believes in the Lord will be put to shame"* (Romans 10:11; 9:33). What's even more amazing is that God chooses a broken woman like me to pour out His life through.

Like Jacob in the Old Testament, I limp, carrying the constant reminder of my thorn in the flesh. It's a symbol of my need for God's mercy and grace. But this limp no longer defines me. I'm learning how to navigate the unmanageable parts of life and to rest in the reality that I am cared for, even in the uncontrollable moments.

A Journey, not a Destination

As we come to the end of this journey, I am reminded that healing is not a destination but a continuous process. Throughout the pages of this book, we have explored together the depths of our wounds, physical, mental, emotional, and spiritual, and the transformative power of God's love and grace. Each chapter has been a testament to the resilience of the human spirit and the relentless pursuit of wholeness.

In the midst of pain and brokenness, we have discovered that healing requires more than time. It demands intentionality, vulnerability, and the courage to confront the deepest parts of ourselves. It is in those raw and honest moments that we find the strength to grieve, to cry out, and to embrace the full spectrum of our emotions. As we allow ourselves to be seen and known, we open the door to God's transformative touch.

The journey of healing is rarely linear. It often involves revisiting old wounds, untangling the lies we've internalized, and learning to hold both strength and vulnerability in the same breath. As the Ugandan wisdom reminds us, we cannot undo the past, but we can allow God to transform our pain into something that nourishes. That sustains. That blesses. My hope is that this book offers you that same invitation: to take what has wounded you and, through God's grace, allow it to become a wellspring of life.

We Are More Than Our Wounds

Our wounds do not define us. They are part of our story, but they are not the whole of who we are. We are beloved children of God, created with purpose and destined for wholeness. In the embrace of His love, we find the courage to face our pain and the hope to keep moving forward.

I hope this book has been a beacon of hope, inspiring you to seek healing, to embrace your story, and to trust in the ongoing work of God's love. Healing is possible. You are never alone.

A Story That Stays with Me

I want to leave you with a story that continues to stir my soul. Brennan Manning (2004, pp. 209-210), in *The Relentless Tenderness of Jesus*, tells of a tender exchange between Saint Francis and Brother Leo:

> One day Saint Francis and Brother Leo were walking down the road. Noticing that Leo was depressed, Francis turned and asked: "Leo, do you know what it means to be pure of heart?"
>
> *"Of course. It means to have no sins, faults or weaknesses to reproach myself for."*
>
> *"Ah,"* said Francis, *"now I understand why you're sad. We will always have something to reproach ourselves for."*
>
> *"Right,"* said Leo. *"That's why I despair of ever arriving at purity of heart."*
>
> *"Leo, listen carefully to me. Don't be so preoccupied with the purity of your heart. Turn and look at Jesus. Admire Him. Rejoice that He is who He is, your brother, your Friend, your Lord and Savior. That, little brother, is what it means to be pure of heart.*
>
> *And once you've turned to Jesus, don't turn back and look at yourself. Don't wonder where you stand with Him. The sadness of not being perfect, the discovery that you really are sinful, is a feeling much too human, even bordering on idolatry. Focus your vision outside yourself on the beauty, graciousness, and compassion of Jesus Christ.*
>
> *The pure of heart praise Him from sunrise to sundown. Even when they feel broken, feeble, distracted, insecure, and uncertain, they are able to release it into His peace. A heart like that is stripped and filled, stripped of self and filled with the fullness of God. It is enough that Jesus is Lord."*

After a long pause, Leo said, *"Still, Francis, the Lord demands our effort and fidelity."*

"No doubt about that," replied Francis. *"But holiness is not a personal achievement. It's an emptiness you discover in yourself. Instead of resenting it, you accept it, and it becomes the free space where the Lord can create anew. To cry out, 'You alone are the Holy One, You alone are the Lord', that is what it means to be pure of heart. And it doesn't come by your Herculean efforts and threadbare resolutions."*

"Then how?" asked Leo.

"Simply hoard nothing of yourself; sweep the house clean. Sweep out even the attic, even the nagging painful consciousness of your past. Accept being shipwrecked. Renounce everything that is heavy, even the weight of your sins. See only the compassion, the infinite patience, and the tender love of Christ. Jesus is Lord. That suffices. Your guilt and reproach disappear into the nothingness of non-attention. You are no longer aware of yourself, like the sparrow aloft and free in the azure sky. Even the desire for holiness is transformed into a pure and simple desire for Jesus."

As I reflect on this story, I'm reminded again of the deep tenderness Jesus offers us, even in our brokenness. His love calls us to stop striving for perfection and instead to rest in His sufficiency. In embracing my own wounds, I've learned to trust that God can bring beauty and purpose through them. I pray that my journey encourages you too: to see your own struggles as sacred ground, where the healing love of Christ meets you and invites you to become a source of healing for others.

All through this book I've shared stories. It is fitting that I close with one.

Birds of a Feather

(Paula's Journal: August 2013)

"Jesus said, *'Look at the birds of the air; they do not sow or reap or store away in barns, and yet your heavenly Father feeds them. Are you not much more valuable than they?'*" (Matthew 6:26).

Aren't the best moments in life the ones where we feel utterly connected? To ourselves, to God, to the rhythm of nature, to the world around us? One such moment unfolded in Damaraland, a rugged, mountainous desert in Namibia that awakens all the senses. Picture this: we're lying in bed at the end of a perfect day, wrapped in the kind of contentment that only follows deep pleasure and adventure.

Our mini-suite is a tent-hut with a traditional African thatched roof, but *"tenting"* hardly does justice to it. Every detail has been curated with such care that it seamlessly blends into the surrounding wilderness, creating a sense of harmony between the indoors and out. An open-air shower and bathroom complete the experience, making even the most ordinary routines feel sacred.That night, as we settle in, Barry glances up at the woven lampshade above our bed and chuckles. *"The attention to detail here is incredible. Look, they've even gone to the trouble of placing tiny, artificial birds up there."* (See Figure 11. *Birds of a Feather.*)

Figure 11. *Birds of a Feather.*

In the morning, we wake to find the birds have vanished. Barry sits up, eyes wide. *"They're real!"* It's a moment, a sheer gift.

We wake before dawn the next morning, eager to witness the departure of our lampshade birds at first light. We lie still, waiting for their first stirrings. One squeezes through the opening at the top of the lampshade, pausing briefly before its mate follows. Together, they dart under the gap between the thatched eave and the tent, vanishing into the desert morning. The sound of their tiny wings leaves us breathless, speechless, filled with wonder and delight. All is gift.

The childlike joy of immersing in Namibia's untamed beauty feels like indulgent self-care, a balm I didn't know I needed. There is something humbling about witnessing the sheer power of nature. It reminds us of our smallness in the grand scheme of things. I feel it deep in my heart: beauty matters. It is grace, freely given, meant to be savoured.

African sunsets still me so profoundly that they bring me to tears. The ferocious might of Victoria Falls, the quiet exhilaration of walking with wild lions in the savannah, these moments slowly unravel the weight of the previous weeks, thawing something frozen inside me. They restore. They beguile and enchant. They awaken a part of my soul I feared might never return, reawakening my spirit to the breathtaking amazement of everything around me. As John Burroughs (1903) wrote, *"I go to nature to be soothed and healed, and to have my senses put in order."* The wild gives its gifts freely, asking for nothing in return.

Deserts and Emptiness

And then, there is the desert. While other travellers set their sights on Europe's well-worn paths, I am drawn to the vast, untamed landscapes of the desert. I've wandered through deserts in Australia, the Middle East, Egypt, Jordan, Israel, India, the U.S., and across Africa. Deserts and wild places enthral me. I've always loved the desert. You sit on a desert sand dune, and it's all quiet and still. But in that silence, you can feel something alive and vibrant.

The desert is no barren wasteland, it seethes with life, holding treasures in its vastness. Perhaps it is the deeper symbolism that beckons me, the call of the inner journey. God leads everyone He loves through the desert; it is His remedy for our restless hearts, always searching for a new Eden. The greatest gift of the desert is His presence. In the barrenness, in the stripping away, He is there. And in the shelter of the Shepherd's love, I find the courage to walk the interior journey.

In my desert, stripped bare, made empty, everything else falls away, and I truly see. And in that emptiness, I am met with abundance. God is easier to find in the wilderness because it is at the edges, where vulnerability is most profound. It is there I begin to grasp what it means to leave everything and follow Jesus. From mess to message. From brokenness to blessing. From wound to witness.
Thanks be to God.

Closing Prayer

Gracious Father,
You who bind up the brokenhearted and call forth beauty from ashes,
I come to You just as I am, bruised, longing, and in need of Your healing touch.

Thank You for the journey You've led me through,
the tender places, the shattered dreams, the slow restoration of what was lost.
Thank You for not rushing me,
for sitting with me in the dust,
and for whispering truth when all I could hear were lies.

Lord Jesus, Wounded Healer,
You bore scars not to shame me but to welcome mine.
You meet me in the places I'd rather hide,
and You name me beloved.

Teach me to rest in the truth that I don't need to be perfect to be loved.
Strip away the striving.

Empty me of self-reliance, of fear, of shame.
And in the hollow spaces, make room for Your mercy.

Holy Spirit, Comforter and Counsellor,
Help me to see my wounds not as disqualifications,
but as the very vessels through which Your light shines.

Make me a gentle presence to others,
not one who fixes, but one who listens,
not one who rescues, but one who bears witness.

Use my story, Lord, for Your glory.
Let the mess become a message.
Let the pain become a path to deeper love.
Let every limp remind me of the grace that holds me.

And when I forget,
when shame rises or sorrow returns,
draw me back again to Jesus,
my refuge, my healer, my hope.

Amen.

Reference List for Book Chapters

Chapter 1 - WHEN CHANGING TOUCHES OLD PAIN

Chapter 2 - WHEN HOPE DISAPPEARED

Brent, L. J., Chang, S. W., Gariépy, J. F., & Platt, M. L. (2013). The neuroethology of friendship. Annals of the New York Academy of Sciences, 1316(1), 1-17. doi: 10.1111/nyas.12315

Gregory, C. (2018). Depression in women: Types, causes, symptoms, and treatments. Psychom. Retrieved from https://www.psycom.net/depression.central.women.html

Jones, A. (1989). Soul making: The desert way of spirituality. USA: HarperOne.

McEvoy, K., Payne, J., & Osborne, L. (2018). Neuroactive steroids and perinatal depression: A review of recent literature. Current Psychiatry Reports, 20(9), 78. doi:10.1007/s11920-018-0937-4.

McLaughlin, M. (1963). The neurotic's notebook (p. 91). Houghton Mifflin.

Piccinelli, M., & Wilkinson, G. (2000). Gender differences in depression: Critical review. British Journal of Psychiatry, 177, 486-492. Retrieved from https://www.cambridge.org/core/services/aop-cambridge-core/content/view/0770B51752F17A5A081F9878B0952608/S0007125000155989a.pdf/gender_differences_in_depression_critical_review.pdf

Rutz, W., & Rihmer, Z. (2009). Suicide in men. suicide prevention for the male person. Oxford Textbook of Suicide Prevention: A Global Perspective. 249-255. doi: 10.1093/med/9780198570059.003.0035

Seligman, E. P. (1991). Learned optimism. New York: Simon & Schuster.

Sorge, B. (2000). Glory: When heaven invades earth. Oasis House.

Chapter 3 - WHAT IS DEPRESSION TRYING TO TELL ME?

Arieti, S., & Bemporad, J. (1978). Severe and mild depression: The psychotherapeutic approach. Basic Books.

Freud, S. (1917). Mourning and melancholia. Standard edition, 14(19), 17.

Fry, S. (n.d.). If you know someone who's depressed, please resolve never to ask them why...

Hamilton, L. K. (2006). Mistral's Kiss (p. 121). Ballantine Books.

Jones, A. (1989). Soul making: The desert way of spirituality. USA: HarperOne.

Malan, D. H. (1979). Individual psychotherapy and the science of psychodynamics. Butterworth-Heinemann.

Malan, D. (2019). Individual psychotherapy and the science of psychodynamics (3rd ed.). USA: CRC Press.

May, G. G. (2007). Addiction and grace: Love and spirituality in the healing of addictions. USA: HarperOne.

Mendelson, E. (Ed.). (2007). W. H. Auden: Collected poems. USA: Modern Library.

Chapter 4 - BURIED GRIEF

Allender, D. B., & Longman, T. (1999). *The cry of the soul: How our emotions reveal our deepest questions about God*. NavPress.

Arieti, S., & Bemporad, J. (1978). *Severe and mild depression: The psychotherapeutic approach*. Basic Books.

Card, O. S. (2005). *Shadow of the Giant* (p. 161). Tor Books.

Crabb, L. (2005a). *Connecting: Healing ourselves and our relationships*. USA: Thomas Nelson.

Crabb, L. (2005b). *Soul talk: The language God longs for us to speak.* USA: Integrity Publishers.

Dessen, S. (2004). *The truth about forever*. Viking.

Dostoevsky, F. (2019). *An honest thief & other stories: "What is hell? I maintain that it is the suffering of being unable to love*." UK: Miniature Masterpieces.

Hamilton, L. K. (2006). *Mistral's Kiss*. Ballantine Books.

Malan, D. (2019). *Individual psychotherapy and the science of psychodynamics* (3rd ed.). USA: CRC Press.

Rumi. (n.d.). *Where there is ruin, there is hope for a treasure.*

St. Ignatius Loyola. (2007). *The spiritual exercises of St. Ignatius of Loyola.* New York: Cosimo Classics.

Chapter 5 - UNDER THE BROOM BUSH

Crabb, L. (2005a). *Connecting: Healing ourselves and our relationships*. USA: Thomas Nelson.

Crabb, L. (2005b). *Soul talk: The language God longs for us to speak.* USA: Integrity Publishers.

Malan, D. (2019). *Individual psychotherapy and the science of psychodynamics* (3rd ed.). USA: CRC Press.

May, G. G. (2007). *Addiction and grace: Love and spirituality in the healing of addictions*. USA: HarperOne.

Mulcahy, S. (2018). *Reflections of the heart.* USA: Balboa Press.

Rohr, R. (1987). *Broken and blessed: A retreat.* Retrieved from http://link.bu.edu/portal/Broken-and-blessed--a-retreat-Richard-Rohr./D_V-h-I4-Hw/

Rumi. (n.d.). *Where there is ruin, there is hope for a treasure.*

Smedes, L. B. (1984). *Forgive and forget: Healing the hurts we don't deserve*. Harper & Row

Chapter 6 - UNDER THE MANGO TREE: REST, REFLECTION AND RESTORATION

Barnes' Notes on the Bible. (n.d.). *Isaiah 61:3.* Bible Hub. Expositor's Bible Commentary. Retrieved from https://biblehub.com/commentaries/isaiah/61-3.htm

Brueggemann, W. (1984). *The message of the Psalms: A theological commentary*. Minneapolis, MN: Augsburg Publishing House.

Campbell, Joseph. *Reflections on the Art of Living: A Joseph Campbell Companion*. Edited by Diane K. Osbon, Harper Perennial, 1991.

Nepo, M. (2013). *Reduced to joy*. USA: Viva Editions.

Singer, T. (n.d.). *Rebuilding your life: A heartfelt journey to starting over*. Thom Singer. Retrieved April 16, 2025, from https://thomsinger.com/blog/rebuilding-your-life/

Chapter 7 - WHAT IS STRESS TRYING TO TELL ME?

Aron, E., & Aron, A. (1997). Sensory-Processing Sensitivity and Its Relation to Introversion and Emotionality. *Journal of Personality and Social Psychology*, 73, 345-68. DOI: 10.1037/0022-3514.73.2.345.

Barton, R. H. (2008). *Strengthening the soul of your leadership: Seeking God in the crucible of ministry*. InterVarsity Press.

Conte, E. (2012). *Advances in Application of Quantum Mechanics in Neuroscience and Psychology: A Clifford Algebraic Approach*. Nova Science Publishers.

Fields, D. (1966). *Where Am I Going?* [Song lyrics]. In C. Coleman (Composer), *Sweet Charity* [Musical]. Retrieved from https://www.dorothyfields.org/quotesby.htm

Fox, K. A. (2018). *Energize your emotions for life.* USA: Wipf & Stock Publishers.

Freudenberger, H. J. (1974). Staff burn-out. *Journal of Social Issues, 30*(1), 159–165. https://doi.org/10.1111/j.1540-4560.1974.tb00706.x

Loder, T. (2004). *Guerillas of Grace: Prayers for the battle* (20th ed.). Augsburg Books.

Mother Teresa. (n.d.). To keep a lamp burning, you have to keep putting oil in it. In *Mother Teresa Quotes*. Retrieved April 16, 2025, from https://www.motherteresa.org/quotes

Poulin, M. J., Brown, S. L., Dillard, A. J., & Smith, D. M. (2013). Giving to others and the association between stress and mortality. *American Journal of Public Health, 103*(9), 1649–1655. https://doi.org/10.2105/AJPH.2012.300876

Stamm, H. (2009). Professional quality of life: Compassion satisfaction and fatigue version 5 (ProQOL). Retrieved from https://psychink.com/ti2012/wp-content/uploads/2012/06/207TICAssign.20111.pdf

Tedeschi, R. G., & Calhoun, L. G. (2006). *Handbook of posttraumatic growth: Research and practice*. Mahwah, NJ: Lawrence Erlbaum Associates.

Uher, R., Tansey, K. E., Dew, T., Maier, W., Mors, O., Hauser, J., Dernovsek, M. Z., Henigsberg, N., Souery, D., Farmer, A., & McGuffin, P. (2014). An inflammatory biomarker as a differential predictor of outcome of depression treatment with escitalopram and nortriptyline. *The American Journal of Psychiatry, 171*(12), 1278–1286. https://doi.org/10.1176/appi.ajp.2014.14010094

Voskamp, A. (2019). *Goodreads.* Retrieved from https://www.goodreads.com/work/quotes/47824463-the-broken-way

Chapter 8 - MY RESTLESS MIND

Australian Bureau of Statistics. (2008). *National survey of mental health and wellbeing: Summary of results, 2007*(Catalogue No. 4326.0). Retrieved from https://www.abs.gov.au/statistics/health/mental-health/national-study-mental-health-and-wellbeing/2007

Australian Broadcasting Corporation. (2015, October 7). *All in the Mind* [Television series episode]. In *Australian Story*. https://www.abc.net.au/news/2015-10-08/all-in-the-mind/6826864

Gluck, S. (n.d.). *HealthyPlace.com Quotes.* Retrieved from https://www.goodreads.com/quotes/10178126-my-anxiety-is-silent-you-wouldn-t-even-notice-a-change

headspace. (2015). *headspace: National Youth Mental Health Foundation*. Retrieved from https://headspace.org.au/:contentReference[oaicite:1]{index=1}

Iliesco, D. (2018). *Adapting tests in linguistic and cultural situations*. UK: Cambridge University Press.

Kelly, W. (1971, April 22). *We have met the enemy and he is us* [Comic strip]. *Pogo*.

Linn, D., Linn, S. F., & Linn, M. (1995). *Sleeping with bread: Holding what gives you life*. Paulist Press.

Mark Twain. (n.d.). "It's not what you eat that gives you indigestion, it's what's eating you." In *BrainyQuote.com*. Retrieved April 16, 2025, from https://www.brainyquote.com/quotes/mark_twain_107495

Martin, E. I., Ressler, K. J., Binder, E., & Nemeroff, C. B. (2009). The neurobiology of anxiety disorders: Brain imaging, genetics, and psychoneuroendocrinology. *Psychiatric Clinics of North America, 32*(3), 549–575. https://doi.org/10.1016/j.psc.2009.05.004

National Park Service. (n.d.). *We have met the enemy and they are ours*. Retrieved April 16, 2025, from https://www.nps.gov/articles/met-the-enemy-4.htm:contentReference[oaicite:8]{index=8}

Oliver, M. (2010). *Swan: Poems and prose poems*. Beacon Press.

Chapter 9 - HOLDING MY FEAR

Becker, R. (2006). *Against pleasure*. In *Domain of perfect affection* (pp. 35–36). University of Pittsburgh Press.

Ciszek, W. J., & Flaherty, D. (1973). *He leadeth me*. San Francisco, CA: Ignatius Press.

Horney, K. (2010). *Neurosis and human growth: The struggle toward self-realization*. New York, NY: W. W. Norton. (Original work published 1950)

Kopp, S. B. (2013). *Blues ain't nothing but a good soul feeling bad: Daily steps to spiritual growth*. Fireside/Parkside Recovery Book.

Manning, B. (2004) *The relentless tenderness of Jesus*. USA: Fleming H Revell.

Milton, J. (1667/2003). *Paradise lost* (B. R. Rajan, Ed.). Penguin Classics. (Original work published 1667)

Nouwen, H. J. M. (1996). *The inner voice of love: A journey through anguish to freedom*. Doubleday.

Rilke, R. M. (2001). *Rilke's book of hours: Love poems to God* (S. Mitchell, Trans.). Riverhead Books.

Rohr, R. (1987). Broken and blessed: A retreat. Retrieved from http://link.bu.edu/portal/Broken-and-blessed--a-retreat-Richard-Rohr./D_V-h-I4-Hw/

Shanley, J. P. (2005). *Doubt: A parable*. Theatre Communications Group.

Simpson, J. A., & Weiner, E. S. C. (Eds.). (1989). *The Oxford English dictionary* (2nd ed., Vol. 20). Oxford, England: Clarendon Press.

Wormald, B. H. G. (1993). Francis Bacon: History, politics and science, 1561 – 1626. UK: Cambridge University Press.

Chapter 10 - WHAT IS ANXIETY TRYING TO TELL ME?

Bouwsma, W. J. (1984). John Calvin's anxiety. *Proceedings of the American Philosophical Society, 128*(3), 252-256.

Bouwsma, W, J. (2020). John Calvin. *Encyclopædia Britannica*. Retrieved from https://www.britannica.com/biography/John-Calvin

Brentnall, J. M. (2005). *John Calvin and anxiety.* Banner of Truth. Retrieved from https://banneroftruth.org/uk/resources/articles/2005/john-calvin-and-anxiety/

Brown, B. (2010). *The gifts of imperfection: Let go of who you think you're supposed to be and embrace who you are*. Hazelden Publishing.

Calvin, J. (1536). *Calvin's Institutes of the Christian religion* (2.2.15-16). Retrieved from https://www.ccel.org/ccel/c/calvin/institutes/cache/institutes.pdf

Epictetus. (2008). *The discourses of Epictetus* (R. Hard, Trans.), Chapter X. Oxford University Press.

Groom, N. (1991). *From bondage to bonding: Escaping codependency, embracing biblical love*. USA: Navpress.

McGrath, A. E. (1990). *John Calvin: A life* (pp. 190-192). HarperCollins Publishers.

Miller, W. R. (1990). *Approaches to counseling and psychotherapy: A casebook* (2nd ed.). Allyn & Bacon.

Chapter 11 - AWAKENING DESIRE

Berry, W. (2022). "I go among trees." *Salt.* Retrieved from https://www.saltproject.org/progressive-christian-blog/2022/9/20/i-go-among-trees-by-wendell-berry

Brother Lawrence, (2017). *The practice of the presence of God*. USA: Leyland Edwards.

Emmons, R. A., & McCullough, M. E. (2003). Counting blessings versus burdens: An experimental investigation of gratitude and subjective well-being in daily life. *Journal of Personality and Social Psychology,* 84, 377-389.

Park, B. J., Tsunetsugu, Y., Kasetani, T., Kagawa, T., & Miyazaki, Y. (2007). Physiological effects of shinrin-yoku (taking in the forest atmosphere or forest bathing): Evidence from field experiments in 2004. *Environmental Health and Preventive Medicine, 12*(5), 168–173. https://doi.org/10.1007/BF02897943

Rippon, J. (1787). *How firm a foundation* (No. 48). In *The Baptist Hymnal* (p. 47). LifeWay Worship.

Watterson, B. (1990). *The authoritative Calvin and Hobbes: A Calvin and Hobbes treasury*. Andrews and McMeel.

Chapter 12 - THE MONSTER WHO WAS SORRY

Bierce, A. (n.d.). *Ambrose Bierce quotes. BrainyQuote*. Retrieved from https://www.brainyquote.com/quotes/ambrose_bierce_121716

Church Publishing. (2000). *Healing from the past*. Church Publishing.

Department of Health & Human Services. (2018). *Health.Vic*. Department of Health & Human Services. Retrieved from https://www.health.vic.gov.au

Gottlieb, M. (1999). *The angry self: A comprehensive approach to anger management*. USA: Zeig, Tucker & Co.

Gottman, J. (2007). *Why marriages succeed or fail: And how you can make yours Last* (1st ed.). USA: Bloomsbury Publishing PLC.

Gottman, J. (2015). *The seven principles for making marriage work*. USA: Potter/Ten Speed/Harmony/Rodale.

Harper Nichols, M. (2020). *All along you were blooming: Thoughts for boundless living*. Grand Rapids, MG: Zondervan.

Hillary, E. (n.d.). *Edmund Hillary quotes. BrainyQuote.* Retrieved from https://www.brainyquote.com/quotes/edmund_hillary_118283

Keen, S. (n.d.), Sam Keen quotes. *BrainyQuote.* Retrieved from https://www.brainyquote.com/authors/sam-kean-quotes

Lisitsa, E. (2013). *The four horsemen: Criticism, contempt, defensiveness, and stonewalling.* The Gottman Institute. Retrieved from https://www.gottman.com/blog/the-four-horsemen-recognizing-criticism-contempt-defensiveness-and-stonewalling/

Mathias, A. (2010). *Biblical foundations for freedom: Destroying Satan's lies with God's truth.* Wellspring Publishing.

Norris, K. (1998). *Amazing grace: A vocabulary of faith.* Riverhead Books.

Nouwen, H. J. M. (1979). *The wounded healer: Ministry in contemporary society.* Image Books.

Simon, P. (1973). *Something so right.* On *There goes Rhymin' Simon* [Album]. Columbia Records.

Strong, J. (1995). *The New Strong's Exhaustive Concordance of the Bible.* Thomas Nelson.

Thayer, J. H. (2011). *Thayer's Greek lexicon.* Electronic Database. Biblesoft, Inc. Retrieved from https://biblehub.com/greek/2836.htm

Twain, M. (n.d.). *Mark Twain quotes. BrainyQuote.* Retrieved from https://www.brainyquote.com/quotes/mark_twain_120156

Chapter 13 - WHAT IS ANGER TRYING TO TELL ME?

Berry, C. R. (2003). *When helping you is hurting me: Escaping the Messiah trap.* New York: The Crossroad Publishing Company.

Department of Health & Human Services. (2018). *Health.Vic.* Department of Health & Human Services. Retrieved from https://www.health.vic.gov.au

Freyd, J. (2002). In the wake of terrorist attack, hatred may mask fear. *Analyses of Social Issues and Public Policy, 2*(1), 5-8.

Johnson, S. (2018). *Escaping conflict and the Karpman drama triangle.* Retrieved from https://bpdfamily.com/content/karpman-drama-triangle

Karpman, S. B. (1968). Fairy tales and script drama analysis. *Transactional Analysis Bulletin, 7*(26), 39–43.

Keller, T., & Keller, K. (2011). *The meaning of marriage: Facing the complexities of commitment with the wisdom of God*. Dutton.

Kenny, E. (n.d.). *He who angers you conquers you* [Attributed quote].

Loder, T. (2013). *My heart in my mouth: Prayers for our lives*. Wipf & Stock Publishers.

Longfellow, H. W. (1857). *Drift-Wood.* Ticknor and Fields.

Seligman, E. P. (1991). *Learned optimism.* New York: Simon & Schuster.

Chapter 14 - WHEN MY STRONGHOLDS BEGAN TO CRUMBLE

Goebbels, J. (1941, January 12). Churchill's Lie Factory. *Die Zeit ohne Beispiel.*

Keen, S. (1992). *The passionate life: Stages of loving.* USA: Harper San Francisco.

Krockel, C. (2016). *War trauma and English modernism.* UK: Palgrave Macmillan UK.

Leaf, C. (2013). *Switch on your brain: The key to peak happiness, thinking, and health*. Baker Books.

McGee, D. (n.d.). David McGee Quotes. *Goodreads.* Retrieved from https://www.goodreads.com/quotes/440648-every-source-of-blessing-is-a-point-of-attack

Mahatma Gandhi, (n.d.). Mahatma Gandhi quotes. *Goodreads.* Retrieved from https://www.goodreads.com/quotes/53582-you-can-chain-me-you-can-torture-me-you-can?utm_source=chatgpt.com

May, G. (1991). *Addiction and grace: Love and spirituality in the healing of addictions*. HarperOne.

Merriam-Webster. (n.d.). Deception. In *Merriam-Webster.com dictionary*. Retrieved April 17, 2025, from https://www.merriam-webster.com/dictionary/deception

Strong, J. (1995). *The New Strong's Exhaustive Concordance of the Bible* (entry G3794). Nashville, TN: Thomas Nelson.

Vachss, A. (1994). You carry the cure in your own heart. The zero – The Official Website of Andrew Vachss. Retrieved from http://www.vachss.com/av_dispatches/disp_9408_a.html

Chapter 15 - WHOSE VOICE AM I HEARING?

Eldredge, J. (2016). *Moving mountains: Praying with passion, confidence, and authority*. Thomas Nelson.

Lawton, C. (Ed.). (2012). *Journeys to mother love: Nine women tell their stories of forgiveness & healing*. CO, USA: Cladach Publishing. In Goodreads. Retrieved from https://www.goodreads.com/work/quotes/21616028-journeys-to-mother-love-nine-women-tell-their-stories-of-forgiveness

Leaf, C. (2015). *Who switched off my brain? Controlling toxic thoughts and emotions*. Baker Books.

Palmer, P. J. (2018). *On the brink of everything: Grace, gravity, and getting old*. Berrett-Koehler.

Tozer, A. W. (n.d.). Hearing God Quotes. Goodreads. Retrieved from https://www.azquotes.com/quotes/topics/hearing-god.html

Willard, D. (1999). *Hearing God: Developing a conversational relationship with God*. InterVarsity Press.

Chapter 16 - ROOTS THAT STILL BLEED

Brandon, N. (2011). *Honoring the self.* USA: Random House Publishing Group.

Catherall, D. R. (2004). *Handbook of stress, trauma, and the family.* UK: Tailor and Francis.

Crabb, L. (1987). *Understanding people.* USA: Zondervan.

Heuertz, C. L. (2017). *The sacred Enneagram: Finding your unique path to spiritual growth*. USA: Zondervan. Retrieved from https://cac.org/daily-meditations/type-four-the-need-to-be-special-2020-03-06/

Horney, K. (1950). *Neurosis and human growth: The struggle toward self-realization*. New York, NY: W. W. Norton & Company.

Oliver, M. (2007). *The uses of sorrow.* In *Thirst* (p. 11). Boston, MA: Beacon Press.

Kingsley, E. P. (1987). *Welcome to Holland.* Retrieved from https://www.dsasc.ca/uploads/8/5/3/9/8539131/welcome_to_holland.pdf

McGee, D. (n.d.). David McGee Quotes. *Goodreads.* Retrieved from https://www.goodreads.com/quotes/440648-every-source-of-blessing-is-a-point-of-attack

Pennington, M. B. (2000). *True self/false self: Unmasking the spirit within*. New York: The Crossroad Publishing Company.

Riso, D. R. & Hudson, R. (1999). *The wisdom of the Enneagram: The complete guide to psychological and spiritual growth for the nine personality types.* USA: Bantam Books.

Rohr, R. (1987). *Broken and blessed: A retreat.* Retrieved from http://link.bu.edu/portal/Broken-and-blessed--a-retreat-Richard-Rohr./D_V-h-I4-Hw/

Sattin, M. (2016). *29: How to heal your triggers and trauma with Peter Levine.* Retrieved from https://www.neilsattin.com/blog/2016/03/29-how-to-heal-your-triggers-and-trauma-with-peter-levine/

Sorge, B. (2000). *Glory: When heaven invades earth*. Oasis House.

Spring, C. (n.d.). Trigger quotes. *Goodreads*. Retrieved from https://www.goodreads.com/quotes/tag/trigger

The Enneagram Institute. (n.d.). *4 The individualist: Enneagram type four*. Retrieved from https://www.enneagraminstitute.com/type-4

van der Kolk, Bessel A. (1994). The Body Keeps The Score: Memory And The Evolving Psychobiology Of Posttraumatic Stress. *Harvard Review of Psychiatry*, 1,(5), 253-265. *Ovid Technologies (Wolters Kluwer Health)*, doi:10.3109/10673229409017088.

van der Kolk, B. A., (2006). Clinical implications of neuroscience research in PTSD. *Annals* of the *New York Academy* of *Sciences 1071*, 277–293. DOI: 10.1196/annals.1364.022

Wegscheider-Cruise, S. (2012). *Learning to love yourself: Finding your self-worth*. USA: Health Communications Inc.

Whyte, D. (2002). *The heart aroused: Poetry and the preservation of the soul in corporate America*. New York: Doubleday.

Zolotushko, L. (2013). *When angels weep 2*. Retrieved from https://pixels.com/featured/when-angels-weep-2-lina-zolotushko.html

Chapter 17 - WHEN REGRET BROKE ME OPEN

Arnold, E., & Moltmann, J. (2014). *Salt and light: Living the Sermon on the Mount* (4th ed.). UK: Plough Publishing House.

Crabb, L. (2006). *The Papa prayer: The prayer you've never prayed.* USA: Thomas Nelson.Hirshfield, J. (1988). *Of gravity and angels* (1st ed.). USA: Wesleyan University Press.

Hirshfield, J. (1988). *Of gravity and angels* (1st ed.). USA: Wesleyan University Press.

Lewis, C. S. (2001). *Mere Christianity.* UK: Harper Collins.

Mark, J. J. (2021). Martin Luther's 95 thesis. *World History Encyclopedia.* Retrieved from https://www.worldhistory.org/article/1891/martin-luthers-95-theses/

May, G. G. (2007). *Addiction and grace: Love and spirituality in the healing of addictions.* USA: HarperOne.

Merton, T. (1971). *Contemplation in a world of action* (p. 178). Garden City, NY: Doubleday.

Nouwen, H. J. M. (1972). *The wounded healer: Ministry in contemporary society.* Garden City, NY: Doubleday.

Peck, S. M. (2010). *The different drum: Community making and peace.* USA: Touchstone.

Rohr, R. & Ebert, A. (2001). The Enneagram: A Christian perspective. USA: Crossroad Publishing.

Rohr, R. (2013). *The sacred wound: Meditation 22 of 53: Richard Rohr's daily meditation.* Retrieved from https://myemail.constantcontact.com/Richard-Rohr-s-Daily-Meditation----August-17--2013.html?soid=1103098668616&aid=VsvGk1wUnuI

Rohr, R. (2019). Yes, and...: Daily meditations. USA: Franciscan Media.

Strong, J. (1995). *The New Strong's Exhaustive Concordance of the Bible* (entry G3794). Nashville, TN: Thomas Nelson.

Tagore, R. (n.d.). Quotefancy. *Retrieved from https://quotefancy.com/quote/955484/Rabindranath-Tagore-When-I-stand-before-thee-at-the-day-s-end-thou-shalt-see-my-scars-and*

Toplady, A. (1776). *Rock of ages*. In *Hymns and spiritual songs*. London: Thomas Cordeux.

Chapter 18 - FROM MESS TO MESSAGE: HOW MY PAIN BECAME PURPOSE

Burroughs, John. *Nature*. 1903. *The Writings of John Burroughs*, vol. 6, Houghton Mifflin, 1903.

Manning, B. (2004) *The relentless tenderness of Jesus*. USA: Fleming H Revell.

Nouwen, H. J. M. (2010). *The wounded healer: Ministry in contemporary society* 2nd ed.). New York: Image Doubleday.

Rohr, R. (1987). *Broken and blessed: A retreat.* Retrieved from http://link.bu.edu/portal/Broken-and-blessed--a-retreat-Richard-Rohr./D_V-h-I4-Hw/

APPENDIX A

Devotional and Prayer Guide: Rejoice. Relax. Rest.

Introduction

In our busy, anxious world, it's easy to forget that God calls us to rest—physically, emotionally, and spiritually. Rest isn't just a lack of activity; it's an intentional time of renewal and healing. As we face the pressures of life, our souls and bodies long for peace. But how often do we truly rest in God's presence? How often do we allow His peace to rule in our hearts, leading to deep, restorative sleep? This guide is designed to help you slow down, rejoice in God's goodness, relax in His presence, and ultimately experience restful sleep, knowing that He is with you.

Rejoice: Remember His Faithfulness

Psalm 4:8 (NIV), "In peace I will lie down and sleep, for you alone, LORD, make me dwell in safety."

Reflection

God's peace is not like the fleeting rest we sometimes experience in our hectic lives. His peace is the deep rest of knowing we are safe in His care. As you reflect on His faithfulness, think of the times you have felt His presence, His protection, and His provision. When anxiety threatens to rob your peace, remember His promises. Trust that He will never leave you nor forsake you. This trust brings a deep inner peace that leads to rest—both in mind and body.

Prayer

Father, thank You for Your faithfulness. Thank You for being the One who sustains me through every season of life. Help me to rejoice in Your goodness and rest in Your promises. I surrender my anxieties to You, knowing that You are in control. May Your peace guard my heart and mind today and always. Amen.

Relax: Find Rest in His Presence

Matthew 11:28-30 (NIV), "Come to me, all you who are weary and burdened, and I will give you rest. Take my yoke upon you and learn from me, for I am gentle and humble in heart, and you will find rest for your souls. For my yoke is easy and my burden is light."

Reflection

Jesus invites us to come to Him with all our burdens, offering rest for our weary souls. He doesn't ask us to carry our struggles alone. When we relax in His presence, we acknowledge that He is in control, and we release our anxieties into His loving hands. True relaxation is found when we take a moment to pause and allow His presence to soothe our hearts, quiet our minds, and restore our souls.

Prayer

Jesus, thank You for inviting me to find rest in You. I come to You with my worries, burdens, and fears, knowing You will give me peace. Help me to relax in Your presence today, trusting that You are gentle and humble in heart. Please calm my thoughts and let Your peace reign in my life. Amen.

Rest: Sleep in His Peace

Philippians 4:6-7 (NIV), "Do not be anxious about anything, but in every situation, by prayer and petition, with thanksgiving, present your requests to God. And the peace of God, which transcends all understanding, will guard your hearts and your minds in Christ Jesus."

Reflection

When anxiety disrupts our peace, it also disturbs our sleep. But God promises that when we bring our anxieties to Him, His peace will guard our hearts and minds. This peace allows us to rest physically and emotionally. If you've struggled with sleepless nights or restless thoughts, now is the time to surrender those worries to God and let Him fill your mind with peace. As you embrace His peace, your body can relax and find the sleep it needs for healing.

Prayer

Lord, I bring my anxieties before You today. I ask You to replace my worry with Your peace. Help me to sleep deeply, knowing that You are watching over me and providing for all my needs. I trust that You will give me rest for my body, mind, and soul. Let Your peace guide me into a restful sleep tonight. Amen.

Sleep Suggestions for Restful Nights

In addition to prayer and meditation on God's Word, here are practical suggestions that can help you find rest at night and improve the quality of your sleep:

1. **Stick to a Sleep Schedule:** Try to go to bed and wake up at the same time each day. This consistency supports your body's natural rhythms and helps you sleep more soundly.
2. **Dim the Lights in the Evening:** Exposure to dim lighting in the evening encourages the production of melatonin, the hormone that promotes sleep. Create a calm, quiet environment as you prepare for bedtime.
3. **Avoid Caffeine and Alcohol:** Caffeine and alcohol can disrupt sleep, so try to limit consumption, especially in the afternoon and evening hours.

4. **Relax Your Mind and Body:** Engage in relaxing activities in the hour before bed. Read a comforting devotional, take a warm bath, or practice deep breathing exercises. Avoid stimulating activities that could keep your mind racing.
5. **Create a Peaceful Sleep Environment:** Use earplugs or a white noise machine to block out disruptive sounds. Consider using a sleep mask to block out light, and keep your room at a comfortable temperature.
6. **Practice Christian Meditation:** Meditating on Scripture can bring peace to your mind before sleep. Reflect on verses that bring you comfort and trust in God's presence with you.
7. **Ask God for Rest:** In your prayers, ask God to provide deep, restorative sleep. Surrender your worries and allow His peace to fill your heart, knowing that He is faithful to restore you.

Closing Prayer

Father, as I reflect on Your Word and Your invitation to rest, I surrender my anxieties to You. Help me to find peace in Your presence and experience the rest You offer. I trust that You will restore my soul and give me the sleep I need to be refreshed for each new day. Thank You for Your faithfulness and love. Amen.

APPENDIX B

Worksheet: Replacing Lies with Truth

1. Identify the Lie

Take a moment to be still and ask the Holy Spirit to reveal any lie you've been believing about yourself, others, or God. Write it down below:

Lie I've Been Believing:

2. Invite the Truth

Now, ask: "God, what is the truth You want me to know?" Wait for a word, a Scripture, or a sense of His heart for you. Write it down below:

God's Truth for Me:

3. Declare the Truth

Say aloud the truth God has revealed to you. Repeat it as needed. Allow the truth to soak into your heart and mind.

4. Surrender the Lie

In prayer, hand the lie to Jesus. Imagine placing it at the foot of the cross. Let it go and receive His love and freedom.

Prayer of Renewal

Lord Jesus,
I bring before You the lie that has held me captive:

"__________."

I no longer want to agree with this lie.
I repent of believing it and living out of it.

I choose now to receive Your truth:

"__________."

Let this truth take root in my mind and spirit.
Renew me. Heal me.
Help me to walk in the freedom You died to give me.

In Your name, Jesus, I pray. Amen.

Acknowledgements

This book was not written alone.

First, I give thanks to God, whose presence I have come to know not in the absence of pain, but within it. In the places where I felt most undone, I discovered that grace was already waiting, steady, patient, and kind. This story exists because of that presence.

I am deeply grateful to my husband, Barry, my companion in life, faith, and work. Thank you for walking beside me through seasons of weariness and renewal, for listening when words came slowly, and for believing in this story even when I was unsure, I could tell it. Your steadiness, humour, and love have been a shelter more times than you know.

To the many clients, students, and colleagues who have entrusted me with their stories over the years, thank you. Your courage in naming pain, sitting with uncertainty, and choosing honesty has shaped me profoundly. While your stories have been carefully reshaped to protect privacy, the truth of what you have shared continues to teach and humble me. This book carries echoes of your wisdom.

I am thankful for the mentors, teachers, and fellow travellers who have influenced my understanding of trauma, faith, and healing. Your insights, spoken in classrooms, whispered in supervision, shared over cups of tea, and lived out in difficult places, have formed the soil from which this work has grown.

To friends and family who offered encouragement, patience, and quiet presence along the way, thank you for holding space when I needed it most. Writing about heartache requires safety, and your kindness helped create it.

Finally, I thank the reader. If you have found your way to these pages, you carry your own story of longing, loss, and hope. My deepest hope is that you feel seen, not fixed; accompanied, not instructed; and gently reminded that even the roots of heartache can hold the beginnings of grace.

Heartache rarely announces itself. It settles quietly into the body, the soul, and the spaces where hope once lived, often long before we have words for it. In *Exploring the Roots of Heartache: The Stories Our Pain Is Trying to Tell*, Dr Paula Davis invites readers into a deeply personal and compassionate exploration of pain, memory, and healing. Drawing from her own journey and decades of walking alongside others as a trauma counsellor, she traces how unacknowledged grief, unmet needs, fear, shame, anger, and longing take root beneath the surface of our lives.

This is not a step-by-step guide or a promise of quick healing. Instead, it is a gentle companion for those who sense that their pain carries meaning, and that listening to it may be the beginning of restoration. Through story, reflection, and spiritual insight, Paula shows how the body remembers what the mind forgets, how fear and anger can become messengers rather than enemies, and how God meets us not beyond our brokenness, but within it.

Written with honesty, tenderness, and hope, this book offers space to pause, breathe, and reflect. For anyone who has felt overwhelmed, weary, or quietly undone, *Exploring the Roots of Heartache* is an invitation to discover that even in the deepest places of pain, grace is already at work, and the roots of heartache may yet give rise to hope.

www.ingramcontent.com/pod-product-compliance
Lightning Source LLC
LaVergne TN
LVHW012339100826
845148LV00018B/2843
9780645117981